The Political Economy of
the New Asian Industrialism

Cornell Studies in Political Economy

EDITED BY PETER J. KATZENSTEIN

The Political Economy of the New Asian Industrialism

EDITED BY

FREDERIC C. DEYO

Cornell University Press

ITHACA AND LONDON

First published 1987 by Cornell University Press.
Second printing 1988.
First published, Cornell Paperbacks, 1987.
Fourth printing 1992.

International Standard Book Number (cloth) 0-8014-1948-4
International Standard Book Number (paper) 0-8014-9449-4
Library of Congress Catalog Card Number 86-29103
Printed in the United States of America
*Librarians: Library of Congress cataloging information
appears on the last page of the book.*

⊗ The paper in this book meets the minimum requirements of the American National Standard for Information Sciences—Permanence of Paper for Printed Library Materials, ANSI Z39.48-1984.

Contents

Contributors

Richard E. Barrett is Associate Professor of Sociology at the University of Illinois, Chicago.

Tun-jen Cheng is Assistant Professor in The Graduate School of International Relations and Pacific Studies, University of California, San Diego.

Soomi Chin is Assistant Professor of Sociology at Kyungpook National University in Taegu, Republic of Korea.

Bruce Cumings is Associate Professor of International Studies at the University of Washington, Seattle.

Frederic C. Deyo is Associate Professor of Sociology at the State University of New York, College at Brockport.

Peter Evans is Professor in the Graduate School of International Relations and Pacific Studies at the University of California, San Diego.

Stephan Haggard is Assistant Professor of Government and Associate in the Center for International Affairs at Harvard University, Cambridge, Massachusetts.

Chalmers Johnson is Walter and Elise Haas Professor of Asian Studies at the University of California, Berkeley.

Hagen Koo is Associate Professor of Sociology at the University of Hawaii, Manoa.

Preface

The newly industrializing countries of East Asia (South Korea, Taiwan, Singapore, and Hong Kong) have experienced very rapid industrial growth over a two-decade period. This growth has been paralleled by a favorable pattern of income equality, low unemployment, and the near elimination of the grinding poverty that debilitates the poorest social strata in other Third World countries. Most remarkable of all, this "economic miracle" has occurred in small countries bereft of the natural and physical resources that have fostered growth elsewhere.

East Asian growth, based in large measure on light export manufacturing, has often been taken to confirm orthodox theories of development, which stress the economic benefits of trade liberalization, private enterprise, and a restricted economic role for the state. More recently, a number of observers have questioned the assumption that the state has played only an indirect and minimal role in development. Increasingly, it has been recognized that, at least in Singapore, South Korea, and Taiwan, comprehensive state intervention has loomed large in the economic restructuring of recent years. One purpose of this book is to seek a more balanced account of East Asian growth, in part through an exploration of the developmental role of the state.

To the extent that the role of the state has been discussed, attention has focused on its economic intervention in guiding development domestically and in managing economic relations externally. Far too little attention has been accorded the sociopolitical and institutional bases for the nearly unique capacity of the East Asian states effectively to implement coherent development strategies. This capacity is rooted in external political alliances, domestic authoritarian rule, and effective economic institutions. A second purpose of this book is to understand these sociopolitical bases for effective state intervention in the marketplace.

The apparently positive developmental consequences of linkages to foreign capital, markets, and technology for domestic growth have seemed to offer greater support to the assumptions of modernization theory than to those of dependencia. For this reason, discussion of sociopolitical aspects of the East Asian experience has not generally engaged the theoretical issues raised by dependencistas. A third purpose here is to present a theoretically balanced account of East Asian development which is selectively informed by both modernization and dependency perspectives and which also affords a critical appraisal of their relative strengths and a basis for their further elaboration.

This book has benefited from the help, suggestions, and support of persons too numerous to list. Special thanks are due Richard Abrams, Gary Gereffi, Janet Salaff, Robert Snow, and Gail Ullman, as well as to Peter Katzenstein, series editor, who gave us the final push to improve a book that seemed already to have exhausted us all. Finally, thanks go to Roger Haydon, manuscript editor; to MIT Press and the World Peace Foundation for permission to reprint the chapter by Bruce Cumings; and to the Institute of East Asian Studies, University of California at Berkeley, for permission to reprint the chapter by Chalmers Johnson.

FREDERIC C. DEYO

Brockport, New York

The Political Economy of
the New Asian Industrialism

Introduction Frederic C. Deyo

The remarkable economic expansion that the East Asian NICs—Taiwan, Hong Kong, Singapore, and South Korea—sustained during the 1970s stands in stark contrast to the experience of most other Third World countries. Equally striking is the association there of rapid industrial growth with relatively equitable income distribution. Although the East Asian "economic miracle" has attracted much attention in the developmental economics literature, however, it has remained largely isolated from the theoretical debates that have informed discussion of sociopolitical aspects of economic development in Latin America and elsewhere (but see Barrett and Whyte, 1982; Gold, 1986). This book seeks to encourage a fuller integration of the East Asian experience of industrialization into the mainstream of development theory through an examination of the social, institutional, and political sources of growth in the East Asian NICs.

After World War II, and into the early 1960s, optimism marked much scholarly theorizing about the economic future of the Third World. As the hegemonic world power, the United States was the home of a widely held orthodoxy that the diffusion of (American) capital, development assistance, cultural values, and political and economic institutions would start the process of economic development and, not incidentally, forestall communist revolution as well (Chirot, 1977). This orthodoxy was systematized and codified in the writings of neoclassical economists, who emphasized the benefits of reliance on the workings of free markets, both domestic and foreign. Among political scientists, sociologists, and some institutional economists, the prevailing orthodoxy found its home in what is loosely termed a modernization perspective. Modernization writers differ widely in disciplinary focus, level of analysis, and theoretical models, but they do share several broad assumptions about socioeconomic development—assumptions that are of particular importance for this volume. Among these is the assertion that international linkages to the states, corporations, markets, and development resources, especially capital and technology, of developed industrial societies have developmentally positive long-term effects, including self-sustaining growth and a mutual stimulation among economic sectors (Rostow, 1971). This assumption is the institutional counterpart of the neo-classical emphasis on the benefits of external economic policies based on the play of market forces. Second is the assertion that though these external linkages may play an important economic role in initiating development, the major determinants of self-sustained growth are to be found within developing countries themselves (Rostow, 1971:144). Once diffusion has cleared away traditional obstacles to development, growth unfolds in an evolutionary fashion. Third is the assumption that over the long run, economic development fosters the diffusion both of democratic participation in an increasingly well-educated and middle-class society and of economic benefits to an ever-broader spectrum of the population (Black, 1966:83).

For many observers the UN Development Decade of the 1960s belied these orthodox assumptions about development. Despite continuing U.S. development assistance and growing levels of direct foreign investment by multinational corporations, the economic gap between industrial and Third World countries continued to widen. Growth sectors in Third World countries did not stimulate more general development, democracy failed to take root, income inequalities worsened over time, and growing economic and political crisis betrayed earlier hopes for social stability. Responses among scholars of development varied greatly. Some argued that government should take a greater economic role, to offset institutional and cultural obstacles to growth or to augment a weak entrepreneurial response with state entrepreneurship. Others sought greater commitment to growth-with-equity policies, which might give as great a priority to agricultural and integrated rural development, the generation of jobs, and the fulfillment of basic needs as to growth itself. (Wilber and Jameson, 1984). Especially prominent was the growing emphasis that modernization theorists placed on the need for strong developmental states (Black, 1966:13–14; Rostow, 1971:25–26). This emphasis was paralleled by an increased insistence on the part of missions from the U.S. Agency for International Development on the creation of government planning machinery. It was stated most forcefully by Samuel Huntington, who argued the need for a ''centralization of power in the bureaucratic polity [to] enhance . . . the capability of the state to bring about modernizing reforms in society'' (1968:167).

As these various departures from orthodoxy signaled a growing intellectual disillusionment, newer, more pessimistic views asserted themselves. One of these, dependency theory, is of particular importance. It originated among Latin American scholars (e.g., Prebisch, 1950), who sought national economic disengagement from the advanced industrial countries, and among neo-Marxist writers on imperialism (Baran, 1968; Galtung, 1971). Although they differed sharply in broader theoretical approach, these two groups of writers did agree that economic linkages between the periphery and the core (the Third World and the industrialized countries) of an evolving world capitalist system produced exploitation and economic stagnation rather than growth in the periphery. This assumption informed a dependency perspective that emerged during the 1960s. At the risk of oversimplification we can identify three major tenets accepted by those working within the tradition.

First, the economic insertion of a Third World country into the expanding world capitalist system encourages specialization in the production of agricultural or mineral commodities for export and a corresponding linkage between these primary export sectors and foreign capital and markets.

Second, while such an insertion brings short-run economic growth, as early production and employment gains are realized, in the longer run a continued reliance on core markets, capital, and techology generates forces that constrain development. A trade pattern dominated by primary exports and manufactured imports generates deteriorating and unfavorable terms of trade for peripheral economies (Prebisch, 1950; Emmanuel, 1972; Amin, 1974). Production oriented toward core markets and often relying on core technologies, capital, and factor inputs creates structural distortions in domestic economies which reflect and perpetuate a predominace of external over internal economic linkages (Chase-Dunn, 1975; Chirot, 1977:34–38, 152). Such distortions hinder industrial diversification and stimulation of other economic sectors by dynamic, externally oriented sectors (Valenzuela and Valenzuela, 1978). Associated with such enclave growth is the emergence of social groups and class segments that benefit from and seek to preserve this development pattern (Galtung, 1971). These groups include relatively well-paid workers, a small sector of the national bourgeoisie, and government bureaucrats. Finally, reliance on core capital and technology, especially through direct foreign investment or foreign assistance, helps foreign interests penetrate domestic economic decision making in firms and state agencies. Economic decisions thus tend to reflect the interests of foreign states and capital despite possibly negative implications for national development (Gereffi, 1978). In addition, reliance on external capital and technology means an outward flow of profits through repatriation, licensing fees, royalties, interest payments, transfer pricing, and other mechanisms by which economic surplus is transferred to core firms.

Third, dependency also has an unfavorable impact on economic equality (Chase-Dunn, 1975; Rubinson, 1976; Bornschier et al., 1978). Multinationals, states, and intergovernmental agencies indirectly push for strong regimes that are capable of controlling unions and restraining wages and levels of public consumption in the interests of capital accumulation (Kaufman, 1979; Street, 1984). The multinationals also use capital-intensive technologies developed in core countries, which generate high-wage employment for only a few workers but little employment for most others (Evans and Timberlake, 1980). Enclave development, moreover, is associated with severe regional and sectoral inequalities.

If neoclassical and modernization orthodoxy has guided the foreign policy and development assistance programs of the United States and other core countries (Chirot, 1977), dependency theory achieved a privileged place in the early development strategies of several Latin American states. The world depression of the 1930s, followed by World War II, made apparent the economic vulnerability and precariousness of a development strategy based on primary exports. The collapse of world markets also made clear the need for state-sponsored economic diversification, especially into manufacturing. This important lesson was subsequently extended to import restrictions and tariffs, currency revaluation, and other policy measures designed to protect and nurture domestic industry. This import-substituting industrialization strategy was most forcefully pursued in Brazil, Mexico, and Argentina, Latin America's three major newly industrializing countries or NICs.

Dependency theory remained useful for an understanding of classic dependency, but the need for reformulation to account for the economic dynamism of the NICs was clear. In response to this need a newer intellectual tradition has evolved, drawing especially on the writing of Fernando Cardoso and Enzo Falleto (1979). Unlike more deterministic dependency accounts, this "dependent development" school recognizes a more complex and contingent relationship between dependency and economic growth. Its revisionist writers seek to understand the ways in which the interaction of domestic and foreign groups, classes, and organizations influence development. Analysis of diverse situations of dependency permits specification of the sociopolitical context of dependency, which itself determines the possibility, nature, and rate of growth (Gereffi, 1983). Classic dependency situations, for example, in which foreign-controlled agricultural or mining enclaves are the leading economic sectors, foster long-term economic stagnation. Conversely, diversified economic growth is encouraged where strong states orchestrate a strategy of domestic industrialization which serves the interests both of multinational companies and of segments of the local bourgeoisie (Evans, 1979).

It is important to note that though this less deterministic variant of dependency theory encourages an empirically more open-ended study of economic growth, it remains wedded to several of the key assumptions of traditional dependency theory. The fact of dependency is still seen as fundamentally constraining development strategies and success (Kaufman, 1979). The outer limits of development are clear in Peter Evans's discussion of Brazil: "dependent development is viable only if it has support from the larger system of imperialism. The entire success of the dependent development is predicated on multinationals willing to invest, [and] international bankers willing to extend credit" (1979:290). "Like classic dependence, dependent development will eventually reach its limits. . . . The Brazilian model cannot survive without its allies from the center'' (p. 329). And growing political disaffection, especially on the part of excluded segments of the national bourgeoisie, suggests a second, political, limitation to continued dependent development.

Shared too by both variants of dependency theory are the assumptions that dependency is self-reinforcing over time, as manifest in deepening economic structural distortions, decisional penetration, and the emergence of dependent classes, and that such development tends to be politically exclusionary and economically inequitable. Such arguments derive strength from studies of rapid industrialization among the Latin American NICs. There industrial expansion, in concert with growing multinational penetration, has been accompanied by rapid but highly inegalitarian growth (Knight and Moran, 1984) and by the imposition during the 1960s and 1970s of repressive political regimes that served to protect the interests of foreign and domestic capital, to reduce populist threats to accumulation and political stability, and to contain the socioeconomic and political tensions generated by uneven and inegalitarian development (Collier, 1979).

The Latin American NICs forced a reconsideration of dependency; the East Asian NICs pose an even more fundamental challenge. In these countries economic growth during the 1960s and 1970s was based largely on production of labor-intensive manufactured goods for world markets. In comparison with the Latin American NICs these countries have by necessity pursued more externally open strategies of development based on trade. Levels of direct foreign investment have not been as dramatic as those in Latin America; nonetheless, rapid and sustained East Asian development has been paralleled by high levels of early external capital assistance, on the one hand, and open, export-oriented development patterns, on the other. And though authoritarian rule by the strong, developmentalist states that typically shepherd dependent development has marked East Asia, economic growth in the region has departed from dependency theory in several ways. Of particular importance has been a capacity to meet the development challenges of changing external circumstances through decisive shifts in strategy and economic structure, attainment of relatively full employment, continued increases in real wages, and low levels of economic inequality (Fields, 1984). These departures have led some observers to invoke orthodox approaches to explain East Asian development. Bela Balassa (1981) has been especially influential in reasserting the neoclassical virtues of open, market-directed strategies for economic growth. But a growing awareness of the significance of state intervention, both in external economic relations and in domestic economic affairs, has led others to explore further the impact on growth of strategies pursued by strong, developmentalist states. The contributors to this book, while they differ sharply in their stance toward dependency theory, fall within this latter, statist tradition.

East Asian development: the role of state strategy

The development literature suggests historical and developmental conditions
under which state economic intervention is an essential component of
growth. These include economic backwardness or lateness (Gerschenkron,
1963), exhaustion or failure of primary-export phases of growth and the
need to nurture import-substituting industry (Prebisch, 1950), cultural or
social obstacles to entrepreneurship or investment (Rostow, 1971), economic structural distortions such as enclave development or lack of domestic economic linkages (Chase-Dunn, 1975; Caporaso, 1978), multinational
domination of key economic sectors (Evans, 1979), and entrenched opposition groups whose conservative power must be broken (Black, 1966; Huntington, 1968:126). In addition, strategic intervention may be important
where development is based on growth in heavy industry or in capital- or
technology-intensive industry, especially since the 1950s among the Latin
American NICs (Kaufman, 1979) and since the 1970s among the East Asian
NICs. Strategy-directed development may also be necessary where changing economic conditions necessitate rapid shifts in economic structure and
external economic relations.

A full specification of these and other conditions cannot be attempted
here, of course, but it is clear that political and economic disabilities encountered in late Third World development are relatively greater than those
encountered in corresponding stages of development in the core. This suggests the special relevance of state interventionist solutions to problems of
contemporary Third World underdevelopment. With few exceptions, Third
World states have since 1945 attempted to accelerate economic development
through more or less coherent growth strategies. Beyond this elemental
proposition, however, some important distinctions must be drawn. First,
such strategies exhibit substantial variation in consistency across policy
instruments and over time. Some strategies may be little more than in-
coherent, shifting, accidental political outcomes of competition among
groups, organizations, or classes. Second, strategies may be little more than
vague pronouncements addressed less to the needs of development than to
those of political legitimation and stability. Where elites lack a commitment
to development or fear imminent political displacement by opposition
groups, development strategies will reflect short-term political needs rather
than longer-term economic ones. Third, and perhaps most problematic, is
the issue of efficacy. Retrospective, strategy-centered interpretations of economic development must either assume or demonstrate that strategies in fact
matter. It is clear that the existence of a strategy that appears to be consistent
with actual economic outcomes does not in itself demonstrate causality
between strategy and performance. Strategies may sometimes follow rather
than precede economic trends. Latin American import-substituting industrialization, for example, was fully articulated as a strategy only after World

War II—after, that is, earlier experiments with ad hoc industrialization policies had encouraged import-substituting industrialization. And governments may sometimes seek to legitimate themselves through the formulation of strategies that "explain" economic success by reference to state action (Wade, 1986).

Finally, there is the question of the relationship between state and strategy. Observers usually associate growth strategies with state intervention, but we can envision cases in which nonstate elites play the major role in generating and implementing development strategies, especially at subnational levels (Walton, 1977) or, as in Hong Kong, where elite unity and economic centralization permit. It is also clear that distinguishing among the complex interactive roles of state and nonstate elites in capitalist development strategies is difficult. Here I draw only a simple distinction between state-led and state-induced strategies. State-led strategies in capitalist economies entail continuing, selective intervention by state agencies in private-sector decision making and market transactions to achieve strategic goals. State-induced but not state-led strategies, on the other hand, emphasize the role of the private sector in implementing strategies within a broad political, legal, infrastructural, and economic framework that the state establishes to pursue its chosen development objectives. In the Latin American context this basic distinction suffices to separate periods of state-led, import-substituting industrial restructuring (e.g., Brazil in the 1950s) from state-induced, neoconservative experiments in economic liberalization (e.g., Chile in the mid-1970s) which depended on state coercion (Foxley, 1983).

The chapters in this book suggest the importance of consistent, developmentalist, state-led strategy for economic growth and restructuring in South Korea, Taiwan, and Singapore. They relate strategy to economic performance through an examination of the institutional linkages between policy and industrial decision making. They examine the broader sociopolitical context that facilitated strategy formulation, asking how state-led industrialization has in turn affected society. Finally, they explore the impact of foreign economic and political linkages on domestic political and economic development.

In Chapter 1, Richard Barrett and Soomi Chin explore the empirical contours of East Asian development through contrasts with other developing countries. Hong Kong, Singapore, Taiwan, and South Korea, they find, collectively evince a unique development pattern led by expansion in a few strategic export industries which has stimulated growth and more jobs in other industries. East Asian industrialization departs from the expectations of those writers in the dependency tradition who argue that external economic dependency is associated with long-run economic stagnation and economic inequality, loss of economic autonomy in economic restructuring and the formulation of development strategy, and a weakening of domestic states. Rather, the East Asian NICs present a pattern not only of continued high growth rates but also of relatively equitable development, a continuing ability to alter domestic economic structures and world market position to adjust to changing economic circumstances, and an enhanced rather than a diminished state power to mobilize and deploy domestic economic resources. An understanding of East Asia's economic successes, the authors conclude, requires the development of middle-range theories that can explain how governments and firms in these open, high-growth economies have successfully adapted to the changing economic environment of the capitalist world system.

Bruce Cumings starts the search for such middle-range theories through an exploration of the historical origins of East Asian industrialism in the broader regional context of Japanese and then American hegemony. For Cumings, the key to an understanding of economic dynamism is strong states using mercantilist policies to lever national economies into higher niches in the world economy. Crucial to the emergence of strong, developmentalist states in Taiwan and South Korea was the Japanese colonial emphasis on economic growth directed by a centralized state, neomercantilist regional development policies, and authoritarian political regimes that precluded the emergence of populist challenge to colonial rule. Under Japanese rule, extensive industrial and infrastructural investment provided a base for subsequent industrial growth. The postwar American hegemony fostered developmentalist, authoritarian, anticommunist states in a newly revived, Japan-centered, capitalist regional economy; organized labor and opposition groups were repressed. Like prewar colonialism, this postwar tutelary control encouraged industrial and development policies to foster economic stability in a geopolitically important region. And as in Japan, industrial policy was implemented through close state-industry linkages. Finally, Cumings notes the importance of growing external autonomy: in the 1970s states began introducing new economic restructuring policies although they lacked core support.

These two essays suggest that Asian economic growth has relied on trade, capital, and technology from core countries. Dependency writers attribute great importance to direct foreign investment as an instrument of foreign control and domestic economic constraint. In Chapter 3 Stephan Haggard and Tun-jen Cheng contrast the role and forms of foreign capital penetration among the Asian and Latin American NICs, as well as the changing relationships of foreign firms with domestic governments and with local enterprise. Multinational corporations dominate these Asian economies, it is frequently assumed, but Haggard and Cheng show that with the exception of Singapore, such corporations have played a less extensive role in the Asian NICs than in industrializing Latin American countries. More important, for long-term development as well as for the avoidance of the usual disadvantages associated with dependency on foreign capital, is the strength of Asian states, which have been able to direct and limit the impact of foreign capital in local economies and whose development projects have played a crucial role in economic growth. The state's role in development increased during the restructuring of the 1970s. In turn the strategic power of states has depended on the one hand on the formation of political coalitions with domestic industry, and on the other on the destruction of the left and curtailment of the power of organized labor and other popular sectors.

Chalmers Johnson and Hagen Koo continue two themes pursued by Haggard and Cheng. The first relates to the institutional basis for effective state policy implementation; the second deals with the political basis for strong, autonomous, developmentalist states. Through a comparison of state-led development in Japan, South Korea, and Taiwan, Johnson argues that state intervention in East Asian capitalist countries has relied on organizational and institutional links between politically insulated state development agencies and major private-sector firms. Through controls over access to credit, export licenses, foreign exchange, and the like, public agencies have been able systematically to manipulate economic incentives in accordance with changing strategic goals. The efficacy of intervention has similarly been amplified through the fostering of powerful, state-linked, private-sector conglomerates, banks, and trading organizations that dominate strategic economic sectors.

Chapter 5 focuses less on the instruments of policy than on the social class and political basis of strong, exclusionary states in Taiwan and South Korea. Koo argues that Japanese colonial rule undermined the strength and independence of landlord and other social classes that in other societies typically penetrate state structures. The Japanese defeat, moreover, was associated with a dissolution of external political and economic linkages. Subsequent reintegration into the U.S.-dominated world state system encouraged the emergence of strong, authoritarian states before reentry into the world capitalist economy. This sequence, Koo shows, fostered strong developmentalist states at the outset of development. The result was a preemptive capacity to control sociopolitical forces associated first with increased foreign investment, then with an emergent industrial bourgeoisie and a growing industrial proletariat.

Cumings and Koo both suggest that if product-cycle virtuosity and effective intervention for development are positive outcomes of the strength and relative autonomy of East Asian states, then the dark underside of autonomy is the political exclusion, often by repression, of groups from the popular sector. The success of labor-intensive industrial development oriented toward exports has been predicated in part on the maintenance of low labor costs. Important to the containment of labor costs has been the political exclusion of organized labor from politics and policy making. Chapter 6 describes the patterns and structures of control through which East Asian regimes have effected such exclusion. Where labor movements were not already weak or controlled, as they were in Taiwan and Hong Kong, labor-intensive manufacturing for world markets has indeed been associated with the imposition or intensification of repressive controls over labor. Such controls contrast with the early corporatist regimes in the Latin American NICs, with their greater emphasis on increased wages and public welfare. Subsequent Asian development in manufactured goods for export, has further consolidated controls through socioeconomic structural changes that have undercut the independence and power of workers' organizations.

In the next chapter Peter Evans argues that this experience of the strong, developmentalist state is in fact consistent with major tenets of dependency theory. In particular, dependency writers have stressed the negative consequences of powerful foreign firms and relatively weak domestic states for long-term economic transformation, and so the weaker position of foreign capital and the relatively stronger position of states in East Asia is fully compatible with the substantially better growth record there than in Latin America. In addition Evans points to the need for fuller attention to the sociopolitical context of dependency in efforts to understand patterns of development.

The concluding chapter presents an integrative summary of the contributions to this volume, underscoring the importance of three keys to an understanding of East Asian development: state coalitional autonomy, institutional consolidation, and the temporal sequence and nature of political and economic linkages to core societies. The interplay of these three factors suggests the usefulness of a strategic capacity model of development, a model that draws on both modernization and dependency approaches.

References

Amin, Samir. 1974. *Accumulation on a World Scale*. New York: Monthly Review.
Balassa, Bela. 1981. *The Newly Industrializing Countries in the World Economy*. New York: Pergamon.
Baran, Paul. 1968. *The Political Economy of Growth*. New York: Monthly Review.
Barrett, Richard, and Martin K. Whyte. 1982. "Dependency Theory and Taiwan: A Deviant Case Analysis." *American Journal of Sociology* 87:1064–1089.
Black, C. E. 1966. *The Dynamics of Modernization: A Study in Comparative History*. New York: Harper & Row.
Bornschier, Volker, et al. 1978. "Cross-National Evidence of the Effects of Foreign Investment and Aid on Economic Growth and Inequality: A Survey of Findings and a Reanalysis." *American Journal of Sociology* 84:651–683.
Caporaso, James. 1978. "Introduction to the Special Issue of *International Organization* on Dependence and Dependency in the Global System." *International Organization* 32:1–12.
Cardoso, Fernando, and Enzo Faletto. 1979. *Dependency and Development in Latin America*. Berkeley: University of California Press.

Chase-Dunn, Christopher. 1975. "The Effects of International Economic Dependence on Development and Inequality: A Cross-National Study." *American Sociological Review* 40:720–738.

Chirot, Daniel. 1977. *Social Change in the Twentieth Century*. New York: Harcourt Brace Jovanovich.

Collier, David, ed. 1979. *The New Authoritarianism in Latin America*. Princeton: Princeton University Press.

Emmanuel, Arghiri. 1972. *Unequal Exchange: A Study of the Imperialism of Free Trade*. New York: Monthly Review.

Evans, Peter. 1979. *Dependent Development*. Princeton: Princeton University Press.

Evans, Peter, and Michael Timerlake. 1980. "Dependence, Inequality, and Growth in Less Developed Countries." *American Sociological Review* 45:531–552.

Fields, Gary S. 1984. "Employment, Income Distribution, and Economic Growth in Seven Small Open Economies." *Economic Journal* 94:74–83.

Foxley, Alejandro. 1983. *Latin American Experiments in Neo-Conservative Economics*. Berkeley: University of California Press.

Galtung, Johan. 1971. "A Structural Theory of Imperialism." *Journal of Peace Research* 8:81–117.

Gereffi, Gary. 1978. "Drug Firms and Dependency in Mexico: The Case of the Steroid Hormone Industry." *International Organization* 32:237–286.

Gereffi, Gary. 1983. *The Pharmaceutical Industry and Dependency in the Third World*. Princeton: Princeton University Press.

Gerschenkron, Alexander. 1963. "The Early Phases of Industrialization in Russia and Their Relationship to the Historical Study of Economic Growth." In Barry Supple, ed. *The Experience of Economic Growth*. New York: Random.

Gold, Thomas. 1986. *State and Society in Taiwan's Economic Miracle*. Armank, N.Y.: Sharpe.

Huntington, Samuel. 1968. *Political Order in Changing Societies*. New Haven: Yale University Press.

Kaufman, Robert. 1979. "Industrial Change and Authoritarian Rule in Latin America: A Concrete Review of the Bureaucratic-Authoritarian Model."

Knight, Peter, and Ricardo Moran. 1984. "Bringing the Poor into the Growth Process: The Case of Brazil." In Charles Wilber, ed. *The Political Economy of Development and Underdevelopment*. 3d ed. New York: Random.

Prebisch, Raul. 1950. *The Economic Development of Latin America and Its Principal Problems*. New York: United Nations.

Rostow, Walt W. 1971. *Stages of Economic Growth*. 2d. ed. New York: Cambridge University Press.

Rubinson, Richard. 1976. "The World-Economy and the Distribution of Income Within States: A Cross-National Study." *American Sociological Reivew* 41:638–659.

Street, James H. 1984. "Values in Conflict: Developing Countries as Social Laboratories." *Journal of Economic Issues* 18:633–641.

Valenzuela, J., and Arturo Valenzuela. 1978. "Modernization and Dependency: Alternative Perspectives in the Study of Latin American Underdevelopment." *Comparative Politics* 10:535–557.

Wade, Robert. 1986. "The Organization and Effects of the Developmental State in

East Asia.'' Paper presented at a conference on development strategies in Latin
America and East Asia, Institute of the Americas, University of California at
San Diego, 4–6 May.

Walton, John. 1977. *Elites and Economic Development.* Austin: University of
Texas Press.

Wilber, Charles, and Kenneth Jameson. 1984. ''Paradigms of Economic Development
and Beyond.'' In Wilber, ed. *The Political Economy of Development
and Underdevelopment.* 3d ed. New York: Random.

Export-oriented industrializing states in the capitalist world system: similarities and differences   Richard E. Barrett and Soomi Chin

The recent successes of a few East Asian states in achieving economic growth through "open," export-oriented industrialization (EOI) strategies have attracted some scholarly attention, but few attempts have been made to interpret these developments in the broader context of theories of economic development or the emergence of an interdependent world economy. This paucity of serious theoretical engagement is reflected in part in the lack of systematic empirical confrontation of important propositions about development with available data on the actual economic experience of these countries. This chapter first offers an overview of major differences between two major perspectives on economic growth: neoclassical/modernization theory and dependency/world systems theory. It then assesses the validity of key propositions suggested by these two general approaches to economic development by examining available data on growth and structural change in the newly industrializing countries of East Asia. The positive development outcomes of the open economic strategies pursued by the East Asian NICs are generally more compatible with the tenets of neoclassical/modernization theory, we suggest, than with those of a dependency/world systems approach.

The dependency/world system model

The world system/dependency model interprets the EOI states as an evolving semiperiphery. As previously semiperipheral nations in Europe, Oceania, North America, and Japan moved into the core over the past three decades, their previous roles were assumed by other nations, including some East Asian states. These states will exhibit an increasing mutual resemblance in their economic, political, and social structures, because the flow of international capital and occasional political and military intervention by core states assign them a similar position in the world system.

In general, dependency and world systems theory predict, industrial development in EOI states will be of a dependent, "artificial" nature. It will often be enclave industrialization, with few linkages to the broader national economy. Second, it will be particularly vulnerable to swings in world economic conditions. Third, this kind of industrialization, where control over capital and markets is heavily influenced by multinational firms, may also result in the domination of national markets by these multinationals, the absence of indigenous entrepreneurship, and economically weakened states. Over the long run these dependency-linked structural problems foster economic stagnation and heightened inequality across regions, economic sectors, and income groups. These basic assertions, it may be noted, continue to dominate the dependency literature, albeit in increasingly qualified form, even though recognition is growing of the possibilities of at least limited vertical mobility within the international economic system (see Friedman, 1982), as well as of the great difficulties in pursuing autarkic development outside that system.

For many First World scholars who take the dependency/world systems models as hypotheses worthy of examination with empirical data, the individual East Asian states have served as interesting counterexamples, or deviant cases, to the causal relationships these models predict (see Amsden, 1979; Chow and Papenek, 1981; Barrett and Whyte, 1982). Few attempts have been made, however, to specify what characteristic forms of social and economic development these states share or to analyze how or why they diverge.

The neoclassical economics/modernization model

The conventional perspective of neoclassical economics/modernization declares that a strategy of export industrialization is a successful adaptation to current world economic conditions and to the factor endowments of these East Asian states (Balassa, 1978). Such open economic strategies, it argues, energize and transform domestic economies through linkages to precisely those external economic factors—capital, markets, and technology—which dependencistas see as inhibiting growth. In addition, some theorists in this tradition expect that the economies and political and social institutions of EOI states will mature and that their industrial structures will converge with those of more developed nations.[1] They expect convergence with the core,

1. Some readers may object to collapsing modernization or convergence theory with the neoclassical theory of economic development. In general we agree with Alejandro Portes's blunt observation of "the almost complete exhaustion of earlier modernization theorizing as a source of insights into the situation of underdeveloped nations or of significant questions for research" (1976:80). Most empirical work in this area has come from economists, and their theories dovetail much better with modernization theory than with the dependency/world system paradigm.

not the semiperiphery; the central dynamic of this model of capitalist development is entropy generated by international capital's search for maximum marginal return and the waning power of national states to restrict investment by multinational firms (see Vernon, 1971).

If this view is correct, then the various economic, political, and social institutions of EOI states may be quite different as the process of development begins, but the logic of industrialization will force changes in the same direction. Export-oriented industrialization will be a temporary stage through which states with certain factor endowments, especially those with a poor natural resource base, will pass. Rapidly changing job structures, ratios of capitalization of industrial jobs, and skill and educational levels of the work force in these East Asian nations will make it difficult for this semiperipheral pattern to become institutionalized.

Neoclassical economists have recently refocused the debate over the EOI model. Core states in the 1980s have adopted more protectionist import policies, and demand for manufactured imports has flagged. The EOI strategy may be a less successful route to economic development in the future (Cline, 1982).

Export-oriented industrialization: a statistical portrait

In this section we contrast data for Taiwan, Hong Kong, South Korea, and Singapore with those for several of the groupings of nations suggested by the World Bank in its recent publications: the low-income nations, the middle-income oil-importing nations, and the nineteen industrial market economies.[2] Such contrasts permit us to determine whether EOI states do in fact comprise a grouping of nations empirically meaningful from the standpoint of world development patterns and trends. Data on economic patterns and trends among the East Asian NICs permit us to assess contrasting propositions about development drawn from the two main perspectives on development.

Rate of economic growth

In general dependency theorists have posited that foreign economic penetration and increasing contact with the capitalist world system lead to long-term economic stagnation (see Bornschier et al., 1978; Barrett and Whyte, 1982). Sustained high growth rates among these nations would argue for the necessity for a better articulation of hypotheses that might explain these

2. The two other groupings, the oil-exporting nations and those nations with centrally planned economies, are so different with regard to trade structures and direction of the economy that it is pointless to use them as a basis for comparison with the EOI states.

exceptions. In fact, several theorists have recognized the problem (see Crane, 1982; Amsden, 1979).

All four EOI states experienced rapid economic growth between 1950 and 1980, as Table 1 shows. During the 1960s all four nations surpassed the average growth rate of gross domestic product (GDP) of low-income, middle-income oil-importing, and industrial market economies. During the 1970s growth rates among the four EOI states appear to have converged, and they appear to have been less affected by the slowdown in world economic growth which hit both middle-income oil importers and the industrial market economies.

Per capital growth in gross national product (GNP) is a better measure of improvements in the standard of living of much of the population. Annual per capita growth in GNP from 1960 to 1982 ranges between 6.6 and 7.4 percent for the East Asian NICs, far above the 3.5 percent average for all middle-income oil importers.

Changes in economic structure and sectoral shifts in employment and GDP

Both dependency and modernization theorists acknowledge that structural transformations of the sources of economic growth and employment provide important yardsticks by which to judge progress. Both see the transition from a largely agricultural to a largely industrial economy as the major aim of development. The role of the service sector in industrialization is less clear; both dependency and neoclassical theorists have warned against a premature ballooning of the service sector but give few measures by which to recognize the phenomenon.

TABLE 1. *Average annual growth rates of gross domestic product (GDP) and per capita gross national product (GNP), 1950–82 (percentages)*

	Average annual growth in GDP			Average annual growth in per capita GNP, 1960–82
Country	1950–60	1960–70	1970–82	
Taiwan	7.6	9.2	8.0[a]	6.6[b]
Hong Kong	9.2	10.0	9.9	7.0
South Korea	5.1	8.6	8.6	6.6
Singapore	N.A.	8.8	8.5	7.4
Low-Income Economies	N.A.	4.5	4.5	3.0
Middle-Income Oil Importers	N.A.	5.9	5.4	3.5
Industrial Market Economies	N.A.	5.1	2.8	3.3

a. 1970–77 data
b. 1960–77 data

Sources. 1950–60 data on growth rate of GDP in East Asian EOI states are from IBRD, 1980. All other data are from World Bank, 1980:110–13, 136–37, and 1984:218–19.

Has there been a structural convergence in the economies of the EOI states? Much of the literature on these states gives the impression that shifts in the sectoral distribution of the labor force and in the origin of gross domestic production have been from the agricultural to the industrial sector. The two city-states of Hong Kong and Singapore are special cases where labor flocked to manufacturing from ill-paid and unproductive commercial and service jobs. Among EOI states in 1960, as Table 2 shows, only Singapore and Hong Kong were above the mean level of proportion of labor force in industry among the middle-income oil importers (16 percent); South Korea had an above-average (66 percent) proportion of the labor force in agriculture. In succeeding years industrial labor forces expanded rapidly, especially in Taiwan, South Korea, and Singapore. A similar, rapid expansion in industrial employment had already occurred in Hong Kong in the 1950s.

Expansion of the industrial labor force in the EOI states has been accompanied by little growth in service jobs. Taiwan, South Korea, and Singapore show the classic pattern of a rapid expansion of industrial employment and a proportional shrinkage in the other two sectors (or at most stability in the service sector). Between 1960 and 1981 service-sector employment expanded by 13 percent in South Korea, but the rate of increase was smaller than the rate at which employment expanded in the industrial sector. South Korea is the only nation among the East Asian NICs to have experienced the kind of explosive urban growth which often accompanies rapid growth of the service sector.

Statistics on trends in distribution by sector of origin of gross domestic product (see Table 3) confirm the general pattern found in the sectoral

TABLE 2. *Distribution of labor force by economic sector, 1960 and early 1980s (percentages)*

Country[a]	Agricultural		Industrial[b]		Service	
	1960	1980s	1960	1980s	1960	1980s
Taiwan	56	19	11	41	33	40
Hong Kong	8	1	52	45	40	53
South Korea	66	34	9	28	25	38
Singapore	8	1	23	36	69	63
Middle-Income Oil Importers	60	44	16	21	24	35
Industrial Market Economies	18	6	38	38	44	56
Low-Income Economies	77	72	9	13	14	15

a. Taiwan data are from 1982; Hong Kong data from 1983; South Korean data from 1981; Singaporean data from 1982. All data for the three World Bank groupings of nations are from 1980.

b. Industrial sector includes mining, manufacturing, construction, and utilities.

Sources. Republic of China, 1983; Singapore, 1985; and World Bank, 1980:146–47, and 1982:146–47.

TABLE 3. *Changing sectoral distribution of gross domestic product in East Asian EOI states, by period or selected years*

	Agriculture	Industry	Service	Total
Taiwan				
1950–60	27.8	32.3	39.9	100.0
1960–70	20.6	41.5	37.9	100.0
1970–77	13.0	50.9	36.1	100.0
1978–82	8.4	45.0	46.6	100.0
Hong Kong				
1950–60	3.7	40.7	55.6	100.0
1960–70	2.9	48.4	48.7	100.0
1970–77	1.8	39.0	59.2	100.0
1982	Nil	28.6	71.4	100.0
South Korea				
1950–60	41.8	21.5	36.7	100.0
1960–70	34.6	30.7	34.7	100.0
1970–77	25.8	38.5	35.7	100.0
1982	16.0	39.0	45.0	100.0
Singapore				
1950–60	3.5	31.2	65.3	100.0
1960–70	2.9	36.1	61.0	100.0
1970–77	1.9	45.5	52.6	100.0
1983	Nil	38.0	62.0	100.0

Note. Unit of measurement is percentage distribution of gross domestic product by sector at current factor cost.

Sources. Taiwan 1978–82 data are from DGBAS, 1983; Hong Kong 1982 data from United Nations, 1985; Singapore 1983 data are from United Nations, 1984. All other data are from World Bank, 1980 and 1984.

distribution of labor. Between 1950 and 1982–83 industry's share of GDP increased among the EOI states (except Hong Kong) while agriculture's share declined. In Taiwan, Hong Kong, and South Korea the service sector's contribution to GDP stayed roughly the same over most of the period; in Singapore it declined. All cases exhibit a rapid increase in the service sector after 1977, suggesting the possibility of recent transition to a postindustrial phase in which service activities predominate.

Income inequality

Neoclassical economic historians argue that though income inequality often increases in the early stages of industrialization, the structural changes resulting from the transition will eventually lead to a more equitable distribution of income. Modernization theorists hold that the shift from a system of reward based on ascription to one based on achievment, which accompanies industrialization, will spread income more evenly between household units. Both groups of theorists argue that the increase in the number of educated individuals leads to more competition for well-paid jobs and the increased supply of educated labor in the job market leads to decreases in the relative incomes that can be obtained from elite positions.

Dependency theorists have generally held that open Third World economies will experience greater income inequality. The mechanisms usually responsible for the association between inclusion in the capitalist world system and heightened inequality include unbalanced or enclave industrial development, the opposition of foreign or indigenous elites to income redistribution, the weak position of the labor movement, the destruction of sideline manufactures in peasant households by cheap imports, and the failure of a middle class to develop (see Bornschier et al., 1978; Barrett and Whyte, 1982). In recent years, however, some dependency theorists have examined whether a nation can avoid some or all of these phenomena while still maintaining contact with the capitalist world system.

Table 4 shows the performance of the East Asian NICs with regard to income distribution. The Gini coefficient, an admittedly imperfect measure, has been used by both dependency and neoclassical theorists as a rough international standard of income inequality (see Adelman and Morris, 1971; Bornschier et al., 1978), and so we present this variable first.

The lower the Gini coefficient, the more equitable is the distribution of income across households. By this measure Taiwan ends the period as the less developed country showing the lowest absolute value (Fields, 1984). The decline of the Gini in Taiwan, from .46 in 1961 to .30 in 1980, is probably the largest decline in the Gini in any nonsocialist nation since 1900.

The trends in the Gini coefficients in the other three nations are less impressive. The Gini in Hong Kong drops from .487 in 1966 to .411 in

TABLE 4. *Measures of income inequality in East Asian EOI states*

Gini coefficients among the East Asian EOI states

Hong Kong	South Korea	Singapore	Taiwan
.487 (1966)	.34 (1964)	.499 (1966)	.46 (1961)
.411 (1971)	.33 (1970)	.452 (1975)	.36 (1968)
.435 (1976)	.38 (1976)	.455 (1980)	.32 (1972)
.447 (1981)			.30 (1980)

Distribution of national income across households, by quintiles of all households (ordered by wealth)

	Hong Kong 1980	South Korea 1976	Taiwan 1971	Taiwan 1981
Lowest 20 percent	5.4	5.7	8.7	8.8
Lowest 40 percent	16.2	16.9	21.9	22.7
Highest 20 percent	47.0	45.3	39.2	36.8

Sources. Gini coefficients from Fields, 1984, except for 1981 data for Taiwan, which are from Kuo, 1983:96–97. Quintile shares of national income are from World Bank, 1980:157, and 1984:272–73.

1971, but in the following decade it rises to .447. In Singapore the Gini declines from .499 in 1966 to .452 in 1975, then rises slightly to .455 in 1980.

In South Korea the Gini is only .34 in 1964, which may well be an underestimate, and it rises to .38 in 1976. Although the South Korean trend is toward greater income inequality, it should be remembered that any Gini in the .30 to .40 range indicates a level of income inequality relatively low by international standards.

Another index of income inequality which is more directly linked to poverty is the proportion of national income received by various quintiles of households in a nation. Table 4 presents the income shares of the poorest 20 percent, the poorest 40 percent, and the richest 20 percent of all households. In Hong Kong in 1980, for example, the poorest 20 percent of all households received 5.4 percent of national income while the richest 20 percent received 47 percent of national income.

If we measure income inequality by the proportion of national income which the poorest 20 to 40 percent of all households receive, Hong Kong and South Korea turn in very good performances and Taiwan's achievements are outstanding. Data on these measures are not available for Singapore, but Gini scores suggest that performance would be about the same as in South Korea or Hong Kong.

A basic needs approach to the measurement of poverty looks at such factors as life expectancy, infant mortality rates, and educational opportunities. It makes the East Asian NICs look even more impressive. All four states have achieved life expectancies far greater and levels of infant mortality far lower than what one would predict for nations with their levels of per capita income. In fact, Paul Streeten cites Taiwan and South Korea as cases where investments in basic human needs and the development of human capital laid "the runway for future take-off into self-sustained growth" (1979:95).

Neoclassical economists stress that a variety of factors are responsible for the low levels of income inequality in the gang of four. In all four states a relatively small wage gap of about 20 percent between agriculture and industry resulted in greater income equality. Insignificant minimum wage laws, weak labor unions, and low pay by both governments and multinational firms inhibited the development of a labor aristocracy in the industrial or urban sector (see Fields, 1984:80–81). Gary Fields sees "the differences in wage-setting processes—supply and demand in the East Asian NICs, institutional wage determination elsewhere—as a major reason for their differential rates of economic success" (p. 81).

Dependency theorists, on the other hand, argue that wage rates in a nascent industrial sector usually make minimal contributions to overall patterns of income inequality at the onset of industrialization. What needs to be explained is how governments were able to pursue economic policies that made the distribution of income more equitable before industrialization or during its early stages.

From this perspective, East Asian NICs are unusual. In Taiwan a foreign army oversaw extensive land reform (1950–53). The Republic of China (ROC) government and the dominant Kuomintang party had no ties to the landlord elite and legitimated their position by rewarding poor farmers and the petit bourgeois who benefited from the export-expansion drive after 1960 (see Amsden, 1979; Crane, 1982). Singapore's ruling party, the PDP, had its roots in labor union activity and owed little to the comprador bourgeois who had profited under British colonial rule (see Deyo, 1981). A different argument applies to Hong Kong: the lack of legitimacy of a colonial government and the propinquity of a large and powerful socialist neighbor may have encouraged the colonial government to try to reduce communist agitation among the lower classes, especially after the 1967 riots, through the provision of social services, subsidized housing, and so on. South Korea, too, could be explained as the result of unique historical circumstances: the Korean War disrupted traditional class relations, the American aid program built up infrastructure and distributed broadly based benefits, while the constant threat from the north made the government more sensitive to the possibility of communist movements among dissatisfied workers or peasants.

In short, few dependency theorists deny that these states have low levels of income inequality. Rather, they argue that all four are the products of unique constellations of national and international forces and are not representative of the "usual" workings of neoclassical labor markets. As such, these states are exceptions to trends in most Third World nations. In addition, some theorists argue that the increasing income inequality that will result from contact with the capitalist world system at either the household (Hammer, 1984) or the personal level (Greenhalgh, 1985) is only now beginning to be seen.

Trade and export expansion

Growth in manufactured exports

States, it is generally assumed, start the EOI process a) in a state of autarky or traditional self-sufficiency, or b) heavily dependent on foreign aid or imports, or c) at the import-substitution stage of industrialization. The process centers on rapid growth in volume of trade and especially of manufactured exports relative to growth in gross domestic product.

For dependency theorists, the shift from the export of raw materials to the export of manufactured goods represents progress in asserting national independence over the acquisition and use of modern technology in competitive export industries; it reduces dependency on core states. Modernization and neoclassical theorists are concerned less with the symbolic nature of success in manufactured exports, more with profit and loss, balance-of-payments questions (dependency theory is almost entirely bereft of hypotheses about monetary policy), and whether the technology employed in production is appropriate (see, e.g., Harberger, 1979). Even these theorists, however, generally acknowledge that the change in export composition provides a rough measure of a nation's ability to produce complex goods in an efficient manner.

The postwar growth in volume of trade as a percentage of GDP in Taiwan and South Korea has been dramatic (IMF, 1982). The city-states of Hong Kong and Singapore, on the other hand, have shown little change in trade dependency from levels they achieved earlier as trading entrepôts. In the 1950s the key development for them was the rise of locally produced manufactures, which began to replace the reexport of other goods as a major source of export income.

More important was growth in manufactured exports (see Table 5), the defining feature of export-oriented industrialization. While all four states— with the possible exception of Hong Kong, which had established a strong manufacturing base in the 1950s—had small export manufacturing sectors in 1960, the East Asian NICs have since experienced a huge growth in the export of manufactures. In general, these very high growth rates for merchandise exports were accompanied by a shift to an increasing proportion of manufactured goods within merchandise exports.

Export partner concentration

Given their market-based view of international trade relations, neoclassical economists generally see no necessary connection between economic

TABLE 5. *Growth rates of merchandise exports, manufactured goods as a percentage of merchandise exports, and amount of manufactured exports*

	Average annual growth rate of merchandise exports		Manufactured goods as a percentage of merchandise exports		Value of manufactured exports in 1981[a]
	1960–70	*1970–82*	*1960*	*1982*	
Taiwan	23.7	9.3[b]	N.A.	89	20,101
Hong Kong	12.7	9.4	80	97	20,076
South Korea	34.7	20.2	14	90	19,188
Singapore	4.2	N.A.	26	56	11,212
Low-income economies	5.4	0.3	21	50	N.A.
Middle-income oil importers	6.7	4.0	17	59	N.A.
Industrial market economies	8.5	5.6	66	73	N.A.

a. In millions of current U.S. dollars
b. 1970–78 data
Sources. World Bank, 1980:125, and 1984:234–35; Republic of China, 1983.

growth and export partner concentration. In fact some neoclassical economists argue that hitching a small national economy to a large, rapidly expanding economy such as the United States or Japan during the 1950–73 era would ensure demand for exports. Dependency theorists, however, have identified this variable as one means by which core states can inhibit growth in peripheral economies (Galtung, 1971; Rubinson, 1977). The early specialization of some EOI states in such export goods as textiles and consumer electronics might lead us to expect an initial trend toward a high export partner concentration. However, this concentration ratio should decline as the market in the chief core partner becomes saturated with the goods concerned and the EOI state broadens its capacity for industrial production and finds more profitable markets elsewhere. The early stages of export-oriented industrialization should thus be associated with rapidly increasing export partner concentration, followed by a gradual decline. However, the huge internal markets of such core states as the United States and Japan make it unlikely that export partner concentration will sink below 20 percent for any of these East Asian EOI states in the near future.

Data on export partner concentration for EOI states between 1962 and 1980 appear in Table 6. Not surprisingly, the United States was the major

TABLE 6. *Export partner concentration in East Asian EOI states, 1962–83 (percentage of total exports going to major partner)*

Year	Taiwan	Hong Kong	South Korea	Singapore
1962	37.7 J	20.7 U	42.8 J	27.5 M
1963	31.7 J	20.3 U	28.6 J	29.1 M
1964	30.9 J	22.0 U	32.0 J	33.4 M
1965	30.6 J	28.8 U	35.2 U	31.2 M
1966	24.0 J	28.3 U	38.3 U	26.9 M
1967	26.2 U	37.4 U	42.9 U	31.4 M
1968	32.3 U	41.4 U	51.7 U	26.3 M
1969	38.0 U	N.A.	50.1 U	22.9 M
1970	39.5 U	35.7 U	46.8 U	21.9 M
1971	43.0 U	35.0 U	49.9 U	22.9 M
1972	42.9 U	33.5 U	46.7 U	20.8 M
1973	38.2 U	28.0 U	31.7 U	18.1 M
1974	36.8 U	26.4 U	33.5 U	16.6 M
1975	34.3 U	26.4 U	30.3 U	17.2 M
1976	37.2 U	29.1 U	32.4 U	15.3 M
1977	38.9 U	32.2 U	31.2 U	15.5 U
1978	39.5 U	30.3 U	32.1 U	16.0 U
1979	35.1 U	27.4 U	29.2 U	14.3 M
1980	34.1 U	26.1 U	26.4 U	15.0 M
1981	36.1 U	27.8 U	26.7 U	15.6 M
1982	39.5 U	28.9 U	28.7 U	17.7 M
1983	N.A.	32.3 U	N.A.	18.1 U

Abbreviations. J = Japan, U = United States, M = Malaysia.

Sources. 1962–66 data are from United Nations, 1966; 1967–69 data are from United Nations, 1970–71; 1970–80 data are from United Nations, 1980. Taiwan data from 1978–82 are from DGBAS, 1983.

export target for Taiwan, Hong Kong, and South Korea throughout the period and became Singapore's major export partner in 1977, 1978, and 1983. Japan was the major export partner for its former colonies in the 1950s, but Taiwan and South Korea both shift to the United States as major export partner in the 1960s.

Export concentration ratios for the EOI states vary throughout the period, from about 15 to 50 percent. All of the EOI states followed a pattern of gradually rising then declining export partner concentration, but they begin at different levels and reach different peak concentrations. Hong Kong at 42 percent, South Korea at 52 percent, and Singapore at 32 percent peak between 1967 and 1969, while Taiwan at 43 percent peaks during 1971–72.

Overall, these data seem to confirm the view that rapid export expansion in merchandise and maufactured goods leads to the early penetration of one major market and the gradual spread of exports to other nations as well. Richard Rubinson (1977) and others have seen export partner concentration as leading to dependency on the part of the exporter. Yet the ability of the states of the gang of four to upgrade their technology and to produce more complex and competitive goods may be at least partially due to their diversification of export partners after the initial export surge.

Government revenue and control

As Francisco Ramirez and George Thomas have pointed out, "Within the world capitalist system, state organization and statist ideology have come to dominate societies. This global phenomenon has led to renewed interest in theories within both Marxist and pluralist [i.e., modernization/neoclassical] perspectives" (1981:139). Although neoclassical economic theory does not emphasize the role of the state in economic development, conventional economic historians have certainly paid attention to the state's role in economic development (see, e.g., Aitken, 1959; Checkland, 1982). In fact the whole "growth with equity" school operates on the assumption that the state has sufficient control over the economy for changes in government policy to have a major impact on the redistribution of income and the nature of economic growth.

Dependency theorists have seen the state as both an exogenous and an endogenous variable in the determination of economic development. Some world systems analysts have maintained that states have some degree of relative autonomy; states are more than simply a "committee of the bourgeoisie" and can act in ways that benefit national economic development as a whole. A nation's dependency on the international capitalist system, on the other hand, is often assumed to reduce the fiscal power of the state, rendering it less effective in aiding national economic development (see Ramirez and Thomas, 1981). Dependency theorists have not considered the possibility that too much state intervention can stifle economic development. The lack of success of two models of economic development outside the world system popular with dependency theorists in the mid-1970s, those of Cuba and pre-Deng China, may inspire more scholarly interest in this topic in the future.

State participation in the economy

Alexander Gerschenkron (1962) and others have suggested that late industrializers such as Germany and Russia experienced greater state participation in economic development, but economists have shed less light on the role of the state in more modern open economies. The state's role in amassing capital for producer goods such as iron or coal, as in the late industrializers, or in fostering import-substitution industries, as in Latin America, is clearly not relevant to nations that have based most of their economic development on the export of light industrial goods (see Aitken, 1959; Collier, 1979).

The East Asian EOI states have been particularly successful, Chalmers Johnson has claimed, in establishing key government organs to direct outward-oriented economic development (1981:9–14). But there is dispute about whether government planning had much effect on economic development in Taiwan (see Little, 1979; Barrett, 1983) and whether the South Korean government's attempts to steer the economy in the 1970s had salutary effects (see Browning, 1981).

Dependency theorists have generally felt that "dependency on foreign interests and foreign economic penetration keep the state weak and prevent it from effectively playing its necessary role in protecting domestic industry and fostering economic growth" (Barrett and Whyte, 1982:1072). As a state's contact with the world capitalist economy grows, we might expect to see the government participating less in its economy.

One problem with state strength or government participation in the economy is that the definition of concepts varies from author to author. Here we use a relatively simple measure, the share of GDP contributed by government revenue (used by Rubinson, 1977), to give a sense of the ability of the state to control domestic resources. In general the dependency model predicts that involvement with the world economy and multinational corporations renders a state less effective in mobilizing resources within its own borders. Modernization theorists and neoclassical economists have a range of views on the issue of state control. Some, with Gerschenkron, see the state in many underdeveloped nations as the only effective institution for the mobilization of capital. Other neoclassical economists fear that a premature ballooning of the government sector will result in high taxes on capitalists and entrepreneurs and a decline in capital formation by the private sector.

IMF data (1982) indicate no decline in state revenue power in South

Korea, Singapore, or Taiwan; data on Hong Kong are not available. In fact IMF data show some *rise* in the state's share of revenue, from 21.6 percent of GDP in 1971 to 23.6 percent in 1982 in Taiwan; from 13.8 percent in 1972 to 19.6 percent in 1981 in South Korea; and from 22.1 percent in 1972 to 30.2 percent in Singapore.

Of course, few conclusions can be drawn from this short time series on government revenue; in the Taiwanese case, for example, the 1982 figure is still below the proportion of GDP devoted to government revenue in the 1950s (see Barrett, 1983), primarily because the earlier period featured extensive state holdings of formerly Japanese industrial enterprises. Similarly, the data tell us little about how revenues were used. Yet overall they do support the idea that these national governments have been increasing their resource bases and have more economic control now than they had at the beginning of the EOI process—a conclusion broadly supportive of neoclassical rather than dependency assertions.

Mobilization of capital

Neoclassical theorists generally stress that the high growth rates of the EOI states could be sustained only by high rates of capital formation relative to gross domestic product. As sociologists of underdevelopment lack a coherent theory of how undistorted or balanced development might take place in less developed countries, except perhaps in the autarkic model of Samir Amin (see Bernstein, 1979:91–94), it is difficult to specify the importance of capital and investment for development beyond the core. Many dependency theorists hold firm to the idea that foreign investors will send their profits home and exacerbate the unequal exchange already inherent in the markets of the capitalist world system. But it is unclear what other sources of capital are available in most less developed countries—except, perhaps, a Stalinist squeeze on the rural sector.

Table 7 presents data on gross domestic investment and gross domestic savings as a proportion of GDP in the East Asian EOI states and the other three groups of nations in 1960 and 1982. In 1960 the EOI states were all below the 21 percent mean among middle-income oil importers of gross domestic investment (GDI) as a proportion of GDP. By 1982 all were above the group's GDI mean of 23 percent. The most impressive increase was in Singapore, where GDI increased from 11 percent to 46 percent of gross domestic product over the two decades.

But of greater importance for an assessment of the changing balance between capital self-sufficiency and dependency are the *sources* of investment capital. Gross domestic savings as a percentage of GDP increased only slightly in Third World countries between 1960 and 1982, but statistics on changes in savings in these East Asian countries tell a different story. It is clear that by world standards the East Asian NICs were outstanding in their

TABLE 7. *Gross domestic saving and gross domestic investment as a percentage of gross domestic product, 1960 and 1982*

	Gross domestic saving		Gross domestic investment		Difference: GDS minus GDI	
	1960	*1982*	*1960*	*1982*	*1960*	*1982*
Taiwan	13	33[a]	20	26[a]	−7	7[a]
Hong Kong	6	25	18	29	−12	−4
South Korea	1	24	11	26	−10	−2
Singapore	−3	41	11	46	−14	−5
Middle-income oil importers	19	19	21	23	−2	−4
Industrial market economies	22	20	21	20	1	0
Low-income economies	18	21	19	24	−1	−3

a. 1978 data
Sources. World Bank, 1980 and 1984.

ability to increase rates of domestic savings and reinvestment during this period of rapid industrialization.

The difference between gross domestic investment and gross domestic savings gives a rough measure of the proportion of investment satisfied by foreign capital. Between 1960 and 1982 the proportion of investment supplied by foreign sources increased in middle- and low-income nations. But the East Asian nations, by contrast, significantly reduced their reliance on foreign sources of capital.

Foreign indebtedness

Capital can usually be obtained from other nations through foreign aid, public or private loans, and direct investment from multinational firms. Over the past fifteen years the East Asian NICs have received relatively little foreign aid compared to other Third World nations, and this aid has not been concentrated in areas of the economy which are closely linked to export industries.[3]

Other foreign capital can enter a nation as loans, often directly to the host state, as direct investment in production facilities in the EOI state, or through working capital made available to local contractors through, for instance, letters of credit.[4] With their high levels of exports, a key factor

3. During the 1950s, of course, all of these nations (Taiwan and South Korea in particular) received aid from the United States and other donors. However, the bulk of this aid went for food, infrastructural improvements, and arms. The composition of aid makes it difficult to argue that aid somehow determined that these nations would become major exporters a decade or so later.
4. Throughout this chapter we deal with foreign control of industry primarily in terms of direct investment and trade. Although subcontracting is clearly another major avenue of foreign control, we slight it here because of the difficulty of obtaining reliable or comparable data.

when international bankers evaluate the creditworthiness of a Third World state, EOI states have the potential to run up heavy foreign debts. However, neoclassical economists might expect EOI states to maintain low and relatively stable debt service ratios; such states, after all, usually eschew "big push" strategies for industrial development and instead emphasize the avoidance of domestic inflation, suppression of consumer demand, and maintenance of low wages in export industries. Treatments by dependency theorists of such key financial actors as the World Bank are relatively underdeveloped, but we can safely assume that dependencistas would view such indebtedness as one more way in which core states subvert and distort economic development in peripheral and semiperipheral states.

Over the past decade, world system analysts have also emphasized the importance of bilateral public and private loans from core banks and governments to peripheral and semiperipheral states. Such loans allow these states access to hard currencies, which can be used for the purchase of core manufactured goods, especially for the military, and even agricultural products.

IMF data (1982) show generally moderate and constant levels of externally held public debt (i.e., debt held by foreign banks and governments) as a percentage of gross domestic product in the EOI states during the 1970s. Taiwan and South Korea were most dependent on foreign loans during this period, at around 10 percent. Singapore's debt dependence declined from 5.6 percent in 1972 to 3.1 percent in 1981; data were not available for Hong Kong. Debt service ratios—ratios of payments required on outstanding debts to the dollar value of exports by the debtor nations—are a good indicator of external financial dependency and vulnerability. Asian Development Bank data on this variable show a pattern very similar to that for externally held public debt during the 1970s. Starting from a low debt service ratio of only 2.3 percent in 1965, South Korea jumped to 19 percent in the early 1970s and gradually declined to 13 percent by the early 1980s. Taiwan remained at roughly 4 percent and Singapore at 1 percent during the 1970s, while Hong Kong's ratio remained consistently below 1 percent throughout the period. South Korea's relatively high debt service ratio suggests that its high but uneven growth strategy has increased its vulnerability to debt crises. Although the country has not actually had such a crisis, the sheer size of its debt led international banking analysts to rank it only slightly below such high-risk countries as Argentina and Brazil in the late 1970s and early 1980s.

Foreign investment

Analysts have stressed how EOI states try to maintain a favorable climate for foreign investment through low taxes on corporate profits, provision of industrial infrastructure, suppression of union activity, and so on. Relatively low risk and high rates of return on investment in ventures in EOI states should lead to reinvestment of profits in these nations. Such considerations raise the matter of the changing proportion of foreign investment, particularly the reinvestment of profits made locally by foreign firms, in gross domestic investment.

One significant source of external capital is direct investment by multinational corporations. Annual data on actual investment by multinational corporations in EOI states are surprisingly difficult to find and often, as in investment in real estate, not particularly relevant to the topic at hand. However, the IMF collects data on debits in investment income, a rough measure of the amount of profit generated by foreign firms in the host country (see Rubinson, 1977). The relative importance of foreign investment in a nation and hence, according to dependency theorists, of the degree of leverage of multinationals over host governments can be gauged by computing this debit in investment income as a proportion of gross domestic investment. Comparative data on three of the EOI states are given in Table 8.

Singapore is clearly the member of the gang of four most dependent on multinational investment: it appears to have become more enmeshed with multinational corporations in 1972–73. Both South Korea and Taiwan show continuing growth in multinational involvement between the late 1960s and 1981. The data suggest a very rapid increase in this indicator of foreign investment during recent years.

These various data on foreign and domestic sources of capital suggest

TABLE 8. *Debits in investment income (as a percentage of gross domestic investment) in East Asian EOI states, 1968–81*

	Taiwan	South Korea	Singapore
1968	2.65	1.16	4.27
1969	3.25	1.95	4.05
1970	4.35	3.24	3.96
1971	4.91	5.03	3.45
1972	5.08	7.14	10.73
1973	4.73	6.34	18.20
1974	3.62	5.77	16.14
1975	6.50	7.55	13.89
1976	6.83	7.41	15.68
1977	7.97	7.63	17.51
1978	N.A.	7.20	20.60
1979	N.A.	7.30	22.00
1980	N.A.	14.70	25.40
1981	N.A.	20.50	24.90

Note. Data on debits in investment income were originally given in Special Drawing Rights, which were converted to U.S. dollars using current exchange rates. Gross domestic investment data were originally given in national currencies and were converted to U.S. dollars using current exchange rates.

Sources. Debits in investment data for 1968–72 are from IMF, 1972; similar data for 1973–81 are from IMF, 1979 and 1985. Gross domestic investment data are from IBRD, 1980 and 1985.

several different strategies for its mobilization. South Korea has had relatively low rates of gross domestic savings, due perhaps to low per capita income levels at the beginning of its export push. It has emphasized heavy foreign borrowing but has not encouraged heavy foreign investment. Other data not presented here show a high year-to-year variability in foreign investment; they suggest that the volatility of Korean politics and of foreign investors' responses to that volatility may have made this government strategy a rational choice.

Singapore has relied heavily on multinational corporations as a source of investment capital. High rates of export earnings, however, have produced debt service ratios that were low and stable. Singapore has had high rates of domestic savings, and its government has controlled more of the gross domestic product than that of any other state except Taiwan.

Taiwan has, in many senses, been most successful at combining high domestic savings rates, a government powerful in terms of its control over revenue, and low dependence on foreign loans or multinational investment. Although the latter two measures of capital dependence have gradually increased for Taiwan during the 1970s, they are still far below those of other EOI states.

Conclusion

Our findings suggest that the open EOI strategies pursued in the East Asian NICs are reflected in uniformly high levels of trade reliance but in more varied levels of penetration by foreign capital. Singapore's dependency on direct foreign investment and South Korea's dependency on loan capital are dramatic instances of foreign capital reliance, but more generally external capital has played an important role in EOI development throughout the region. Less easily documented is the extent of reliance on foreign technology, a particularly important factor for development during economic restructuring.

Although these levels of foreign capital reliance are not remarkable by Latin American standards, they do define a pattern of moderate, sustained external economic reliance. But they are accompanied by other data showing strong economic performance marked by rapid, continuing, and relatively equitable growth, successful structural transformation, and very high levels of employment. In addition there are indications of declining economic dependency, including diversification of trading partners and a growth in domestic savings. Finally, in growing state control over domestic revenues we see an apparent strengthening of the economic power of the state. Though hardly definitive, these data generally run counter to dependencista predictions of long-term stagnation, growing inequality, deepening dependency, and a weakening of the state. To the extent that economic dynamism is seen as following from open economic development strategies centering on trade and linkage to foreign capital, these findings offer at least partial support for those working within a neoclassical perspective.

We have provided little analysis of political or social changes within these states or of changes in their core trading partners. A full analysis of trends in trade and investment would require us to address the strategies of multinational firms in the United States and Japan (see Cohen, 1975; Ozawa, 1979; Barnett and Muller, 1974); the goals of the International Monetary Fund and international banks (see Aronson, 1979); and the development of multinational corporations based in the EOI states themselves (see Kumar and McLeod, 1981). If we are to move beyond theory building through categorization to convincing crossnational analysis, then, as Christopher Chase-Dunn (1982) suggests, we must link these institutional changes and the motives of these important actors to their consequences for development in the EOI states.

References

Adelman, Irma, and Cynthia T. Morris. 1971. "Anatomy of Patterns of Income Distribution in Developing Countries." Final research report. U.S. Agency for International Development, CSD-2236.

Aitken, Hugh G. J., ed. 1959. *The State and Economic Growth*. New York: Social Science Research Council.

Amsden, Alice. 1979. "Taiwan's Economic History: A Case of 'Etatisme' and a Challenge to Dependency Theory." *Modern China* 5:314–380.

Aronson, Jonathan D., ed. 1979. *Debt and the Less Developed Countries*. Boulder: Westview.

Balassa, Bela. 1978. "Exports and Economic Growth: Further Evidence." *Journal of Development Economics* 5:181–189.

Barnett, Robert, and Ronald Muller. 1974. *Global Reach*. New York: Simon & Schuster.

Barrett, Richard E. 1983. "State and Economy on Taiwan, 1960–1980." Mimeo.

Barrett, Richard E., and Martin K. Whyte. 1982. "Dependency Theory and Taiwan: Analysis of a Deviant Case." *American Journal of Sociology* 87:1064–1089.

Bernstein, Henry. 1979. "Sociology of Underdevelopment versus Sociology of Development?" In David Lehman, ed. *Development Theory: Four Critical Studies*. London: Cass.

Bornschier, Volker, et al. 1978. "Cross-national Evidence of the Effects of Foreign Investment and Aid on Economic Growth and Inequality: A Survey of Findings and a Reanalysis." *American Journal of Sociology* 84:651–683.

Browning, E. S. 1981. "East Asia: In Search of a Second Economic Miracle." *Foreign Affairs* 60:123–147.

Chase-Dunn, Christopher. 1982. "The Uses of Formal Comparative Research on Dependency Theory and the World-system Perspective." In Harry Makler,

Alberto Martinelli, and Neil Smelser, eds. *The New International Economy*. Beverly Hills: Sage.

Checkland, S. G. 1982. "Stages and the State: How Do They Relate?" In Charles P. Kindleberger and Guido di Tella, eds. *Economics in the Long View*. New York: New York University Press.

Chow, Steven C., and Gustav Papenek. 1981. "Laissez-faire, Growth and Equity: Hong Kong." *Economic Journal* 91:466–485.

Cline, William R. 1982. "Can the East Asian Model of Development Be Generalized?" *World Development* 10:81–90.

Cohen, Benjamin J. 1975. *Multinational Firms and Asian Exports*. New Haven: Yale University Press.

Collier, David, ed. 1979. *The New Authoritarianism in Latin America*. Princeton: Princeton University Press.

Crane, George T. 1982. "The Taiwanese Ascent: System, State and Movement in the World-economy." In Friedman, ed., 1982.

Deyo, Frederic C. 1981. *Dependent Development and Industrial Order*. New York: Praeger.

DGBAS (Directorate-General of Budget, Accounting, and Statistics). 1983. *Statistical Yearbook of the Republic of China*. Taipei: Executive Yuan.

Fields, Gary S. 1984. "Employment, Income Distribution and Economic Growth in Six Small Open Economies." *Economic Journal* 94:74–83.

Friedman, Edward, ed. 1982. *Ascent and Decline in the World-System*. Beverly Hills: Sage.

Galtung, Johan. 1971. "A Structural Theory of Imperialism." *Journal of Peace Research* 8:81–117.

Gerschenkron, Alexander. 1962. *Economic Backwardness in Historical Perspective*. Cambridge: Harvard University Press.

Greenhalgh, Susan. 1985. "Sexual Stratification: The Other Side of Growth with Equity in East Asia." *Population and Development Review* 11:265–314.

Hammer, Heather-Jo. 1984. "Comment on 'Dependency Theory and Taiwan: Analysis of a Deviant Case.'" *American Journal of Sociology* 89:932–937.

Harberger, Arnold C. 1979. "Perspectives on Capital and Technology in Less-developed Countries." In Kenneth P. Jameson and Charles K. Wilber, eds. *Directions in Economic Development*. Notre Dame: University of Notre Dame Press.

IBRD (International Bank for Reconstruction and Development). 1980 and 1985. *World Tables*. Washington, D.C.

IMF (International Monetary Fund). Annual. *Government Finance Statistics*. Washington, D.C.

Johnson, Chalmers. 1981. "Introduction: The Taiwan Model." In James C. Hsiung, ed. *Contemporary Republic of China: The Taiwan Experience, 1950–1980*. New York: Praeger.

Kumar, Krishna, and Maxwell G. McLeod, eds. 1981. *Multinationals from Developing Countries*. Lexington: Lexington Books.

Kuo, Shirley. 1983. *The Taiwan Economy in Transition*. Boulder: Westview.

Little, Ian. 1979. "An Economic Reconnaissance." In Walter Galenson, ed. *Economic Growth and Structural Change in Taiwan*. Ithaca: Cornell University Press.

Ozawa, Terutomo. 1979. *Multinationalism, Japanese Style*. Princeton: Princeton University Press.

Portes, Alejandro. 1976. "On the Sociology of National Development." *American Journal of Sociology* 82:55–85.

Ramirez, Francisco O., and George M. Thomas. 1981. "Structural Antecedents and Consequences of Statism." In Richard Rubinson, ed. *Dynamics of World Development*. Beverly Hills: Sage.

Republic of China. 1983. *Statistical Abstract of the Republic of China*. Taipei: Executive Yuan.

Rubinson, Richard. 1977. "Dependence, Government Revenue, and Economic Growth, 1955–1970." *Studies in Comparative International Development* 12:3–28.

Singapore. 1985. *Singapore Monthly Digest of Statistics*. Singapore.

Streeten, Paul. 1979. "A Basic-needs Approach to Economic Development." In Kenneth P. Jameson and Charles K. Wilber, eds. *Directions in Economic Development*. Notre Dame: University of Notre Dame Press.

United Nations. Annual. *Yearbook of International Trade Statistics*. New York.

United Nations. 1984. *United Nations Statistical Yearbook*. New York.

United Nations. 1985. *Monthly Bulletin of Statistics*. July. New York.

Vernon, Raymond. 1971. *Sovereignty at Bay: The Multinational Spread of U.S. Enterprises*. New York: Basic.

World Bank. Annual. *World Development Report*. New York: Oxford University Press.

The origins and development of the Northeast Asian political economy: industrial sectors, product cycles, and political consequences Bruce Cumings

East Asia today is the center of world economic dynamism. Japan in 1980 became number two in the world in gross national product (GNP). Its achievement is complemented by the "gang of four," South Korea, Taiwan, Singapore, and Hong Kong. These four East Asian developing countries now account for almost twice the export totals of the entire remainder of the Third World, and their growth rates are usually the highest in the entire world. Singapore and Hong Kong are difficult to categorize: are they nations? industrial platforms? city-states? My concern in this chapter will be with the northeastern portion of the East Asian basin: Japan, Korea, and Taiwan.

These four nations (including the two Koreas) in 1978, before the second oil shock, accounted for a combined GNP of about $1.06 trillion, a population of 190 million, an annual growth rate of 10 percent, and perhaps $232 billion of world trade. This compared to a U.S. GNP in 1978 of about $2 trillion, a population of 218 million, a growth rate of 4 percent, and world trade of $326 billion. Apart from the United States, no other region had a higher GNP—the combined GNP of the European Economic Community in 1978 was $1.95 trillion, less than double the Northeast Asian figure, and the average growth rate in the EEC was 2.9 percent. The Soviet Union had a larger population but a lower GNP, and a growth rate estimated at 3.1 percent.

Since the onset of export-led growth in the mid 1960s the GNPs of both Taiwan and South Korea have grown by an average of about 10 percent per year, with manufacturing expansion often doubling that figure. North Korea, according to official statistics, had the highest rate of agricultural growth in the entire world in the period 1970–78, and since the Korean War its industrial production has grown at the highest rate in the socialist world.[1] In the space

I would like to thank the following people for helpful comments: Peter Gourevitch, Albert Hirschman, Peter Katzenstein, Stephen Krasner, James Kurth, Jeffrey Paige, and Immanuel Wallerstein.

1. U.S. Central Intelligence Agency (CIA), *Handbook of Economic Statistics 1979* (Washington, D.C.: National Foreign Assessment Center, 1980).

of one generation these countries have transformed their economic structures such that the agrarian sector, including upwards of 60 percent of the population in 1960, now accounts for less than 20 percent of GNP. It is little wonder that American developmentalists speak of miracles in Taiwan and South Korea, or that socialist economists like Joan Robinson speak of a miracle in North Korea. For reasons of space, however, I shall limit this analysis primarily to South Korea and Taiwan.

A glance back before World War II suggests that we may need a longer perspective to capture the true dimensions of this growth. Japan's interwar annual growth rate of 4.5 percent doubled the rates of interwar Europe; colonial manufacturing growth in Korea, 1910–1940, averaged 10 percent per annum, and overall GNP growth was also in the 4 percent range, as was Taiwan's. No nation's heavy-industrial growth rate was steeper than Japan's in the period 1931–1940; in the textile sector, Japan's automation was ahead of Europe's in 1930. Yet new research now suggests that both Korea and Taiwan experienced higher GDP growth rates than Japan between 1911 and 1938 (Japan, 3.36%; Korea, 3.57%; Taiwan, 3.80%).[2]

In the past century Japan, Korea, and Taiwan have also moved fluidly through a classic product-cycle industrialization pattern, Korea and Taiwan following in Japan's wake. Japan's industrialization has gone through three phases, the last of which is just beginning. The first phase began in the 1880s, with textiles the leading sector, and lasted through Japan's rise to world power. In the mid-1930s Japan began the second, heavy phase, based on steel, chemicals, armaments, and ultimately automobiles; it did not begin to end until the mid-1960s. The third phase emphasizes high-technology "knowledge" industries such as electronics, communications, computers, and silicon-chip microprocessors.

Within Japan each phase, in good product-cycle fashion, has been marked by strong state protection for nascent industries, adoption of foreign technologies, and comparative advantages deriving from cheap labor costs, technological innovation, and "lateness" in world time. Each phase involved a bursting forth into the world market that always struck foreign observers as abrupt and unexpected, thus inspiring fear and loathing, awe and admiration.

For Japan the product cycle has not been mere theory; it has melded with conscious practice to make Japan the preeminent example of upward mobility in the world system through successive waves of industrial competition. In the 1930s Kaname Akamatsu elaborated his famous "flying geese" model of industrial development in follower countries, predating Raymond Vernon's

2. G. C. Allen, *Japan's Economic Policy* (London: Macmillan, 1980), p. 1; see also Kazushi Ohkawa and Henry Rosovsky, *Japanese Economic Growth: Trend Acceleration in the Twentieth Century* (Stanford, Calif.: Stanford University Press, 1973), pp. 74, 82–83. For the comparisons of growth rates with Korea and Taiwan see Mataji Umemura and Toshiyoki Mizoguchi, eds., *Quantitative Studies on Economic History of Japan Empire* [sic], *1890–1940* (Tokyo: Hitotsubashi University, 1981), p. 64.

work by several decades.[3] Time-series curves for imports, import-substitution for the domestic market, and subsequent exports of given products tend to form a pattern like wild geese flying in ranks. The cycle in given industries— textiles, steel, automobiles, light electronics—of origin, rise, apogee, and de- cline has not simply been marked, but often mastered, in Japan; in each industrial life cycle there is also an appropriate jumping off place, that is, a point at which it pays to let others make the product or at least provide the labor. Taiwan and Korea have historically been receptacles for declining Japanese industries. Adding agriculture gives a pattern in which in the first quarter of this century Korea and Taiwan substituted for the diminishing Japanese agricultural sector, exporting rice and sugar in great amounts to the mother country (Taiwan was annexed in 1895, Korea in 1910). By the mid-1930s Japan had begun to export iron and steel, chemical, and electric- generation industries, although much more to Korea than to Taiwan. In the 1960s and 1970s, both smaller countries have received declining textile and consumer electronic industries from Japan (as well as from the United States), and in the 1980s some Japanese once again speak of sending steel and autos in the same direction.

Thus if there has been a miracle in East Asia, it has not occurred just since 1960; it would be profoundly ahistorical to think that it did. Further- more, it is misleading to assess the industrialization pattern in any one of these countries: such an approach misses, through a fallacy of disaggregation, the fundamental unity and integrity of the regional effort in this century. Yet ahistorical disaggregation is the most common approach; it is reinforced by the many differences between the three countries, and by the dominant modernization school in U.S. academic circles, which has produced by far the greatest quantity of literature on East Asian development. The three countries speak different languages, have different histories, different cultures (albeit all traditionally influenced by China), and, in Korea and Japan, two highly homogeneous but quite different ethnic constituencies. Modernization theory and these basic differences have reinforced a tendency, at least since 1945, to view each country apart from the others and to examine single- country trajectories. Furthermore, critical and radical (or nonmodernization) developmentalists have tended to ignore East Asia, focusing instead on Latin America and Africa. Those that do study East Asia usually study the Chinese revolution, which produced many things but not stunning industrial development.

A country-by-country approach is incapable of accounting for the re- markably similar trajectories of Korea and Taiwan. Thus, specialists on Korea argue that its development success "is unique in world history";[4]

3. Kiyoshi Kojima, *Japan and a New World Economic Order* (Boulder, Colo.: Westview, 1977), pp. 150–51.
4. L. L. Wade and B. S. Kim, *Economic Development of South Korea: The Political Economy of Success* (New York: Praeger, 1978), p. vi.

Taiwan specialists make similar claims. Thus, Taiwan specialists cite the apparent "paradox" of Taiwanese development—that it developed in a fashion that contradicts the assumptions of dependency theorists—while not breathing a word about Korea.[5] Both groups of specialists omit the essential Japanese context of Korean and Taiwanese development. Conventional neo-classical economists attribute growth in Taiwan or Korea to specific attributes of each nation: factor endowments, human capital in the form of a reasonably educated workforce, comparative advantage in labor cost, and so on. Modernization theorists offer a diffuse menu of explanations for Taiwan or Korea, ranging from the discipline or "rationality" of traditional Confucianism, through various cultural arguments, the passion for education, U.S. aid and advice, and the presumed "natural" workings of the product cycle, to the diffusion of advanced education, science, and technology.[6] Political arguments about the alleged big power of small states, while addressing one facet of East Asian political development, beg the question why Korea and Taiwan but not Guatemala or Burma. Product-cycle arguments, unlike the others, do have the virtue of linking Japanese with Korean and Taiwanese development, but their proponents do not explain why the cycle has conformed to theory in Northeast Asia so much better than elsewhere.

This chapter asserts that an understanding of the Northeast Asian political economy can only emerge from an approach that posits the systemic inter-action of each country with the others, and of the region with the world at large. Rapid upward mobility in the world economy has occurred, through the product cycle and other means, within the context of two hegemonic systems: the Japanese imperium to 1945, and intense, if diffuse, American hegemony since the late 1940s. Furthermore, only considerations of context can account for the similarities in the Taiwanese and South Korean political economies. Simultaneously, external hegemonic forces have interacted with different domestic societies in Korea and Taiwan to produce rather different political outcomes: this, too, has been characteristic throughout the century. Korea was more rebellious in 1910; it is more rebellious today. I seek, therefore, to explain both the similarities in economic development and the differences in political consequences in the three countries.

Some theoretical considerations

The concept of the product cycle offers a useful way to understand change and mobility within and among nations. This theory of the middle range

5. See Susan Greenhalgh, "Dependency, Distribution and the Taiwan 'Paradox,' " and Denis Simon, "U.S. Assistance, Land Reform, and Taiwan's Political Economy" (both papers presented at the Taiwan Political Economy Workshop, Columbia University, New York, 18–20 December 1980).

6. For a good example of this line of reasoning see chap. 2 in Edward S. Mason et al., *The Economic and Social Modernization of the Republic of Korea* (Cambridge: Harvard University Press, 1980).

has the virtue of being compatible with liberal, neomercantile, and Marxist or world system theories. That is, the neoclassical liberal can make the Ricardian assumption that a system of open exchange (free trade) provides the structure in which nations maximize their comparative advantages and thus create a world-ranging and mutually beneficial division of labor. The mercantilist can make the Listian assumption that free trade is the ideology of the early-arriving hegemonic nation, and that to catch up the follower nation needs not laissez-faire but a strong state, not open systems but protectionist barriers. For a world system analyst the product cycle is one among several means of upward and downward mobility; the core assumption is the existence of a capitalist world economy that, at least in our time, is the only world-ranging system. Thus, the core power pursues an imperialism of free trade, and rising powers use strong states, protectionist barriers, or a period of withdrawal and self-reliant development (the Stalinist or socialist option) as means to compete within the world system.[7]

All three theories assume that the product cycle is a middle-range explanation for the waxing and waning of industrial sectors, and that it is imbedded in some larger structure—an international division of labor or a world economy. All likewise assume intense competition—a race—for development; nations swim upstream, against the current, or are carried backward. Both Liberal and Marxist theory postulate a utopia to end the struggle: a world of free trade and the greatest good for the greatest number, or societies submitted to a rational plan under a world socialist government. Mercantilists are content to postulate a survival of the fittest, by whatever means necessary.

The world system perspective posits a tripartite division of the globe: core, semiperiphery, and periphery. A tripartite hierarchy appeals to many analysts: Aristotle was the first to note the social stability provided by a broad middle class, and Charles Kindleberger pointed out many years ago that in a hierarchy of top, middle, and low the middle functions "to discipline the third member in forms of behavior which he should adopt toward the first. The relations of the middle class to the wealthy and to the working classes may partake of this character. . . ."[8]

Immanuel Wallerstein, a sociologist by academic origin, casts onto the global system the classic role of the middle class in providing social stability,

7. For references, see David P. Calleo and Benjamin M. Rowland, *America and the World Political Economy* (Bloomington: Indiana University Press, 1973), and Jacob Viner, "Power versus Plenty as Objectives of Foreign Policy in the Seventeenth and Eighteenth Centuries," *World Politics* 1 (October 1948), on mercantilism and neomercantilism; Raymond Vernon, *Sovereignty at Bay: The Multinational Spread of U.S. Enterprises* (New York: Basic Books, 1971), on the product cycle and free trade; Immanuel Wallerstein, "The Rise and Future Demise of the World Capitalist System: Concepts for Comparative Analysis," in Wallerstein, ed., *The Capitalist World-Economy* (New York: Cambridge University Press, 1979), for the world system approach.

8. Charles P. Kindleberger, "Group Behavior and International Trade," *Journal of Political Economy*, February 1951, p. 42.

disciplining and mediating those below to serve the interests of those above, and being an agency of change, through class or individual social mobility.[9] This is the role for the semiperiphery in the world; the means of upward mobility are wars, diplomacy, alliances, product cycles, and so on.[10]

What about the "world upper class," or core? I use the term *hegemony* to refer to core-state behavior. By hegemony I do not mean the Gramscian notion of class ethos, nor a crude Marxist notion of ruling class or imperial domination, nor the diffuse contemporary Chinese usage, referring to big-power domination in all its manifestations. Nor do I use it in Robert Keohane and Joseph Nye's sense "in which one state is able and willing to determine and maintain the essential rules by which relations among states are governed."[11] I mean by hegemony the demarcation of outer limits in economics, politics, and international security relationships, the transgression of which carries grave risks for any nonhegemonic nation.

In the postwar American case, hegemony meant the demarcation of a "grand area."[12] Within that area nations oriented themselves toward Washington rather than Moscow; nations were enmeshed in a hierarchy of economic and political preferences whose ideal goal was free trade, open systems, and liberal democracy but which also encompassed neomercantile states and authoritarian politics; and nations were dealt with by the United States through methods ranging from classic negotiations and trade-offs (in regard to nations sharing Western traditions or approximating American levels of political and economic development) to wars and interventions (in the periphery or Third World), to assure continuing orientation toward Washington. The hegemonic ideology, shared by most Americans but by few in the rest of the world, was the Tocquevillean or Hartzian ethos of liberalism and internationalism, assuming a born-free country that never knew class conflict. Not a colonial or neocolonial imperialism, it was a new system of empire begun with Wilson and consummated by Roosevelt and Acheson. Its very breadth—its non-territoriality, its universalism, and its open systems (within the grand area)—

9. Wallerstein, "Rise and Future Demise."

10. Like most interesting concepts, these categories of core, semiperiphery, and periphery have problems of definition and scope, but they are useful for locating nations in the world economy. A similar set of categories is Krasner's tripartite distinction between makers, breakers, and takers among nations. See Stephen D. Krasner, "US Commercial and Monetary Policy: Unravelling the Paradox of External Strength and Internal Weakness," in Peter J. Katzenstein, ed., *Between Power and Plenty: Foreign Economic Policies of Advanced Industrial States* (Madison: University of Wisconsin Press, 1978), pp. 51–52.

11. See C. Fred Bergsten, Robert O. Keohane, and Joseph S. Nye Jr., "International Economics and International Politics: A Framework for Analysis," in Bergsten and Lawrence B. Krause, eds., *World Politics and International Economics* (Washington, D.C.: Brookings, 1975), p. 14; also Keohane and Nye, *Power and Interdependence: World Politics in Transition* (Boston: Little, Brown, 1977), pp. 42–46.

12. The "grand area" was a concept used in Council on Foreign Relations planning in the early 1940s for the postwar period. See Laurence H. Shoup and William Minter, *Imperial Brain Trust: The Council on Foreign Relations and U.S. Foreign Policy* (New York: Monthly Review Press, 1977), pp. 135–40.

made for a style of hegemony that was more open than previous imperialisms to competition from below. Indeed, we may eventually conclude that this was its undoing.

This form of hegemony establishes a hierarchy of nations, therefore, but not one that is frozen: it may render obsolescent the development of underdevelopment. Instead, far more than the German hegemony in Eastern Europe that Albert Hirschman analyzed or the Japanese unilateral, colonial hegemony, it is open to rising talent from below and particularly to disparities of attention (what Burke, speaking of England and the American colonial revolution, called "wise and salutary neglect") that give leverage and room for maneuver to dependencies. As Hirschman put it more recently, the dependent country "is likely to pursue its escape from domination more actively and energetically than the dominant country will work on preventing this escape."[13] Finally, this form of hegemony also fused security and economic considerations so inextricably that the United States has never been sure whether economic competition from its allies is good or bad for grand-area security. As a result, inattention often becomes catatonia (witness U.S. policy toward Japan in the past decade). A diffuse hegemony, then, it perhaps merits a diffuse definition: we know it in the doing, and we mark it more in retrospect. American postwar hegemony grew less out of specific human design (although Dean Acheson as architect would come close) than out of the long-term reaction of hegemonic interests to the flow of events.

These various terms and concepts are applicable to the international system. But Kindleberger notes in a seminal paper that foreign-policy actions and reactions are imbedded "deep in the structure of society." In one nation (e.g., Germany) class may be important in understanding foreign economic policy; in another (e.g., Britain) it may not.[14] Likewise, in nations the state may be strong or weak, and empirical investigation suggests that this bears little relationship to Wallerstein's strained argument that state power recedes as one climbs down the hierarchy from core to periphery. In Japan, Taiwan, and Korea, much of their success and their variance from one another may be explained by reference to state and society. For the strength of states, we can use Alexander Gerschenkron's sequencing argument and Stephen Krasner's simple scheme: strong states can formulate policy goals independently of particular groups, they can change group or class behavior, and they can change the structure of society.[15] (After all the inflated verbiage, this is fundamentally what Nicos Poulantzas had in mind when he referred

13. Albert O. Hirschman, *National Power and the Structure of Foreign Trade* (1945; rpt. Berkeley: University of California Press, 1980), pp. ix–x; Burke is quoted in Hirschman.

14. Kindleberger, "Group Behavior," pp. 43–44, 46. The *locus classicus* for such reasoning is now James R. Kurth, "The Political Consequences of the Product Cycle: Industrial History and Political Outcomes,"*International Organization* 33 (Winter 1979), pp. 1–34.

15. Krasner, "US Commercial and Monetary Policy," p. 60; Alexander Gerschenkron, *Economic Backwardness in Historical Perspective* (Cambridge: Harvard University Press, 1962).

to the "relative autonomy" of capitalist states.)[16] Japan, as Krasner notes, rates as very strong on this scale; so, in the later periods, do South Korea and Taiwan. Indeed, these three strong states go far toward explaining their product-cycle virtuosity.

Finally, there is society, by which I mean both the conventional notion of a system structured by groups and classes and Karl Polanyi's sense of society being the human web that reacts to market penetration, capitalist relations, and industrialization in varying but always critical ways around the globe.[17] Attention to society and its reactions can avoid the reductionism of some Wallersteinians who place inordinate emphasis on the structuring effect of the world system on national societies, as if they are putty to be shaped and molded. In fact, in the Northeast Asian case the three different societies deeply affect the development of the national and regional political economies.

The origin of the Northeast Asian political economy, 1900-1945

However much it may pain the majority of Korean nationalists and the minority of Taiwanese nationalists, the place to begin in comprehending the region's economic dynamism is with the advent of Japanese imperialism. Japan's imperial experience differed from the West's in several fundamental respects.[18] It involved the colonization of contiguous territory; it involved the location of industry and an infrastructure of communications and transportation in the colonies, bringing industry to the labor and raw materials rather than vice versa; and it was accomplished by a country that always saw itself as *dis*advantaged and threatened by more advanced countries— Japan was "weak and puny," Professor Etō Shinkichi has written, and this perception affected the entire colonial enterprise. All of these characteristics made themselves felt most strongly in Korea, the closest and always the most important of Japan's possessions.

Japan entered upon colonization late, in a world with hundreds of years of colonial experience and where, as King Leopold of Belgium said three years before the Meiji Restoration, "the world has been pretty well pillaged already." Most of the good colonial territories were already spoken for; indeed, for several decades Japan faced the possibility of becoming a dependency, perhaps even a colony, of one of the Western powers. With imperial attention mostly focused on China and its putative vast market, however, Japan got

16. Nicos Poulantzas, *Political Power and Social Classes* (London: NLB, 1975), part 4.
17. Karl Polanyi, *The Great Transformation* (New York: Farrar & Rinehart, 1944).
18. See Bruce Cumings, *The Origins of the Korean War: Liberation and the Emergence of Separate Regimes* (Princeton: Princeton University Press, 1981), chap. 1. On Taiwan see Samuel Ho, *The Economic Development of Taiwan 1860-1970* (New Haven: Yale University Press, 1978), pp. 26, 32; he puts a similar emphasis on the role of the colonial state in Taiwan.

what E. H. Norman called a "breathing space" in which to mobilize its resources and resist the West. Its success was manifest in victories over China
and Russia within the decade 1895 to 1905, but that should blind us neither
to Japan's perception of its position as poised between autonomy and dependency in a highly competitive world system nor to the very real threats
posed by the West. While the British and the Americans marveled at Japanese
industrial and military prowess at the turn of the century, the Kaiser sent
his famous "yellow peril" mural to the Tsar and the French worried about
Japanese skills being tied to a vast pool of Chinese labor, posing a dire threat
to the West. In such circumstances the Japanese were hardly prone to worry
about the sensitivities of Taiwanese or Koreans but rather to see them as
resources to be deployed in a global struggle; and, of course, Japan never
lacked for Westerners (including socialists like Sydney and Beatrice Webb,
and hardy Americans like Theodore Roosevelt) who were quick to justify
Japanese aggression.[19]

The relative lateness of the endeavor imparted several additional characteristics: first, a posthaste, anticipatory quality in colonial planning; second,
an extraordinary interest in and mimicking of previous colonial experience;
third, a rather quick anachronism to the whole enterprise; last, little choice
but to colonize contiguous neighbors.

Many have spoken of Japan's defensive reform and industrialization after
1868; and so it was with Japan's colonial expansion—offensive to Taiwanese
and Koreans, it looked defensive to Japanese planners in a predatory world.
And, much like reform at home, the colonial effort had an anticipatory,
preconceived, planned aspect. The characteristic figure in this architectonic
endeavor was therefore not an adventurous Cecil Rhodes type but an ad-
ministrator and planner like Gōto Shimpei, who played the architect in the
Taiwan colony.

Like MITI in the Japanese economy today, the colonizers exercised sharp
"administrative guidance" in shaping colonial society. These planners would
both mimic the West and seek to avoid its errors. Thus, Itō Hirobumi discovered the secret of the German state, colonial administrators studied French
policies of assimilation, architects designed railroad stations in the classic
style for Seoul and Taipei. When Europeans witnessed Japanese behavior,
they were looking into a mirror of their own behavior.

There was also something anachronistic about Japanese imperialism, perhaps not in the seizure of Taiwan but certainly by 1910 with Korea, and a
fortiori 1931 with Manchuria. Japan since the 1880s has always seemed in
some vague way to be about twenty years behind European and American
developments, and therefore to be persisting in the lathered pursuit of things

19. Jean-Pierre Lehmann, *The Image of Japan: From Feudal Isolation to World Power,
1850–1905* (London: Allen & Unwin, 1978), p. 178; J. M. Winter, " The Webbs and the Non-
White World: A Case of Socialist Racialism," *Journal of Contemporary History* 9 (January
1974), pp. 181–92.

the West was tiring of; today, for example, an automobile boom runs in Japan some two decades after the boom began ending in the United States. By 1910 strong anti-imperialist movements had developed in England and the United States, and shortly thereafter Woodrow Wilson was not only calling for self-determination in colonies but pursuing an American neo-imperialism that envisioned organizing great spaces in the world for free trade and competition, thereby branding the exclusive possession of colonial territory as outmoded or immoral, or both. Another great power, Russia, emerged from World War I with an equally potent idea: self-determination and national revolution for colonial peoples. Wilson and Lenin both changed the rules of the game for latecomers like Japan. The swashbuckling, sword-carrying colonist suddenly looked like a museum exhibit to the modern world that Japan took as its constant reference after 1868. Thus, seeking to anticipate every eventuality, Japan met an unanticipated consequence: progressives proclaimed Japan to be a backward exemplar of 19th-century ideas.

In order to acquire colonies in the first place, Japan had to maximize its comparative advantages by seeking territory close to home. The West, always stretched in East Asia, could in judo-like fashion be dispatched in the near reaches of Japan. Thus, unlike most colonial powers Japan colonized neighboring countries, making feasible a close, tight integration of colony to metropole. Contiguity also facilitated the settling of colonial migrants, especially from among an insular, homogeneous people who abhor distance from the native source, and could raise the potential of extraordinarily rapid exchange-time in market relations. Japan quickly enhanced this potential through laying railroads, opening ports, and making heavy investments in communications.

Lateral expansion also meant that Japan preferred the military, in the form of a land army resident in the colony, as its coercive force—not a navy or a tiny cadre of colonial ministers, *à la* Britain. As Hannah Arendt once suggested, lateral imperialism is usually more repressive, and this was true of Japanese colonialism.

In Korea and Taiwan the colonial power emphasized not only military and police forms of control but also development under strong state auspices. This was particularly true after the Depression, when Japan used a "mighty trio" of state organization, central banking, and *zaibatsu* conglomerates to industrialize Korea and parts of Manchuria. Although strong in both colonies, the state in Korea bulked even larger in the economy than in Taiwan, as figures on government capital formation show.[20] Much like its role in the decades after the Meiji Restoration, the state substituted for an absent or at most incipient entrepreneurial class. As David Landes writes of Japan,

It was the State that conceived modernization as a goal and industrialization as a means, that gave birth to the new economy in haste and

20. Umemura and Mizoguchi, *Quantitative Studies*, pp. 70–77.

pushed it unrelentingly as an ambitious mother her child prodigy. And though the child grew and developed its own resources, it never overcame the deformity imposed by this forced nurture.[21]

The deformations were even more marked in Korea and Taiwan, where the colonial state stood above and apart from societies that had not yet reached Japan's level of social, political, and economic development. Thus, a highly articulated, disciplined, penetrating colonial bureaucracy substituted both for the traditional regimes and for indigenous groups and classes that under "normal" conditions would have accomplished development themselves. The colonial state replaced an old weak state, holding society at bay so to speak; this experience goes a long way toward explaining the subsequent (post 1945) pronounced centralization of Taiwan and both Koreas, and has provided a model for state-directed development in all three.

Japan's administrative and coercive colonialism took two quite different societies and political economies, and molded them into look-alikes.[22] The first act was a major cadastral survey and land reform: 1898–1906 in Taiwan, 1910–18 in Korea. North-South trunk railroad lines were laid. Ports were opened. In Taiwan, cane sugar and to a lesser extent rice were promoted; by 1938 Taiwan was second only to Cuba in sugar exports. Korean rice exports expanded by leaps and bounds in the 1920s. Yet agricultural growth was stronger in Taiwan than in Korea; colonial administrators remarked that what could be done with economic incentives in Taiwan required coercion in Korea.

Here we have our first important societal reaction to hegemonic penetration. Whereas Taiwan had for the most part only an aboriginal population until the 18th century, and a small class of Chinese absentee landlords by the end of the 19th century (the *ta-tsu-hu*), Korea had a powerful landed class of centuries' duration, in which property holding and aristocratic privilege were potently mixed.[23] The Japanese found it expedient to root landlords more firmly to the ground, as a means of disciplining peasants and extracting rice for the export market. The landlord class therefore persisted through to 1945, although by then it was tainted by association with imperial rule. In Taiwan, by contrast, land reform at the turn of the century eliminated absentee lords and fostered a class of entrepreneurial landowners, emerging "from below" as they had in Japan. By 1945 most Taiwan landowners held less land than their Korean counterparts and were far more productive. Whereas tenancy

21. David S. Landes, "Japan and Europe: Contrasts in Industrialization," in William W. Lockwood, ed., *The State and Economic Enterprise in Japan* (Princeton: Princeton University Press, 1965), p. 182.

22. Cumings, *Origins*, chaps. 1 and 2; Ho, *Economic Development*, pp. 28–57; also Ching-yuan Lin, *Industrialization in Taiwan, 1946–1972: Trade and Import-Substitute Policies for Developing Countries* (New York: Praeger, 1973), pp. 13–28.

23. James B. Palais, *Politics and Policy in Traditional Korea* (Cambridge: Harvard University Press, 1975), pp. 1–19.

increased markedly in Korea, it actually decreased in Taiwan between 1910 and 1941. Samuel Ho has concluded that by 1945 agriculture in Taiwan was quite scientific, and change had occurred "without disrupting the traditional system of peasant cultivation."[24] Korea, on the other hand, had frequent peasant protests and rebellions, guerrilla movements in the border region, and above all a huge population movement off the land that severely disrupted the agrarian political economy.[25] In other words, Korea betrayed most of the features associated with colonial underdevelopment, Taiwan did not. It may be that the very existence of Korea, and subsequently Manchukuo, gave Taiwan its own "breathing space" within the regional imperium. In any case, its experience did not conform to the predictions of dependency theorists. And, of course, Taiwan produced a weak nationalist impulse, Korea an extraordinarily strong one.

In the 1930s Japan largely withdrew from the world system and pursued, with its colonies, a self-reliant, go-it-alone path to development that not only generated remarkably high industrial growth rates but changed the face of Northeast Asia. In this decade what we might call the "natural economy" of the region was created, although it was not natural, its rational division of labor and set of possibilities have skewed East Asian development ever since. Furthermore, during this period, Japan elaborated many of the features of the neomercantile state still seen today. One prescient writer in the mid 1930s speculated that Japan's heavy industrialization spurt was so impressive that "if world trade were not restricted by tariff walls and import quotas . . . Japan might become the largest exporter in the world—and in a very short time." Guenther Stein saw in this spurt "the beginning of a new epoch in the industrialization of the world."[26] He was right on both counts. (This is not the usual dating: the watershed years of 1945–50 are presumed to have remade Japan, but, as we shall see, they did not.)

The definitive work by Kazushi Ohkawa and Henry Rosovsky sees two "long swings" of Japanese industrial growth in this century, one in the 1930s and the other in the post-1955 period; the first was only marginally less successful. The 1930s' development rested on the "two sturdy legs" of cheap labor and "a great inflow of technology," followed by massive state investments or subsidies to *zaibatsu* investors. Exports were still mostly "light," mainly textiles; but iron and steel, chemicals, hydroelectric power, aluminum, and infrastructure (transport and communications) grew markedly in the imperium.[27] What is so often forgotten is that this spurt located industry in the colonies as well.

Japan is among the very few imperial powers to have located modern heavy industry in its colonies: steel, chemicals, hydroelectric facilities in

---

24. Ho, *Economic Development*, pp. 43, 57.
25. Cumings, *Origins*, chaps. 8–10.
26. Guenther Stein, *Made in Japan* (London: Methuen, 1935), pp. 181, 191.
27. Ohkawa and Rosovsky, *Japanese Economic Growth*, pp. 180–83, 197.

Korea and Manchuria, and automobile production for a time in the latter. Even today, China's industry remains skewed toward the Northeast, and North Korea has always had a relatively advanced industrial structure. Samuel Ho remarks that, by the end of the colonial period, Taiwan "had an industrial superstructure to provide a strong foundation for future industrialization"; the main industries were hydroelectric, metallurgy (especially aluminum), chemicals, and an advanced transport system. By 1941, factory employment, including mining, stood at 181,000 in Taiwan. Manufacturing grew at an annual average rate of about 8 percent during the 1930s.[28]

Industrial development was much greater in Korea, perhaps because of the relative failure of agrarian growth compared to Taiwan but certainly because of Korea's closeness both to Japan and to the Chinese hinterland. By 1940, 213,000 Koreans were working in industry, excluding miners, and not counting the hundreds of thousands of Koreans who migrated to factory or mine work in Japan proper and in Manchuria. Net value of mining and manufacturing grew by 266 percent between 1929 and 1941.[29] By 1945 Korea had an industrial infrastructure that, although sharply skewed toward metropolitan interests, was among the best developed in the Third World. Furthermore, both Korea and Taiwan had begun to take on semiperipheral characteristics. Korea's developing periphery was Manchuria, where it sent workers, merchants, soldiers, and bureaucrats who occupied a middle position between Japanese overlords and Chinese peasants; as Korean rice was shipped to Japan, millet was imported from Manchuria to feed Korean peasants in a classic core-semiperiphery-periphery relationship. As for Taiwan, its geographic proximity to Southeast Asia and South China made it "a natural location for processing certain raw materials brought in from, and for producing some manufactured goods for export to, these areas."[30]

The Japanese managed all this by combining a handful of *zaibatsu*, several big banks, and the colonial state structures. They also foisted upon Koreans and Taiwanese an ideology of incorporation emphasizing a structural family principle and an ethical filiality: the imperium was one (not-so) happy family with Emperor Hirohito as the father. Although the colonized peoples (especially Koreans) remember this period with intense loathing—the forced Emperor worship, the alien Shintō beliefs, the requirement to speak Japanese and take Japanese names—the fact remains that as Taiwan and Korea have industrialized in the postwar period they have fostered *zaibatsu*-like conglomerates, with extensive family interpenetration, and ideologies of familial hierarchy and filial loyalty (the "New Life" movement in Taiwan, the "New Spirit" movement in 1970s South Korea, a corporate familism in North Korea).[31]

28. Ho, *Economic Development*, pp. 70–90; Lin, *Industrialization in Taiwan*, pp. 19–22.
29. Mason et al., *Economic and Social Modernization*, pp. 76, 78.
30. Lin, *Industrialization in Taiwan*, p. 19.
31. Bruce Cumings, "Corporatism in North Korea," *Journal of Korean Studies* 4 (1983).

Although Taiwan seemed to emerge from the last phase of colonialism relatively unscathed, with few disruptions, Korea was profoundly transformed. The period from 1935 to 1945 was when Korea's industrial revolution began, with most of the usual characteristics: uprooting of peasants from the land, the emergence of a working class, widespread population mobility, and urbanization. Because the Japanese industrialized from above, however, social change accompanying this revolution was greatest in the lower reaches of society. The social and regional conflicts that racked Korea in the 1945–53 period have their origins in the immense population shifts, agrarian disruptions, and industrial dynamism of the final phase of the Japanese imperium. This was truly a decade-long pressure cooker; the lifting of the lid in 1945 deeply affected Korea.[32] But Japan, too, was deeply changed by the experience. Japan was remade in this period.

The modern Japanese state, well described in its contemporary features elsewhere,[33] was initially the great work of the Meiji oligarchs. But it was in the 1930s that it took on many of the neomercantile features that persist today: its virtuosity in moving through the product cycle, from old to new industries; the extraordinary role for the bureaucracy and key agencies like MITI, exercising "administrative guidance" throughout the economy; the peculiar vehicles for credit, which account for much of the mobility in and out of industries; the role of large conglomerates; the systematic exclusion of labor from most important decision making; and the high rates of exploitation of poorly paid female labor.

The imperatives of late development in a predatory world shaped Japan more in the 1930s than in any other period, amid the general breakdown of the world system. Sharp competition precipitated remarkable unity at home. The militarist aggression and street politics of the young radicals blind us to the formidable coalition that came together within Japan during the decade. Chalmers Johnson argues that this period saw the emergence of three key features. The first was national planning and industrial strategy that extended to most major industries in Japan. Its only American counterparts are isolated experiences like the Manhattan Project or the space program. The second was the structural features of the MITI function in the years 1939–43 (even though MITI had not yet appeared), including key managerial personnel ("old cadres") who persisted long into the postwar period. And the third was the role for the state and credit institutions that is by now the mark of the Japanese model.[34] G. C. Allen has argued that Japan owed industrial success in the 1930s to "structural adaptability" that

32. Cumings, *Origins*, chaps. 1 and 2.
33. T. J. Pempel, "Japanese Foreign Economic Policy: The Domestic Bases for International Behavior," in Katzenstein, *Between Power and Plenty*, pp. 139–90.
34. Chalmers Johnson, "A Japanese Model?" (Paper presented at the Japan Seminar, University of Washington, School of International Studies, Seattle, May 1981); also Johnson, *MITI and the Japanese Miracle* (Stanford, Calif.: Stanford University Press, 1982), pp. 305–24.

came from systematic state subsidization and protection of new industries, and credit institutions that treated investment funds in very mobile fashion. Allen suggests that Japan's ability to centralize credit institutions and industry "under a single control" was a great comparative advantage at the time, although such concentration was also a measure of the immaturity of the Japanese economy: with capital weak and many producers still in traditional sectors, the state had to select and foster large industries and banks. Like Johnson, he finds "an identifiable thread of continuity" from this period to the contemporary era.[35] Ohkawa and Rosovsky also trace the practice of administrative guidance to the 1930s, with state planning agencies being central to the surveying of the foreign technology scene, the import of technology, licensing, allocation of foreign exchange to importers, and so on.[36] These early agencies, and their MITI successor, in effect were the directors of Japan's movement through the product cycle.

Behind everything in Japan there seems to have been a bank. In the 1930s the Big Four *zaibatsu* controlled four of the six biggest banks; their integrated financial power made it possible to mobilize and direct capital, achieving great and rapid adaptability. The banks, official and semi-official, along with the *zaibatsu*, "provided the chief means by which the government promoted industries of national importance."[37] Thus, the forerunners of MITI provided the goals, and the banks and corporations the means, for directing and riding the product cycle.

The prewar *zaibatsu* were family-interpenetrated conglomerates that used feudal-holdover ideologies to incorporate workers "as fellow clansmen who devote themselves to the services of their overlord." By the end of the 1930s, Mitsui, Mitsubishi, and Sumitomo controlled half the copper and coal production, half the total ship tonnage, 70 percent of flour milling, 90 percent of paper production, most of the aircraft industry, nearly all sugar refining, and, with some smaller and newer *zaibatsu*, nearly all of the colonial industrialization in Korea, Manchuria, and Taiwan.[38] The *zaibatsu* and the state combined to accomplish a thorough repression and incorporation of labor, leading in the 1940s to a forced military-style discipline in the factories that long left its mark on the working class. Women were particularly exploited: they received much lower wages than men for similar work, and predominated in the older textile sector. Finally, at the bottom were more than a million Korean laborers in Japan, men and women harshly regimented for the most difficult sorts of industrial work and subjected to invidious racial discrimination.

In the postwar period Japan was shorn of a few features of its 1930s political economy. But in Taiwan and, later, South Korea the 1930s model

35. Allen, *Japan's Economic Policy*, pp. 42–50, 119–20.
36. Ohkawa and Rosovsky, *Japanese Economic Growth*, pp. 221–23.
37. Allen, *Japan's Economic Policy*, pp. 50, 102, 128.
38. Ibid., pp. 51–54.

reappeared, in nearly all its aspects, including militarization and harsh repression of labor.

The postwar settlement and the emergence of a new hegemony

In September 1945, as U.S. occupation forces filtered into Japan, an American officer walked into a Mitsui office in Tokyo and introduced himself. A man in the office pointed to a map of the Greater East Asian Coprosperity Sphere and said, "There it is. We tried. See what you can do with it!"[39] It was not until 1948 that the United States would seek to do much with it, however. In the period 1945–47 in Korea, Japan, and Taiwan, society reacted strongly against the effects of imperial militarism and industrial midwifery. American occupation in Japan led by a 19th-century liberal also reacted strongly in the early years against the political economy of prewar Japan, seeking to destroy the Japanese Imperial Army, break up the *zaibatsu*, eliminate rural landlords, and bequeath to the world a reformed and chastened Japan that would never again mix aggression with economic prowess. Unions and leftist parties were unleashed and, with Occupation "New Dealers," mustered a challenge to the prewar system strong enough, at minimum, to establish the countervailing power that enables us to call postwar Japan a democracy. Although the main emphasis was on democratization and an end to militarism, narrower interests also asserted themselves. The first head of the Economic and Scientific Section of the Occupation, for example, was Robert C. Kramer, a textile industrialist; he and representatives of American textile, rayon, ceramics, and other industries threatened by Japanese competition opposed reviving Japan's economy, particularly in its potent prewar form.[40] American allies, especially the British, also urged that commitments to reform and reparations be carried through, thereby to weaken Japan's competitiveness in world markets.

From the early 1940s, however, one sector of American official opinion opposed a punitive occupation, for fear that this would play into the hands of the Soviets and make a reintegration of Japan with the world economy impossible. In essence, such people, who included a Japanophile faction in the State Department,[41] wanted a Japan revived to *second-rank* economic status and enrolled in an American-managed free trade regime. Such recommendations remained in the background, however, while Japan's Ameri-

39. John Emmerson, *The Japanese Thread* (New York: Holt, Rinehart & Winston, 1978), p. 256. I am indebted to Michael Schaller for providing me with this quotation.
40. Jon Halliday, *A Political History of Japanese Capitalism* (New York: Pantheon, 1975), pp. 183–84.
41. Akira Iriye, "Continuities in U.S.-Japanese Relations, 1941–1949," in Yonosuke Nagai and Iriye, eds., *The Origins of the Cold War in Asia* (Tokyo: University of Tokyo Press, 1977), pp. 378–407.

can emperor, Gen. Douglas MacArthur, masterfully imposed a benevolent tutelage upon the Japanese people.

All this began sharply to change in late 1947, leading to what we might call the Kennan Restoration. George Kennan's policy of containment was always limited and parsimonious, based on the idea that four or five industrial structures existed in the world: the Soviets had one and the United States had four, and things should be kept that way. In Asia, only Japan held his interest. The rest were incontinent regimes, and how could one have containment with incontinence? Kennan and his Policy Planning Staff played the key role in pushing through the "reverse course" in Japan.

American policy in the mid-20th century resonated with Jacob Viner's description of British policy in the 18th: it was governed "by joint and harmonized considerations of power and economics."[42] Security and economic considerations were inextricably mixed. A revived Japan was both a bulwark against the Soviets and a critical element in a reformed and revived world economy. What is surprising, in the multitude of formerly classified American documents now available on early postwar Asian policy, is how powerful were the economic voices. In particular, a cluster of bankers and free traders, now dubbed the "Japan Crowd," were instrumental in the ending of the postwar reforms in Japan and the revival of the regional political economy that persists today.[43] Economics bulked so large because, as Charles Maier points out, the defeated Axis powers (Japan and West Germany) were to become world centers of capital accumulation and growth, not of political or military power.[44] Thus Japan's economy was reinforced, while its political and military power (beyond its borders) was shorn. The result is that in the postwar world economy Japan resembles a sector as much as a nation-state. Until the 1970s it was a distinctly secondary sector when compared to the United States, that is, it was returned to semiperipherality as (it was hoped) a permanent second-rank economic power.

The coalition that brought the reverse course to Japan has been well detailed elsewhere. In brief it included, in addition to Kennan, Dean Acheson, Dean Rusk, Max Bishop and others within the government, several journalists, and a powerful lobby of American firms and individuals who had had large investments in prewar Japan: General Electric, Westinghouse, Goodrich, Owens-Libby, American Can, and others.[45] Percy Johnston, head of the pivotal Johnston Committee whose report in April 1948 was instrumental in the reverse course, was chairman of the Chemical Bank; the "Dodge Line" of fiscal austerity was run by a Detroit banker; many Wall Streeters, including

42. Viner, "Power versus Plenty," p. 91.

43. John G. Roberts, "The 'Japan Crowd' and the Zaibatsu Restoration," *Japan Interpretor* 12 (Summer 1979), pp. 384–415.

44. Charles S. Maier, "The Politics of Productivity: Foundations of American International Economic Policy after World War II," in Katzenstein, *Between Power and Plenty*, p. 45.

45. Halliday, *Political History*, p. 183.

the American maker of the Japan Peace Treaty, John Foster Dulles, supported a revival of Japan's economic prowess. As good free traders from the new hegemonic power, they had nothing to fear from Japan. The old hegemonic power, Great Britain, fought unsuccessfully against the changes.

As thinking about a revived Japan evolved in 1948–50, two problems emerged: first, how could Japan's vital but second-rate status be assured; second, how could a prewar political economy that got raw materials and labor from the Northeast Asian periphery survive in the postwar world without a hinterland? George Kennan raised these problems in a 1949 Policy Planning Staff meeting:

> You have the terrific problem of how the Japanese are going to get along unless they again reopen some sort of empire toward the south. . . .
> If we really in the Western world could work out controls . . . foolproof enough and cleverly enough exercised really to have power over what Japan imports in the way of oil and other things . . . we could have veto power over what she does.[46]

Thus, once the decision to revive Japan was made, two questions predominated: the hegemonic problem and the hinterland problem. The CIA in May 1948 suggested Northeast Asia as the new (old) hinterland:

> As in the past, Japan for normal economic functioning on an industrial basis, must have access to the Northeast Asiatic areas—notably North China, Manchuria, and Korea—now under direct, indirect, or potential control of the USSR.[47]

A high official in the Economic Cooperation Administration, a few months later, suggested the same hinterland, and a drastic method of recovering it. Without North China and Manchuria, he argued, Japan would have "no hope of achieving a viable economy"; it (and Korea) would be "doomed to military and industrial impotence except on Russian terms." Therefore, "Our first concern must be the liberation of Manchuria and North China from communist domination."[48] This rollback option, however, was delayed; the victory of Mao's forces throughout China and the possibility in 1949 that Washington might be able to split Moscow and Peking (Acheson's policy) combined to suggest a hinterland for Japan in Southeast Asia.

In July 1949, the CIA asserted that the United States had "an important interest" in "retaining access to Southeast Asia, for its own convenience and

46. See Kennan's remarks in "Transcript of Roundtable Discussion," U.S. Department of State, 6, 7, and 8 October 1949, pp. 25, 47, in Carrollton Press *Declassified Documents Series*, 1977, 316B.
47. U.S. Central Intelligence Agency, ORE 43-48, 24 May 1948, in HST/PSF file, Memos 1945–49, box 255, Harry S. Truman Library, Independence, Missouri.
48. Economic Cooperation Administration, unsigned memorandum of 3 November 1948, in Dean Acheson Papers, box 27, Harry S. Truman Library.

because of the great economic importance of that area to Western Europe and Japan." It argued that "the basic problem with respect to Japan is to recreate a viable economy. This in turn requires a stabilization of the situation in Southeast Asia and a *modus vivendi* with Communist China." The latter requirement might be satisfied if China could be drawn away from "vassalage toward the USSR."[49] Southeast Asia was the preferred candidate for Japan's hinterland. It would provide markets for Japan's textile and light industrial exports, in exchange for raw materials Japan badly needed. The problem was that France and Britain sought to hold the countries in the region exclusively, and nationalist movements resisted both the Europeans and a reintroduction of the Japanese. Thus, "Anglo-American consensus over Japan dissolved" as the United States played the hinterland option. Japan was a threat to sterling bloc trade and currency systems, and was "perforce in the dollar bloc"; the United States wanted Japan to earn dollars in the sterling bloc, which would have the dual virtue of supporting Japan's revival while encouraging Britain's retreat from empire.[50]

The Occupation also rearranged Japan's monetary and trade policies to support a revival of trade. The yen was fixed in 1949 at the rate of 360 to $1.00, from which it did not depart until 1971; the rate was artificially low to aid Japanese exports. The Dodge Line pursued a strict policy of fiscal restraint. In the same year (1949) the Occupation removed price floors on Japanese exports, raising fears of "dumping" in Southeast Asia.

Particularly important is the *triangular* structure of this arrangement: United States (core), Japan (semiperiphery), and Southeast Asia (periphery). This structure was clearly articulated in the deliberations leading up to the adoption of NSC 48/1 in late December 1949, a document so important that it might be called the NSC 68 for Asia. (With this the United States made the decision to send aid to the Bao Dai regime in Vietnam, not after the Korean War began.) The first draft argued the virtues of a "triangular" trade between the United States, Japan, and Southeast Asia, giving "certain advantages in production costs of various commodities"—that is, comparative advantage in the product cycle. It also called for a positive policy toward Communist-held territory in East Asia: the goal was "to commence the rollback of Soviet control and influence in the area." The final document changed this phrase to read, "to contain and where feasible to reduce the power and influence of the USSR in Asia."[51] The roll-back contingency expressed both

49. Central Intelligence Agency, ORE 69-49, "Relative US Security Interest in the European-Mediterranean Area and the Far East," 14 July 1949, in HST/PSF file, Memos 1945–49, box 249, Harry S. Truman Library.

50. Calleo and Rowland, *America and the World Political Economy*, pp. 198–202.

51. Draft paper, NSC 48, 26 October 1949, in NSC materials, box 207, Harry S. Truman Library. For a fuller elaboration see Bruce Cumings, "Introduction: The Course of American Policy toward Korea, 1945–53," in Cumings, ed., *Child of Conflict: The Korean-American Relationship, 1945–1953* (Seattle: University of Washington Press, 1983).

the fear of continuing communist encroachment, what with the fall of China in 1949, and the search for a Japanese hinterland.

The Korean War effectively drew the lines of the "grand area" in East Asia. When the war broke out, the Seventh Fleet was interposed between Taiwan and the mainland, suggesting once again an integration of Taiwan with Japan and the world economy. South Korea was almost lost in the summer of 1950. Then, after the Inch'on landing, the course of the fighting opened the realm of feasibility suggested in NSC 48/1; the "contain and reduce" phraseology was used in the State Department to justify the march north and, in passing, to wrench North Korea's industrial base away from the communists. Roll-back met several hundred thousand Chinese "volunteers," however, and that debacle froze the situation. The geopolitical lines, or hegemonic outer limits, were thus fixed and they have survived. Taiwan and South Korea were in, North Korea and Manchuria were out. It remained only to reintroduce Japanese economic influence, which the Kennedy administration did in the early 1960s in both Taiwan and South Korea.

Acheson would remark in 1954 that "Korea came along and saved us," and the *us* included Japan. The Korean War not only boosted the Japanese economy but provided MacArthur with justification for reviving police and military and for excluding labor and the left within Japan. The strategic lines of the new Northeast Asian political economy, however, brought the peculiar nature of American hegemony to the fore. There is a paradox at the heart of it: nonterritorial in contrast to Old World imperialism, organizing great spaces and knocking down barriers to trade, it has outer limits sufficient to keep countries *in* the system but not sufficient to protect the home economy against destructive competition, and not sufficient to maintain effective dependency relationships or a frozen hierarchy. The system permits upward mobility. The United States retrieved South Korea and Taiwan from oblivion in 1950, but invoking the threat of oblivion to keep them in line in later years was unthinkable. The United States keeps Japan on a food, oil, and security dependency, maintaining a light hold on the Japanese jugular; yet to squeeze would be disastrous. Outer limits are not enough to bring recalcitrant allies to heel. Furthermore, within those outer limits a dependent but strong state obtains leverage over the American "weak state," weak in the sense of competing centers of power and economic interest that can be played off against one another.[52] Thus, the postwar settlement simultaneously gave Japan, in particular, dependency and autonomous capability.[53]

Japan is ultradependent on the United States, or on American firms, for oil and security, and significantly dependent on the United States for food.

52. Krasner, "US Commercial and Monetary Policy," pp. 63–66; Hirschman, *National Power*, passim.

53. Jon Halliday, "Japan's Changing Position in the Global Political Economy" (Paper presented at the annual meeting of the Association for Asian Studies, 1979, Los Angeles).

During the Occupation, the Petroleum Board that set policy was made up
of members mostly drawn from American oil majors, and even in the mid
1970s Japan was receiving about 70 percent of its oil deliveries from the
majors.[54] In the 1960s and 1970s the United States also supplied 60 to 70
percent of Japan's food imports, and in the 1950s used the PL480 program
to sell grain in Japan, Taiwan, and South Korea. All three have been protected
markets dependent upon American grain. And since 1945 Japan has had
no military capability remotely commensurate with its economic power.
Even today analysts cannot decide if Japan is a superstate or a puny dependency. When Ezra Vogel began a Harvard seminar on Japan by saying
that "I am really very troubled when I think through the consequences of
the rise of Japanese power," Samuel Huntington responded that Japan has
"these really fundamental weaknesses—energy, food, and military security."
It is, he thought, "an extraordinarily weak country."[55] The paradox of the
postwar Northeast Asian settlement is that both are right.

Within Japan, after the reverse course took hold, was a formidable political
economy for competition in world markets. The *zaibatsu* were less smashed
than reformed, prospering again by the mid 1950s if in less concentrated
form. More important, they were now under *state* influence and control,
something that prewar bureaucrats had longed for; the role of the big banks
was also enhanced.[56] With the *zaibatsu* weakened, the military smashed,
and the landlords dispossessed, but with the bureaucracy untouched (the
Occupation governed through the existing bureaucracy with few reforms or
purges), the Japanese state had more relative autonomy than in the prewar
period. Indeed, it was the great victor of the Occupation. Autonomy enabled
Japan to pursue neomercantile policies of restricting entry to Japanese markets, resisting the intrusion of foreign capital, and providing various incentives
and subsidies to restructure the industrial base in the 1950s, and conquer
foreign markets in the 1960s and 1970s.

T. J. Pempel and Jon Halliday both note the low level of internationalization
of the Japanese economy. Total foreign assets in Japan in the mid 1970s
were only about 2 to 3 percent of total assets, few non-Japanese multinationals
operated there, and the major markets for foreign imports remained food
and oil. Halliday argues that Japan's "successful isolation" has precipitated
greater elite unity than in countries like the United States: Japan does not
have major conflicts between firms with national and those with international
interests, therefore foreign interests cannot invoke much leverage in domestic

54. See ibid.; also Martha Caldwell, "Petroleum Politics in Japan: State and Industry in a
Changing Policy Context" (Ph.D. diss., University of Wisconsin, 1980), chap. 2.
55. Ezra F. Vogel, "Growing Japanese Economic Capabilities and the U.S.-Japan Relationship"
(Summary of the 1st meeting of the American Discussion Group on U.S. Policy toward Japan,
Harvard University, 13 December 1979; hereafter cited as *Harvard Seminar 1979*).
56. Johnson, "A Japan Model?" Also Allen, *Japan's Economic Policy*, pp. 108–9.

Japanese politics. Moving out of declining into advanced sectors is much easier because powerful domestic business interests rarely clash, and a labor force lacking influence at the commanding heights can be eased out of old industries and retrained for new ones. Japan's monetary isolation lessens the influence of foreign lenders, while reliance on bank rather than share capital also promotes mobility and flexibility.[57] Finally, as in the prewar political economy, labor is corralled by docile unions, paternalism, and a large reservoir of workers in traditional sectors. Ohkawa and Rosovsky call Japan a businessman's "heaven on earth" in regard to labor, while Pempel says labor is "a fundamentally excluded sector"; they also note that women continue to bear inferior and exploited positions in the workforce, and that the state still does not spend significant amounts on social welfare.[58]

Postwar Korea and Taiwan

The immediate postwar settlement in Taiwan and Korea fundamentally expressed the differences in the two *societies*. Taiwan "drifted aimlessly" in the late 1940s, having to reorient its trade away from Japan and toward China (until 1949); it sold sugar, cement, aluminum, and food to this now-enlarged periphery.[59] But it remained "an extremely well-ordered society," with "fewer signs of social disintegration" than any place on the Asian mainland.[60] Like Japan, the state emerged stronger after the inflow of the Kuomintang (KMT) and the China mainlanders in 1945–49. The potent colonial bureaucracy was preserved nearly intact; Japanese personnel in many cases stayed on well into 1946, training Taiwanese replacements, and native bureaucrats who had served in the colonial administration continued in office. When the mainlanders took over they added a powerful military component to give the state even more autonomy from society: the Kuomintang had finally found a part of China where its bureaucracy was not hamstrung by provincial warlords and landlords. Thus, for the first time, the Nationalists were able to accomplish a land reform; they could do so because none of them owned any land in Taiwan. The reform, in turn, aided the productivity of agriculture because redistributed land went primarily to entrepreneurial, productive, relatively rich peasants. Furthermore, a disproportionate number of experts, technicians, and well-educated professionals fled the mainland, adding to Taiwan's already significant human capital. The result, once the Seventh Fleet drew the outer limit in 1950, was a state with

57. Pempel, "Japanese Foreign Economic Policy," pp. 163–64; Halliday, "Japan's Changing Position"; Halliday, *Political History*, p. 283.
58. Ohkawa and Rosovsky, *Japanese Economic Growth*, pp. 118, 235–36; Pempel, "Japanese Foreign Economic Policy," pp. 149–55.
59. Ho, *Economic Development*, p. 103; Lin, *Taiwan's Industrialization*, pp. 27–28.
60. Ho, *Economic Development*, p. 104.

significant relative autonomy but now far more dependent on the United
States than in any previous period of Nationalist rule.

Korea, of course, was divided in 1945. In the North a quick and efficient
social and anticolonial revolution occurred under Soviet auspices, the ultimate
(but also the predictable) societal response to nearly half a century of Japanese
imperialism. The South, however, festered for five years through dissent,
disorder, major rebellions in 1946 and 1948, and a significant guerrilla movement in 1948 and 1949. Southern landlords succeeded in recapturing the
state in 1945 and 1946, under American auspices, and used it in traditional
fashion to protect social privilege rather than to foster growth. They prevented
major land reform until the Korean War began, and showed no interest in
developing the economy. Instead, they ruled through draconian police and
military organizations. As in Taiwan there was considerable continuity in
the bureaucracy from the colonial period, but the Japanese officials had
mostly fled when the war ended and those Korean functionaries who remained
were largely unable to function, since they were often hated more than the
Japanese overlords. The southern state entered a general crisis of legitimacy
in the late 1940s: marked by the worst Japanese excesses but unable to carry
forward colonial successes, the regime seemed doomed.

When civil war erupted in June 1950 the North had an easy time of it,
sweeping the southern regime away until it met massive American intervention. But paradoxically, the three-month northern occupation of the south,
which included a revolutionary land reform in several provinces, cleared the
way to end landlord dominance in the countryside and to reform landholding
on the Taiwan model once the war terminated in 1953. By 1953 South
Korea further resembled Taiwan. Its colonial heavy industry had been am-
putated by Korea's division, most of it now in the north and beyond reach;
like Taiwan, southern Korea was the home of light industry and the best
rice-producing provinces. During the war many northerners had fled south,
also disproportionately including the educated and professional classes. By
the war's end the South had a standing army of about 600,000, compared
with 75,000 in 1950, so it approximated the distended Nationalist Army.
Finally, Syngman Rhee, like Chiang Kai-shek, had won an ironclad commitment of American defense from communism. So, to put it concisely, by
1953 Taiwan and South Korea once more resembled each other, but what
was accomplished with ease in Taiwan required a war in Korea.

Import-substituting industrialization

With the underbrush of the early postwar period cleared away, Taiwan
and South Korea (ROK) once again began marching in tandem. The Korean
War gave Taiwan a head start on postcolonial industrialization on the typical
import-substituting pattern, but by 1953 the ROK was doing the same. Both
were enmeshed in a system of American hegemony that brought them eco-

nomic and military aid on an unheard-of scale, but Taiwan's low societal response and the KMT's high relative autonomy gave it more bargaining power with the United States. The Rhee regime, on the other hand, was penetrated from below by superannuated landlords who retained political influence and from above by a huge American political, economic, and military presence. In the years immediately succeeding the devastation of the war, society was quiet and Rhee ruled through a diffuse authoritarian system that was cruel in its domestic political consequences but incapable of mustering the autonomy to direct growth, and unable to withstand the social onslaught that came in 1960. The now-senile Rhee was toppled, the colonial-linked police and military came undone, and the way was clear for a dynamic authoritarian system.

Since 1945 South Korea has received some $13 billion in American military and economic aid, and Taiwan some $5.6 billion ($600 per capita in the ROK, $425 per capita in Taiwan).[61] To gauge the true dimensions of this munificence comparative figures are helpful. The ROK's total of nearly $6 billion in U.S. economic grants and loans, 1946–78, compares with a total for all of Africa of $6.89 billion and for all of Latin America of $14.8 billion; only India, with a population seventeen times that of South Korea, received more ($9.6 billion). U.S. military deliveries to Taiwan and the ROK in 1955–78 (that is, excluding the Korean War) totaled $9.05 billion. All of Latin America and all of Africa received $3.2 billion; only Iran got more, and most of that was pumped in after 1972 (the figure is $10.01 billion). Soviet economic aid to LDCs, 1954–78, was $7.6 billion in drawn aid, that is, little more than American aid to the ROK alone. Total drawn aid for all LDCs from all socialist countries, 1954–78, was $13.4 billion, about 25 percent greater than the total for Taiwan and the ROK since 1945. Soviet military deliveries to all LDCs, 1955–78, totaled $25.3 billion, about 280 percent of the total for Taiwan and the ROK.[62]

During the 1950s U.S. aid accounted for five-sixths of ROK imports. Aid was lavished on Japan as well, and special U.S. military procurements from Japan alone in the period 1952–56 totaled $3.4 billion, one-fourth of American commodity imports at that time.[63] Samuel Ho estimates for Taiwan that foreign savings, much of which was U.S. aid, totaled 40 percent of gross domestic capital formation.[64] This significant figure is low when compared to the ROK; Taiwan's higher rate of domestic savings can be accounted for by less postwar disruption and the Kuomintang's having taken China's gold reserves to the island. Taiwan has also had an additional source of aid and investment unavailable to the ROK, overseas Chinese.

61. CIA, *Handbook 1979*; also Ho, *Economic Development*, pp. 108–11; also Mason et al., *Economic and Social Modernization*, p. 165.
62. CIA, *Handbook 1979*.
63. Allen, *Japan's Economic Policy*, p. 130.
64. Ho, *Economic Development*, p. 237.

The United States, of course, did not just give military and economic aid to Taiwan and the ROK but deeply influenced economic programs and the societies themselves. Often it was difficult to know if natives or Americans were writing the plans and policies; the aid missions pushed through land reform on Taiwan and forced it through in Korea; here, in short, was by far the best example in the world of what Wallerstein has called "development by invitation." If the principle of upward mobility in this system is "many called, few chosen," Taiwan and the ROK were clearly part of the chosen few.[65] Japan, too, was chosen, if at a higher level in the system: not only were aid totals high, but the United States allowed a "simultaneous technological infusion" in the 1950s that brought backward Japanese industries up to speed and started new ones.[66] American hegemony also had an element of indulgence in the halcyon years of the 1950s—U.S. officials tolerated import substitution in Taiwan and the ROK while chiding both for having the state too involved in the economy (i.e., the typical policy of Republican administrations). Thus, the three Northeast Asian political economies had in the 1950s a rare breathing space, an incubation period allowed to few other peoples in the world. The period set the stage for the breakthroughs of the 1960s, and it may be a capitalist analogue to the radical tonic of withdrawal and reorientation by socialist state machineries and societies.

Taiwan and Korea pushed remarkably similar import-substitution programs, although the Taiwan program was less fitful. The key industries were textiles, cement, flat glass, and so on, protected by and nurtured behind a wall of tariffs, overvalued exchange rates, and other obstacles to foreign entry.[67] In both countries capitalist parvenus, usually mainlanders in Taiwan and northerners in the ROK, interpenetrated the state, official monopolies, and banks, making windfall profits in import-substituting industries through such connections. Both the KMT and the Rhee regime, after all, grew out of agrarian-bureaucratic traditional systems and had pursued so-called "bureaucratic capitalism," with its "total interpenetration of public and private interests."[68] Favored capitalists took over formerly Japanese-held industries in Taiwan and the ROK, laying the basis for many of the conglomerates that would appear in the 1960s and 1970s (especially in Korea). The phase of "easy" import substitution started two or three years earlier in Taiwan and came a cropper in 1958–59; it did the same in the ROK in 1960–62. In both countries a new export-led industrialization began in the early 1960s.

65. Immanuel Wallerstein, "Dependence in an Interdependent World," in Wallerstein, *Capitalist World-Economy.*

66. Ohkawa and Rosovsky, *Japanese Economic Development,* p. 92.

67. On Korea, see Mason et al., *Economic and Social Modernization,* pp. 7–8; also Paul W. Kuznets, *Economic Growth and Structure in the Republic of Korea* (New Haven: Yale University Press, 1977), pp. 48–71; on Taiwan see Lin, *Taiwan's Industrialization,* pp. 3–4, and Ho, *Economic Development,* p. 106.

68. Alice H. Amsden, "Taiwan's Economic History: A Case of Etatisme and a Challenge to Dependency Theory," *Modern China* 5 (July 1979), p. 362.

In the 1950s both regimes had absurdly swollen military machines—about 600,000 soldiers in each army, ranking among the highest military/civilian ratios in the world. The United States footed much of the tab in Korea, less so in Taiwan because Americans opposed Taiwan's pretensions to retake the mainland. Thus, Taiwanese defense spending ran at about 12 percent of GNP, Korean at about 4 percent. These large militaries served two important purposes: first, as a perimeter defense for the hegemonic "grand area." Without such military machines and expenditures Japan would have had to spend much more than its less than one percent of GNP on defense. As Paul B. Simpson said of the U.S. aid program to the ROK in the 1950s:

> If we were to characterize the program simply, we would say that the Korean consumer has been subsidized by ICA and U.S. military expenditures in return for the maintenance of a large military establishment. The attitude one adopts toward this Korean military program very largely determines one's attitude toward the U.S. aid program in Korea.[69]

Second, the military in both countries gave disciplined training and basic literacy to a mass of young people, while rearing officers and managers who later populated state bureaucracies and big corporations. Of course, both distended militaries have continually devastated democratic impulses.

In the Korean case the military also played a decisive role in the switch from import substitution to export-led growth. The downfall of Syngman Rhee carried the bureaucratic capitalists with it. After the military coup in 1961 those who had profited from import substitution were marched through the streets, carrying sandwich signs with slogans like "I was a parasite on the people." A transition that occurred with difficulty in several Latin American nations transpired quickly, if violently, in South Korea; managed from the top down, it cleared away social and political obstacles to the new program.

The export-led phase and the emergence of BAIRs

Readers who know Latin America and especially the work of Guillermo O'Donnell will have noticed that Taiwan and Korea went through industrialization in phases that resemble the sequence in Brazil, Argentina, and other states, even though the import-substituting phase was much shorter in East Asia. It would have continued longer had it not been for opposition by American aid officials (which demonstrates their superior influence in this region of overwhelming American hegemony). But this phase did not have the political characteristics it had in Brazil and elsewhere. Politics did not stretch to include workers, peasants, or plural competition for power.

69. Paul B. Simpson, "Report on the University of Oregon Advisory Mission," mimeo. (Eugene: University of Oregon, 1961), p. 49. I am indebted to Tony Michel for bringing this quotation to my attention.

The political sequence of inclusion followed by exclusion, as the "easy" phase ended and export-led development began, was absent.[70] Labor was excluded in the 1950s and remained excluded in the 1960s; nor did the squeezed middle class of bureaucrats and small businessmen achieve representation in either Taiwan or South Korea. It is possible to argue, however, that the Korean state was more penetrated by society in the 1950s, both because new capitalists gained some influence as the landlord interests receded and because the United States and a small stratum of Korean liberals insisted on a formal democratic structure that was occasionally implemented, if only through students massing in the streets. The democratic facade could occasionally be invoked. Taiwan, of course, has been ruled under martial law since 1947 in a single-party system; the KMT's internal organization principles were on Leninist lines. Its politics could easily translate into the new state requisites for export-led development and deepening import substitution. In Korea, however, such a state had to be reinforced: bureaucratic, secret police, and party power needed to be strengthened.

In both countries the export-led program was decided by the United States. Edward Mason and his associates say that in Korea the United States "basically dictated" the reform programs; Ian Little says that in Taiwan A.I.D. pressure was one of the "clearest cases in economic history of cause and effect."[71] Therefore, early 1960s' policies in Taiwan and the ROK tended to be very similar. Taiwan promulgated a nineteen-point reform package in 1960, containing extensive reforms of monetary, fiscal, taxation, and trade practices. Korea pursued the same package after Park Chung Hee's coup in 1961. It involved downward revaluation of currencies to cheapen exports, drastic lowering of tariff barriers that had protected native industries, tax holidays, exemptions, and reductions across the board for firms willing to export, and state guarantees for foreign investment and foreign loans. Implemented by 1963 or 1964, the package was followed by accelerated depreciation schemes, discounts and subsidies for transportation costs, and monopoly rights for certain firms, usually linked explicitly to export performance.[72] Taiwan established its big Free Export Zone (FEZ) at Kaohsiung in 1965, and Korea followed suit with its Masan FEZ. Both regimes developed

70. Guillermo A. O'Donnell, *Modernization and Bureaucratic-Authoritarianism in South American Politics* (Berkeley: University of California Institute for International Studies, 1973); see also the articles by O'Donnell, Fernando Henrique Cardoso, Robert Kaufman, James Kurth, Albert Hirschman, and Jose Serra in David Collier, ed., *The New Authoritarianism in Latin America* (Princeton: Princeton University Press, 1979). Serra, Hirschman, and, in part, Kaufman challenge the O'Donnell theses.

71. Mason et al., *Economic and Social Modernization*, p. 47; Ian M. D. Little, "An Economic Renaissance," in Walter Galenson, ed., *Economic Growth and Structural Change in Taiwan* (Ithaca: Cornell University Press, 1979), p. 474. See also Ho, *Economic Development*, p. 195.

72. Mason et al., *Economic and Social Modernization*, pp. 96, 129–32; Kuznets, *Economic Growth*, pp. 73, 96–97; Lin, *Taiwan's Industrialization*, pp. 83–93.

long-range planning agencies and multiyear plans; American experts continued riding herd on the planning function (a sort of transnational planning).

Both regimes pursued their comparative advantage in relatively well-educated and skilled, but low-paid, labor. Paul Kuznets notes that Korea's comparative advantage derived from these factors and that labor was "abundant and unorganized"; Wade and Kim estimate Korean labor productivity as higher than American in light industries such as textiles and electronics, at 20 percent the cost. In the FEZs, however, labor-cost savings for foreign firms may be substantially higher: one source puts Korean productivity at 2.5 times American at 10 percent of the cost, for a factor of 25 in cost savings.[73] One Taiwan analyst has argued for the virtues of "splitting up the production process" on a worldwide basis, since capital has much greater mobility than labor.[74] This is, of course, the point. The result of the early 1960s' reforms was that Taiwan and the ROK became suppliers of labor to an increasingly far-flung division of production; in the mid 1960s multinational corporations, the World Bank, and the IMF replaced U.S. aid missions as the conduits to the world economy. This pattern, most marked in East Asia, is well known and need not detain us. More important were the political consequences.

By the mid 1960s both Taiwan and South Korea possessed strong states that bear much comparison to the prewar Japanese model, and to the bureaucratic-authoritarian states in Latin America. Termed NICs (Newly Industrializing Countries) in much of the literature, the Taiwan and Korean variants deserve a more accurate acronym. I shall call them BAIRs, or Bureaucratic-Authoritarian Industrializing Regimes. These states are ubiquitous in economy and society: penetrating, comprehensive, highly articulated, and relatively autonomous of particular groups and classes. Furthermore, especially in Korea, state power accumulated considerably just as the ROK began a deepening industrialization program in steel, chemicals, ships, and automobiles. Taiwan has developed planning agencies and bureaucracies to go with its existing strong state, but with society weak the state has had neither the occasion nor the necessity to deepen or change its features: once strong for retaking the mainland and guaranteeing KMT power, it is today strong for economic development. The best Latin American analogy for Taiwan would be Mexico, where deepening industrialization occurred within the context of an established authoritarian system; Korea is closer to Argentina, where deepening required a much stronger state. In any case, by the mid 1960s Taiwan and South Korea had joined the world: we no longer need area-specific, idiosyncratic explanations for their politics. They now

73. Kuznets, *Economic Growth*, p. 103; Wade and Kim, *Economic Development*, p. 100; Suh Sang Chul, "Development of a New Industry through Exports: The Electronics Industry in Korea," in Wontack Hong and Anne O. Krueger, eds., *Trade and Development in Korea* (Seoul: Korea Development Institute, 1975).
74. Lin, *Taiwan's Industrialization*, p. 134.

have the politics that their economies—and powerful external forces—demand.

In the creation of the Korean BAIR, there was a poignant moment for American political scientists. Amid Kennedy administration pressure to go civilian and respect human rights, the ROK promulgated a new constitution in 1963. Harvard scholar Rupert Emerson journeyed to Seoul and advised Koreans, in classic American fashion, to disperse power through a strong legislature, a two-party system, and various checks and balances. Five years later Samuel Huntington published a book that cited the ROK for precisely the opposite: he applauded the regime for its accumulation of central power and its stability amid rapid economic and social change. Huntington's concern for order transcended liberal categories: the problem was not to hold elections but to create organizations.[75] Although his preferred vehicle was the party, the logic fitted a strong state power by whatever means necessary. The book was translated into Korean and is widely read there. Huntington's logic was possibly the first piece of political advice from an American that did not fall on deaf ears in Korea.

Shortly after the coup, Park and his allies organized the Democratic Republican Party (DRP) and the Korean Central Intelligence Agency (KCIA). During much of the 1960s the DRP was the designated vehicle for a stable politics; its internal structure mimicked the KMT with its democratic centralism. But when Park's power was shaken in the period 1969–71 (he nearly lost the 1971 election to Kim Dae Jung in spite of manipulation), the KCIA emerged as the preferred organization of order. An arm of the executive, it penetrated nearly every arena of Korean life, with agents in factories, central and local government offices, and university classrooms. Organized with the help of the U.S. CIA, and always working in close liaison with the Seoul CIA station, it was an example of transnational politics to go with the transnational economics. Unfortunately for Park Chung Hee, the KCIA became so strong that every director came to challenge his power (Lee Hu-rak, Kim Jae-gyu, Kim Hyong-uk) until finally its chief shot Park to death over dinner one evening in October 1979.

In the economic sphere the Koreans in the early 1960s set up an Economic Planning Board (EPB), which took on many of the functions of MITI. It took over from a previous ministry the entire budgeting function; it decides which industries and firms to promote, which to phase out; it closely supervises both the development and the implementation of planning; along with an official trade promotion agency (KOTRA) it surveys the world for needed markets, capital, and technology. The main difference from Japan is that the EPB brings in foreigners (Americans and Japanese) as "senior partners" in consultation and planning.[76] Many other state agencies are involved in

75. Samuel Huntington, *Political Order in Changing Societies* (New Haven: Yale University Press, 1968), pp. 7, 25, 258–61.

76. Mason et al., *Economic and Social Modernization*, pp. 16–17.

export promotion, and in both Korea and Taiwan, the achievement of some export target is cause for patriotic hoopla and celebration (this has become the national pastime of these two BAIRs).

Until the mid 1970s, American analysts tended to deny that an authoritarian politics might have much to do with economic growth in Taiwan and the ROK. But more recent writing has discarded the previous assumptions of the modernization literature, that development could proceed amidst or would promote democracy. Kuznets, for example, argues that "because this [Korean] regime has been authoritarian and has no economic interest base, it could hold down wages and consumption, largely ignore rural interests, and concentrate on rapid development through industrialization."[77] He errs only in suggesting that the state has no base. The state's relative autonomy from particularistic economic interests, combined with the exclusion of workers and farmers, gives it the capacity to look after the whole in the interest of, but not necessarily at the behest of, certain of the parts. In this structural sense it resembles the relative autonomy of the Japanese state.

A Harvard project on the Korean economy also breaks with the assumption of inevitable democratic development. The authors find that "Korea, Inc." is "undoubtedly a more apt description of the situation in Korea than is 'Japan, Inc.'" The state is senior, the corporations lesser partners: "It is the government that is Chairman of the Board [of Korea, Inc.], with business holding a few directorships."[78] The Korean *zaibatsu* (the Koreans pronounce it *chaebol*, but the term is the same) have grown up with the new BAIR. Ten of them now appear on *Fortune*'s international 500. Like prewar Japanese *zaibatsu*, there is great family interpenetration: the Harvard project found that of current *chaebol* chief executives, 61.4 percent are firm founders, 7.9 percent are direct descendants of founders, 12 percent are relatives of founders, and only 18.8 percent are unrelated to the founding family.[79] As a Gerschenkronian analysis would suggest, "feudal holdovers" have been an important aspect of late development in East Asia: in the case of prewar Japanese *zaibatsu*, Korean *chaebol*, and the Taiwanese state (the President being the son of Chiang Kai-shek), it is the traditional family structure that provides a basis for organizing industry. The power of this analysis is confirmed in the Northeast Asian socialist case, where the North Korean state is highly interpenetrated by Kim Il Sung's family and where his son has been chosen as successor.

As in Japan, Korean and Taiwanese big firms exercise paternalistic sway over workers with company dormitories, recreation and hospital facilities, uniforms, and company songs. The different labor markets in Korea and Taiwan mean, however, that there is no permanent employment, working

---

77. Kuznets, *Economic Growth*, p. 85; see also pp. 105–7.
78. Mason et al., *Economic and Social Modernization*, pp. 16, 263, 485.
79. Ibid., p. 277.

hours are much longer (52 hours per week in the big firms, longer in small firms), and wages are much lower in relation to living cost.

Yet there is no question but that the state is the maker and at times the breaker of the conglomerates. They prospered and grew as the economy grew, in close consort with state support. They do not have the credit power of the Japanese *zaibatsu*. At the core of the latter was always a bank, but in Korea and Taiwan it is the state that provides credit. This is one of its greatest weapons. State bureaucracies like the EPB control domestic credit and favor certain export-oriented firms, and they mediate foreign credit through licensing schemes. Thus, they have almost total control over access to investment capital; the *chaebol* are all structured with very low equity and huge debt components.[80] Most are in technical bankruptcy at any given time. Thus, when the Yolsan conglomerate added to Park Chung Hee's difficulties by (reportedly) flirting with the opposition leader Kim Dae Jung in 1979, the president pulled the plug and Yolsan collapsed, taking several small banks with it. Samuel Ho notes the same sort of autonomy for the state in Taiwan: it can move in and out of sectors, promote this or that industry, because it is "relatively neutral to sectoral or regional interest."[81] It is this relative autonomy and promotion of sectoral mobility that makes these BAIRs resemble the Japanese model.

Another similarity with the Japanese model is the exclusion of labor, the exploitation of women, and the low state expenditures on social welfare— all three, of course, are bound to be more extreme in the periphery than in the core. Social spending is minimal in both countries. In 1973, expenditures on social insurance, public health, public assistance, welfare, and veterans' relief represented 0.97 percent of GNP in the ROK, 1.2 percent in Taiwan; this compares with 3 percent in Malaysia and 5.3 percent in Japan.[82] Such figures capture the tradeoff between Japan and Korea and Taiwan: the latter two spend 4 to 10 percent of GNP on defense, and Japan can hold defense expenditures under one percent; but Japan, by virtue of its "New Deal" during the Occupation and its democratic system, must spend 5 percent on social programs (still low by world standards). In any case both the ROK and Japan until recently escaped with spending about 6 percent of GNP on defense and welfare combined. Korean and Taiwanese workers pay the cost in the periphery.

Exploitation of labor, particularly females, is so marked that it is foolish to deny it (even though many American specialists continue to do so). In both the Kaohsiung and the Masan FEZs 80 percent of the workforce is female, and teenage girls are about 60 percent of that total. Most of the work is unskilled assembly, done by girls recruited from peasant families. Their

80. Ibid., pp. 19, 486.
81. Ho, *Economic Development*, p. 251.
82. Mason et al., *Economic and Social Modernization*, p. 22.

wage rates are at the bottom of the heap in world scales—one-third of Japan's level, one-fifth to one-tenth of the U.S. level, even one-half of the level in Hong Kong, where similar practices prevail. The state guarantees foreign firms not only various investment subsidies and profit remissions, but prohibition of union organization. In the Kaohsiung FEZ about 85 percent of the 150 or so firms are wholly or partially foreign-owned (including holdings by overseas Chinese).[83] FEZ products include light electronic assemblies (like calculators), textiles, and simple manufactured items like nuts and bolts. Thus these are basically platforms of world production located in countries that can provide cheap and controlled labor. In Korea and Taiwan strikes are usually prohibited (even though they may occur), and unions are company- or state-managed in good corporate fashion.

All in all the BAIR provides a potent mix, fusing state and economic power in pursuit of comparative advantage in world markets. To the extent that hegemonic outer limits are not invoked, relative autonomy is at any given time greater in Taiwan and Korea than it is in Japan or the United States. Thus both states sought in the early 1970s to use their autonomous power to upset transnational and free-trade interests by once again import substituting, this time in heavy industry. Both sought not simply to deepen their industrial structures but to deepen their self-reliance and independence vis-à-vis their hegemonic partners. One key enabling factor was the massive reentry of Japanese capital (loans and investments) into the ROK and Taiwan in the mid 1960s. Accomplished relatively easily in Taiwan, in Korea, as we would predict, society reacted strongly and the "normalization" had to be rammed down the throats of protesting students and legislators in 1964–65. But Japan's reentry gave both regimes a strong proxy to play off against American power and capital: a single hegemony began to turn into a dual hegemony.

Park Chung Hee declared in 1972 that "steel = national power," a pithy slogan that symbolizes the deepening industrialization of both countries. The Third Five-Year Plan, 1971–76, inaugurated this phase. During 1969 to 1971 domestic capital formation rose markedly in the ROK, to account for 26 to 30 percent of gross domestic product, compared to 17 to 18 percent in the United States and 36 to 40 percent in Japan during the same years; the manufacturing sector rose from 11 percent to 30 percent between the early 1960s and the mid 1970s. A similar and coterminous deepening occurred in Taiwan. Economist Anthony Michel has also noted that Korean economic nationalists were dominant in constructing the Third Five-Year Plan, by-passing the EPB, which is transnationally penetrated by Western economists with theories opposed to industrial deepening.[84] The ROK got a new integrated

83. Lin, *Taiwan's Industrialization*, pp. 139–44; Choe Boum Jong, "An Economic Study of the Masan Free Trade Zone," in Hong and Krueger, *Trade and Development*.

84. Kuznets, *Economic Growth*, p. 67; Mason et al., *Economic and Social Modernization*, p. 99; Greenhalgh, "Dependency, Distribution"; seminar paper by Anthony Michel, University of Washington, Seattle, 5 May 1983.

steel mill (developed and installed by Japanese technicians), supertanker shipbuilding capacity, heavy chemical factories and refineries, and an auto industry (with GM, Ford, and Japanese technology) that produced 38,000 cars by 1978. American planners and economists resisted these developments, arguing that heavy industry is unsuited to the factor endowments and small domestic markets of both countries; surplus, idle capacity would be the inevitable result.[85] In other words, Korea and Taiwan were violating a rational international division of labor.

The ROK and Taiwan were able to obtain needed financing and technology for these enterprises from the Japanese, in part because the new programs provided the structure necessary to receive declining Japanese heavy industry. This simultaneously increased Taiwanese and Korean autonomy in the world at large while deepening dependency on Japan. The United States was opposed and, indeed, during the same period the Nixon administration dealt the sharpest blows since 1949 to both countries by limiting shoe and textile imports, floating the dollar, recognizing People's China, and pulling a division of U.S. troops out of the ROK. This set the agenda of conflict for the present: would the Northeast Asian political economy continue as a joint hegemony or as an increasingly Japanese preserve?

By the early 1970s, Korea and Taiwan were both in transition between peripheral and semiperipheral status;[86] in a sense they had recovered their structural position of the last years of the Japanese empire. Vietnam was a periphery for both, as each sent construction teams and other industrial personnel, and Korea sent some 300,000 soldiers over a seven-year period (1966–73). The Vietnam War played for the ROK the role that the Korean War played for Japan; labeled "Korea's El Dorado," it accounted for as much as 20 percent of foreign exchange earnings in the late 1960s.[87] Procurements for the war were also important for Taiwan, and, by the 1970s, Taiwan was exporting capital goods, technicians, and foreign aid to several Southest Asian nations.[88] Both countries sent construction teams to the Middle East to recycle petrodollars after the 1973 oil shock. By the late 1970s both nations were competing for an intermediate position in the world economy, continuing to export labor-intensive goods to advanced countries and capital-intensive goods to LDCs.[89] Firms in both countries sought to go multinational, looking for cheaper labor in Bangladesh, Mexico, and elsewhere, while continuing to supply construction to the Middle East. In these tactics Taiwan and the ROK have been more successful than other industrializing regimes

85. Kuznets, *Economic Growth*, p. 152; Lin, *Taiwan's Industrialization*, p. 137.
86. Daniel Chirot, *Social Change in the Twentieth Century* (New York: Harcourt Brace Jovanovich, 1977), pp. 218–20.
87. David C. Cole and Princeton N. Lyman, *Korean Development: The Interplay of Politics and Economics* (Cambridge: Harvard University Press, 1971), p. 135; also Kuznets, *Economic Growth*, p. 71.
88. Greenhalgh, "Dependency, Distribution."
89. Lin, *Taiwan's Industrialization*, pp. 131–32.

such as Brazil and Argentina. Korea, however, had to bolster its state power and did so in dramatic fashion: the early 1970s were the period of the Yusin Constitution (*yusin* in Korean is *isin* in Japanese, the same characters used to refer to the post-1868 Meiji reforms), KCIA penetration of society, a clump of "emergency decrees," and increasing use of vile tortures against dissidents.

Although Taiwan and Korea sought to escape dependency in the 1970s, what they succeeded in doing was exchanging one form of dependency for another, or enhancing one and reducing the other. The U.S. role has declined; experts no longer dictate to the regimes, as they did in the early 1960s, but "offer suggestions." The direct dependency of the 1950s and early 1960s has changed into an indirect dependency, increasingly like Japan's, within the U.S. hegemony. Both countries remain captive grain markets for the United States, both continue to get much of their oil shipped in and refined by U.S. multinationals, and both remain highly dependent on the United States for security (with Taiwan moving into a less determinate position after the U.S.-China normalization). In both countries direct aid ended in the mid 1960s, but PL480 grain and other supports continue to flow as a trade-off for "voluntary" textile export restraint. In the period 1951–74 Korea alone received $8 billion in U.S. food shipments, most of it under PL480, and surplus American grain has been essential in keeping wages low in Korea and Taiwan.[90]

Japan, by contrast, lacking a military or resource component to foster peripheral dependency, has pursued a trade hegemony that could be a textbook example of Hirschman's schema for Germany in interwar Eastern Europe. Japan's trading practices toward Taiwan and the ROK fit almost perfectly with his outline of techniques a dominant country uses to create an "influence effect" dependency: create groups with vested interest in trade, direct trade toward poorer countries, trade with countries with little mobility of resources, induce discrepancies between production for export and for the home market, and so on.[91] Northeast Asia exemplifies Hirschman's rule that dependency will emerge where country A takes a large percentage of trade from country B, but country B's trade is a small part of country A's total trade. He illustrates this by reference to Bulgaria's trade with Germany: 52 percent of its imports came from and 59 percent of its exports went to Germany, but that trade only amounted to 1.5 percent of German imports and 1.1 percent of German exports.[92] In the 1970s, Japan accounted for about 25 percent of ROK exports and 38 percent of its imports; Japan and the United States combined accounted for 70 percent of ROK imports and about two-thirds of its exports.[93] Direct Japanese investment in Korea bal-

90. Wade and Kim, *Economic Development*, p. 10; Kuznets, *Economic Growth*, p. 103.
91. Hirschman, *National Power*, pp. 34–35.
92. Ibid., p. 30.
93. Mason et al., *Economic and Social Modernization*, pp. 138, 497; Kuznets, *Economic Growth*, p. 73.

looed after the 1965 normalization, which was itself accompanied by a munificent package of loans and credits totaling about $300 million. Within a few years Japanese direct investment outstripped the American total; in the period 1972–76, for example, Japanese investment was more than four times the American total ($396 million to $88 million). Japan's ten largest trading firms handled as much as 50 percent of exports and 60 percent of imports to and from Korea between 1963 and 1972.

Taiwan's trade is similarly skewed; but Taiwan is less dependent on financing from Japan and the United States, whereas the ROK's dependence on Japanese financing since 1965 is, according to Kuznets, "characteristic of Korea's earlier satellite role within the Yen Bloc."[94] Both countries remain almost entirely dependent on American and Japanese multinationals for foreign markets and technology transfer.[95] Although an indirect dual dependency continues to exist, the Japanese are more aggressive than the Americans: as Ezra Vogel argues, the Japanese try "to induce as much technological dependence on Japan . . . as possible."[96] In Taiwan and Korea this takes the form, for example, of letting them assemble color television sets while jealously guarding the technology necessary to make a color picture tube.

Many are called but few are chosen: Korea's export-led trap

Export-led development on the Korean and Taiwan model places four critical obstacles in the way of upward mobility in the world system. First, LDCs need to break into the system of economic exchange at a point other than comparative advantage in labor, that is, in marketing, better technology, or better organization. Yet multinationals provide most of the markets and use "steady-state" or obsolescent technologies—as Lin puts it, technology "is stable in the product-cycle sense."[97] Second, limited factor endowments and the small domestic markets that characterize such offshore production inhibit second-stage industrialization and cause early problems of surplus capacity. Third, rising competition from poorer states means that there is a critical but a short and slim lead over competing LDCs. Multinationals, especially the smaller textile firms, may simply move production facilities to countries offering better labor costs. Finally, core-country protectionism will arise to the extent that declining sectors have representation in the polity. In the late 1970s, Taiwan and Korea met all these problems compounded by inflated oil prices.

In the event, Taiwan was chosen but the ROK was not. Taiwan is beginning to manufacture computers for export (Atari moved a big factory there in

94. Kuznets, *Economic Growth*, p. 85.
95. Lin, *Taiwan's Industrialization*, p. 173.
96. Vogel, *Harvard Seminar 1979*.
97. Lin, *Taiwan's Industrialization*, p. 134.

1983), while Korea suffered a loss of 6 percent of GNP in 1980, the first loss since the export-led program began. In 1978, the Korean threat to advanced country industries seemed so palpable that Japanese newspapers were filled with wary editorials about "the Korean challenge," and a middle-level State Department official stated in my earshot that a prime goal of U.S. policy toward Korea was to "manage its articulation with the world economy so that we don't get another Japan there." According to some sources, the Carter administration put off its troop withdrawal plan both to maintain influence in Korea and to stave off ever-increasing Japanese dominance. In June 1979, Jimmy Carter visited Park Chung Hee and toasted him for his stable rule. Six months later Park was assassinated amidst a general political and economic crisis. The timing of the economic crisis may be explained by the second oil wave of early 1979, but the cause of the crisis lay deep in the structure of Korea's economic activity. The late 1970s saw increasing protectionism, declining technology transfer, and a greater need to borrow to meet oil expenses and service previous debt. Furthermore, in dialectical fashion, the remedy that Korea had used to ride out the first oil wave—dispatching construction teams to the Middle East—caused a skilled labor shortage that bid up wages within Korea, thus jeopardizing the ROK's comparative advantage. At the same time, an outward-turning People's China began eating into Korean textile markets. The big steel, shipbuilding, and automobile factories met the very obstacle that free traders had predicted: when ships and cars could not be sold abroad, the small domestic market could not help out. Korean automobile production in late 1979 and 1980 came to a virtual standstill. Thus, as the economist Yung Chul Park stated, all these problems threatened to "bring the export-led industrialization to a rather abrupt end."[98] Korean EPB planners stated publicly that the economy was "uncontrollable" and in a "quandary."

The economic difficulties detonated a political crisis, beginning with vastly enhanced opposition power deployed around Kim Dae Jung. He in turn drew support from textile workers, small businesses and firms with national rather than international interests, and his native southwestern Cholla region, which, historically rebellious and leftist, had been left out of much of the growth of the previous fifteen years. Major urban insurrections occurred in the southeastern cities of Pusan and Masan in the autumn of 1979. Some 700 labor strikes were recorded in 1979–80, and in April 1980 miners took over a small town east of Seoul and held it for several days. In May, hundreds of thousands of students and common people flooded the streets of Seoul, leading to martial law, which in turn touched off a province-wide rebellion in South Cholla and the capture of the provincial capital by rebels who held

98. A good summary of the recent economic problems of the ROK's export-led program can be found in Yung Chul Park, "Recent Economic Developments in Korea" (Paper presented to the Columbia University Seminar on Korea, 24 April 1981).

it for a week. Korea seemed to be on the verge of disintegrating as Iran had done, but unlike Iran the military did not fracture and a new general, Chun Doo Hwan, executed a multistage coup: within the military in December 1979, within the KCIA in April 1980, and throughout the state apparatus in summer 1980. Through withering repression the strong societal reaction was quieted, but at the cost of a deep radicalization of remaining protesters.

In the aftermath of this rebellious period, the Korean state intervened continuously to revive the economy's comparative advantage in the world system. The state sponsored the sectoral reorganization of several large conglomerates, on the principle of one *chaebol* for each industrial sector. For the first time the ROK publicly referred to the "organic" nature of its perimeter defense relationship with Japan, as justification for demanding at least $6 billion in Japanese loans and aid. (In early 1983 Korea and Japan agreed upon a $4 billion package of loans and credits, clearly marking Japan's increasing role as compared to that of the United States.) Finally, the state accomplished a thorough repression of labor in outlawing strikes and unions, closely watching any and all organizing activity, and driving down wages. Thus in 1981 labor productivity increased 16 percent while wages went down 5 percent in real terms. GNP growth of 6.4 percent recovered the loss of 1980.[99] Yet the period 1978–83 has seriously weakened the ROK in its struggle with Taiwan for advantageous position in the world economy.

In 1979, the World Bank reported that "the burden of external debt is being steadily reduced," and agreed with Korean planners that a growth rate for exports of 16 percent and for GNP of 9 to 10 percent per year could be sustained through the 1980s. It noted that "confidence in Korea's ability to meet its external debt service obligations is based on the continuation of rapid export growth."[100] Since the 1980 downturn the economy has grown only in the 5 to 6 percent range, debts have more than doubled since 1979 to a total external debt of $42 billion (third largest in the world), and export growth has tumbled badly. Growing by double-digit rates throughout the 1970s, and by 17 percent in the bad year of 1980 (to $17.2 billion), exports reached $21 billion at the end of 1981 and by mid 1983 were no higher than $22 billion on an annual basis. In other words, export growth has been flat since 1981. Taiwan's exports have not been booming, either, but its external debt is no more than $7 billion and the slowing of export growth has had no apparent effect on internal politics.

Thus, in 1983 as in the rest of this century, Taiwan continues its smooth

99. See "South Korea's New Leader: Off and Running," *Far Eastern Economic Review*, 30 January–5 February 1981; *Christian Science Monitor*, 5 January 1982; *Tonga Ilbo* (East Asia Daily), 26 December 1981.

100. World Bank, *Korea: A World Bank Country Economic Report*, Parvez Hasan and D. C. Rao, coordinators (Baltimore: Johns Hopkins University Press, 1979), pp. 8–9, 47. This is also a good source on World Bank criticism of Korea's deepening industrialization strategy during the Third Five Year Plan.

development, in spite of losing major security guarantees and in spite of structural obstacles to its development. South Korea, on the contrary, plays out its history of economic dynamism mixed with spasmodic social reaction. Today, its development program hangs in the balance.

Conclusions

I have sought to demonstrate the shaping and conditioning effects of economic forces on three distinct societies, peoples, and cultures, and the effects of industrial product cycles on a regional political economy. Japan, Taiwan, and South Korea have come to have similar economic structures (although in different temporal sequences), and all three, with markedly different traditional polities, have adopted quite similar political models and roles for the state. The BAIR model—relative state autonomy, central coordination, bureaucratic short- and long-range planning, high flexibility in moving in and out of industrial sectors, private concentration in big conglomerates, exclusion of labor, exploitation of women, low expenditures on social welfare and, in prewar Japan and contemporary South Korea and Taiwan, militarization and authoritarian repression—is found in all three nations. When one is compared to another the differences will also be salient, but when all three are compared to the rest of the world the similarities are remarkable.

I have also argued that industrial development in Japan, Korea, and Taiwan cannot be considered as an individual country phenomenon; instead, it is a regional phenomenon in which a tripartite hierarchy of core, semiperiphery, and periphery was created in the first part of the 20th century and then slowly recreated after World War II. The smooth development of Taiwan has its counterpart in the spasmodic and troubled development of Korea, and neither can be understood apart from Japan. Not only was Taiwan's society less restive and its state less penetrated by societal constraint, but it also had breathing space occasioned by Japan's greater attention to Korea and Manchuria before 1945, and American "development by invitation" after 1950. In short, the developmental "successes" of Taiwan and Korea are historically and regionally specific, and therefore provide no readily adaptable models for other developing countries interested in emulation.

The evidence also strongly suggests that a hegemonic system is necessary for the functioning of this regional political economy: unilateral colonialism until 1945, U.S. hegemony since 1945. Today there is increasing competition between American and Japanese hegemony over semiperipheral Taiwan and South Korea, but as years pass there may well be sharper competition over a new hinterland, People's China. Will the United States or Japan, or both, organize Chinese labor in the world system? And as Chinese labor-intensive exports increase, whither Taiwan and South Korea? Past history suggests that a triangular structure works best, and so Taiwan and the ROK should move into a middling position between China on the one hand and the United States and Japan on the other. The Chairman of the Korea Exchange Bank, Choon Taik Chung, said in 1981 that "within ten years, Korea will be the bridge . . . between mainland China and the United States." Already, some synthetic textiles made in South Korea are being shipped to China for finishing, taking advantage of cheaper labor cost; the finished product is then sold in American markets. Within Japan, there are voices arguing that Japan should slowly transfer its auto and steel industries to South Korea and Taiwan, placing emphasis instead on high-technology "knowledge industries."[101] The continuing world competitiveness of Japanese auto and steel exports in the early 1980s seems to have slowed this transfer, but it will probably continue. Still, international politics and domestic social forces (especially in Korea) complicate the replication and deepening of this "natural" tripartite hierarchy.

The China connection comes to the heart of the problem. In a recent discussion Raymond Vernon said the Japanese capabilities for exploiting that opportunity are "some orders of magnitude greater than the capacity of the U.S." to deal with it. Jon Halliday argues that Japan is far better positioned than the United States to benefit from the economic opportunities of the 1980s in Northeast Asia.[102] In a situation of stable U.S. hegemony, such as existed from 1951 to 1970 in the region, Japan and the United States could profit equally from such opportunities. Today, in an era of limits, this is not the case. The world system does not provide open access for all. It can tolerate only one or two hegemonies, and only one or two Japans. For the smaller and weaker countries, core-power rivalry spells trouble in the intermediate zone. For Japan, the coming period, like the interwar period, will test its ability both to be successful economically and to live at peace with the world around it: tragically, in the past its striving toward core-power status resembled less flying geese than a moth toward a flame.

Americans, as Vogel suggests, "haven't begun to think about the implications of living in a world where Japan is the most powerful industrial power."[103] They must also decide if they can live at peace with a formidable Japan. And they must contemplate the obvious fact that, in the late 20th century, the race is passing to those who are best organized for competition in a merciless world system. We see this reflected in a poignant observation by Raymond Vernon:

> The concept of free access of every country to every market and the gradual reduction of trade barriers and the openness of capital markets, served us well, given our internal political and economic structure, and

101. Lecture by Norman Thorpe, Seoul correspondent for the *Asian Wall Street Journal*, Seattle, Wash., 8 January 1982; also John Marcom Jr., "Korea Dents Japanese Dominance in Steel," *Asian Wall Street Journal*, 28 December 1981.
102. Raymond Vernon, in *Harvard Seminar 1979*; Jon Halliday, "The Struggle for East Asia," *New Left Review* no. 124 (December 1980), pp. 3–24.
103. Vogel in *Harvard Seminar 1979*.

given our position in the world from 1945 on. All my preferences, all my values argue for retaining this system, for as long as one can. But one observes the way in which Japan has organized itself . . . with a certain unity of purpose, which can easily be exaggerated, but nonetheless at the same time should not be overlooked. One looks at the way in which state enterprises are being used somewhat—*somewhat* . . . by the other advanced industrial countries and now by the developing countries in very considerable degree. Observing these various forms of interference with the operation of market mechanisms, I find myself reluctantly pushed back constantly to the question whether we have to opt for a set of institutional relationships and principles that reflect a second best world from our point of view. We have to somehow organize ourselves. . . .[104]

104. Vernon in ibid.

State and foreign capital in the East Asian
NICs Stephan Haggard and Tun-jen Cheng

Economists have been attracted to the success of the East Asian newly industrializing countries—South Korea, Taiwan, Hong Kong, and Singapore. Treating political and historical factors as residual and emphasizing the benefits of "correct" policy choices, however, they have produced incomplete explanations of East Asian growth (Chen, 1979; Balassa, 1981). In this chapter we attempt a more institutional approach to the development of the East Asian NICs, focusing in particular on the role of foreign capital. Two axes of comparison inform the analysis.

First, we argue that critical differences *among* the four cases should not be overlooked; the purported East Asian model is not of a piece (Johnson, 1980, 1981; Wade and White, 1985). These differences include not only obvious ones between city-states and larger countries but also variations in relations between government and local and foreign firms and in national responses to the international economic turbulence of the 1970s and early 1980s.

Second, we argue that the common pursuit of an export-oriented development strategy differentiates the East Asian NICs from the large, import-substituting NICs of Latin America, including Brazil, Mexico, and Argentina. Our analysis thus permits us to assess the applicability of dependency theory to East Asia. Developed initially with reference to Latin America, the concepts of dependency and dependent development seek to capture the internal distortions and external vulnerabilities of countries pursuing successive stages of import-substituting industrialization under the auspices of a

This capter was originally prepared for delivery at the 1983 Annual Meeting of the American Political Science Association, Chicago, September 1–4, 1983. We thank Alice Amsden, Kent Calder, Bruce Cumings, Fred Deyo, Peter Evans, Jeff Frieden, Gary Gereffi, Tom Gold, Jeff Hart, Chi Huang, Chalmers Johnson, Ethan Kapstein, Byung-Kuk Kim, Hagen Koo, Tom Ilgen, Chung Lee, Jamie Mackie, Sylvia Maxfield, Chung-in Moon, John Ravenhill, and Robert Wade for comments on earlier drafts, and Maura Barry and Lucia Tsai for research assistance.

"triple alliance" of local, foreign, and state capital (Cardoso, 1973; Evans, 1979).[1]

All developing countries exhibit some sort of division of labor between local firms, multinational corporations, and state-owned enterprises. The explanatory problem is to account for sectoral variations and differences in the relative power of the three actors across countries. Such an explanation requires us to address critical domestic variables that dependency analysts ignore, including development sequencing, the political and economic strategies of state elites, and the interests and forms of representation of domestic social groups. We advance three sets of arguments.

In the first section we examine the role of foreign capital, and particularly direct investment, in East Asian development. The adoption of an export-oriented strategy for growth fostered, except in Singapore, domestic manufacturing firms capable of competing internationally. Despite generous government incentives, foreign direct investment dominated only a few sectors and played a comparatively small role in overall capital formation and even in exports. This pattern of economic development contrasts sharply with the Latin American model of successive rounds of import substitution financed in part by large external indebtedness and resulting in a strong multinational presence.

The second section examines the political basis of export-led growth. We explain the nature of this broad policy regime by examining the nature of the state, the ideologies and influence of technocrats, and the coalitional bases of national development.

The politically insulated nature of the state in the East Asian NICs requires that we pay particular attention to the development projects of technocratic elites. The degree of state intervention across the four countries varies. In South Korea, Singapore, and Taiwan the state has played a central role in orchestrating export-led growth, while Hong Kong has maintained a laissez-faire posture. Nonetheless, technocrats in each country have been influenced by economic ideologies that emphasize the advantages of private-sector, export-led growth. In each case technocrats have had wide leeway to design economic policy and firm, consistent, and high-level political support to implement it.

Technocrats have been constrained, however, by the prior development of domestic business. In South Korea, Taiwan, and Hong Kong political elites could build a viable economic strategy around previously developed national firms; they did not have to intervene extensively in production or rely heavily on foreign firms to substitute for entrepreneurial weakness. In

1. The triple alliance model also sought to capture a set of innovations in the organization of production which involved all three partners (Evans, 1981). In certain sectors, such as petrochemicals, this arrangement appears common to both import-substituting and export-oriented NICs, suggesting that certain sectoral rather than national factors might explain these institutional arrangements.

Singapore, by contrast, the national bourgeoisie was extremely weak; foreign firms came to play a dominant role there. Similarly in Latin America the choice of an industrial strategy of "deepening" necessarily entailed a larger role for foreign and state-owned enterprises.

Another coalitional argument concerns the relative weakness of labor and of leftist and populist forces. In all four cases, state elites had increased freedom of maneuver in pursuing a probusiness strategy because of the absence of effective political and labor opposition.

In the third section we raise more explicitly the question of external vulnerability and dependency. The dependency tradition locates the major external constraint on dependent development in the multinational corporation. But this notion is incomplete and misleading. No account of East Asian growth is possible without attention being paid to the influence of empire and international security alliances; yet dependency theorists, no less than liberal economists, have been oddly negligent of high politics. International political relationships and the transnational networks they produce, from British and Japanese colonialism to the postwar system of American alliances, have influenced choice of growth strategies. Moreover, the outward orientation of the East Asian NICs means that orientation changes in world markets and protectionism in the advanced industrial states can have profound effects on economic performance. Wages in the East Asian NICs have risen steadily, gradually undermining competitiveness in the light, labor-intensive manufactures that initially led growth. A second tier of would-be NICs has sought to establish a presence in a similar range of industries. Common competitive pressures have increased state attention to the upgrading and diversification of industry and exports. Though approaches to industrial adjustment have varied across the East Asian NICs, they have invariably involved another change also: an effort to lure new foreign investment into desired sectors.

Foreign capital and development sequencing

Development crises and the convergence on export-led growth

The role of foreign capital in East Asian NIC growth has varied during the different phases of postwar development. The city-state sequence in Hong Kong and Singapore involved a transition from entrepôt to manufacturing center, though commercial and service activities retained importance and grew in significance during the 1970s. The development pattern in South Korea and Taiwan, on the other hand, is characterized by a transition first from primary commodity exporter under colonial control to import-substituting industrialization (ISI), second to a strategy of export-led growth.

These postwar transitions were forced by development crises, one of the entrepôt model, the other of ISI. Both were resolved by a turn to export-oriented industrialization. In South Korea, Taiwan, and Singapore the change in development strategy was acccompanied by an effort to lure foreign investors. The reforms came at a historically auspicious moment, allowing the four countries to exploit rapid growth in world trade and the emergence of new forms of foreign investment.

It is no exaggeration to say that American aid sustained the Korean and Taiwanese economies in the fifties, supplementing domestic capital formation and allowing increased imports. In both cases, reconstruction, the severing of traditional export markets, high levels of inflation, and chronic balance-of-payments deficits dictated the choice of import substitution supported by a policy package that typically included stringent import controls and an overvalued exchange rate.

Dependence on aid was high. In South Korea aid financed nearly 70 percent of total imports between 1953 and 1962 and equaled 80 percent of total fixed capital formation (Cole, 1980). Economic assistance totaled $5.74 billion between 1946 and 1976, but 45 percent of this amount came during the critical years of import-substituting reconstruction, 1953 to 1961. Taiwan tells a similar story. Of a current-account deficit of $1.3 billion between 1953 and 1962, aid financed approximately $1.1 billion, or 85 percent (Jacoby, 1966). Total economic aid commitments between 1951 and 1965, including PL480 food aid, were almost $1.5 billion. Between 1952 and 1962 U.S. aid financed 38 percent of gross domestic capital formation.[2] In Taiwan a relatively small portion of aid was channeled into industry, but even there American assistance proved critical in stimulating new investment by financing the import of intermediate inputs.

In East Asia, in contrast to Latin America, direct foreign investment played a negligible role during this ISI phase. Manufacturing in Brazil and Mexico saw substantial direct investment in the 1950s, to service large internal markets in line with an industrial strategy of deepening in consumer durables and intermediate goods (Evans and Gereffi, 1981). South Korea and Taiwan were too small and politically risky to attract much investment interest.

Japanese investment had been extensive in the imperial period, contributing to the development of an industrial and infrastructural base in both countries. In Taiwan food processing, in particular sugar refining, was the major industry before the 1930s. After the mid-thirties the colonial administration took steps to broaden the island's industrial base to include some manufactures, fertilizer, and processing of raw materials (Ho, 1978). In Korea state-chartered firms supported the imperial policy of developing the

---

2. These enormous sums are in addition to military aid, which totaled over $6 billion in Korea from 1946 to 1979, yielding a commitment of approximately $13 billion. The comparable figure for Taiwan is $5.6 billion (Central Intelligence Agency, 1980).

country as a logistical base for Japan's expansion into China. Between 1925 and 1939 the share of mining and manufacturing in total output jumped from 19 percent to 45 percent. Heavy and chemical industries played a leading role in this development, though most were located in the North (Chang, 1982:chap. 2). After the war Japanese properties fell into the hands of the new governments, giving them a key political resource.

In the fifties foreign investment played a greater role in Taiwan than in South Korea; Korea's economic relations with Japan were severed altogether until normalization in the mid-sixties. Even so, foreign investment from 1952 to 1959 totaled less than $30 million in Taiwan. Of eighty-six cases of direct investment in Taiwan across the 1950s, fifty-eight cases were by overseas Chinese (Gold, 1981:170; Schive, 1978). The importance of such investment in Hong Kong and Singapore, as well as Taiwan, is difficult to gauge but remains a continuous and unique factor in their postwar development.[3] The flight of large amounts of capital followed the Chinese Revolution and provided an important source of external finance in the early postwar development of both Taiwan and Hong Kong. Through 1980 overseas Chinese investors were responsible for 54 percent of all cases of foreign investment in Taiwan but only 35 percent of total capital and a negligible proportion of technology licensing arrangements.[4]

In sum, the 1950s in Taiwan and South Korea were characterized by the pursuit of an ISI strategy required by war and reconstruction, financed largely by American aid, and supplemented only marginally in Taiwan by overseas Chinese, Japanese, and American direct investment. Both countries benefited from the nationalization of prewar Japanese investment. Though economists have emphasized the inefficiencies of import substitution (Balassa, 1981:chap. 1), the postwar phase of ISI allowed existing and new firms to consolidate strong domestic positions free from competition, from imports, and from foreign investment.

This pattern differs significantly from the entrepôt model of Hong Kong and Singapore. Strategically located to act as service centers for vast hinterlands, Singapore and Hong Kong have been outward-looking from the beginning. Early trading, shipping, and banking services began as British and Chinese foreign investments but developed into firms with a distinctly local identity. Singapore's agency houses integrated vast investments in plantations and mining across Malaya and the Netherlands East Indies with the

3. Although overseas Chinese capital has played only a very small role in South Korea's development, an unknown portion of "Japanese" foreign investment in the country is believed to be held by Koreans living in Japan.
4. Thomas Gold (1981:170) has shown that direct investment in Taiwan by overseas Chinese resembles local investment in sectoral composition, being concentrated in real estate, light industry, and the service sector. It often takes joint-venture form and is motivated in part by the ability to repatriate capital legally.

city's commercial and banking services.[5] Hong Kong–based firms such as Jardine Mathieson and the Hong Kong and Shanghai Bank had been important in the China trade since the 19th century.

The entrepôt is by nature hyperdependent. Economic activity is completely contingent on economic and political conditions in the hinterland and trends in the international economy. This dependence results in periodic entrepôt crises that forced Hong Kong and Singapore to industrialize just as the Depression had forced Latin America to industrialize.

The Chinese Revolution and the strategic embargo by the United Nations associated with the Korean War provided such a stimulus in Hong Kong. Entrepôt trade fell off significantly after 1949, while capital and capitalists were flowing into the colony from Shanghai.[6] Hong Kong's internal markets were relatively small, and so manufacturing could only be export-oriented. By the end of the 1950s domestically produced exports, particularly textiles and apparel, had surpassed reexports, making Hong Kong the first of our four countries to enter the export game. It could be argued, however, that Hong Kong had in fact gone through a period of disguised ISI on the mainland. It was under sheltered conditions that the entrepreneurial capabilities of the Shanghai capitalists had developed—not to mention their fixed capital and plant, some of which ultimately found its way to Hong Kong (Coble, 1980).

Singapore's pattern differs somewhat. Anti-Chinese sentiment in the late fifties in Indonesia undoubtedly attracted some flight capital to Singapore (Lim, 1977), but the money was not carried by the same entrepreneurial cadre that had fled the Chinese Revolution for Hong Kong. As a result, local investment was, and remains, heavily concentrated in the tertiary sector and real estate (Buchanan, 1972). A second difference concerns Singapore's relations with its hinterland. The long-term unviability of the entrepôt model argued for some form of economic association with Malaya,[7] for as Indonesia and Malaysia developed, they would become less content to channel trade through Singapore. The economic premise of the brief association with

5. In the mid-1950s the twelve largest houses still handled a quarter of Malaya's imports and exports (Puthucheary, 1960:52–53). By 1937 total foreign investments in Malaya totaled over $500 million (Callis, 1978:48–58).

6. Estimates vary, but capital inflow was very substantial. Po S. Wong (1958:5) estimates that HK\$1 billion entered between 1949 and 1951, while Edward Szczpanik (1958:153) cites HK\$1.7 billion between 1947 and 1951. Shou-eng Koo estimates that the total transfer of funds by overseas Chinese through 1965, from all sources, including particularly Indonesia and the Philippines, where anticommunist sentiment had erupted into periodic anti-Chinese violence, was HK\$6–7 billion. If we accept estimates by the Chinese University of Hong Kong, the U.S. Department of Agriculture, and the Hong Kong government, then such transfers would equal approximately 40 percent of gross domestic capital formation for the 1949–65 period.

7. This argument was advanced by World Bank missions in 1955 and 1961 (Hughes, 1969).

Malaya (1963–65) was that the advantages of infant industry protection and access to a large market would outweigh the decline of the entrepôt trade. Import barriers were raised in 1964 and 1965, but the full implementation of the common market faltered. Nevertheless, it was during this import-substituting "window" that foreign manufacturing investment first entered Singapore.[8]

Both Singapore and Hong Kong have retained entrepôt functions, as discussed below. Most notably, investment by the largest oil multinationals has made Singapore the third largest refining center in the world after Houston and Rotterdam (Siddayo, 1977).[9] The share of Hong Kong's trade conducted with China has increased in the wake of China's economic reforms, while both Singapore and Hong Kong have grown into major international financial centers.

In each of the four East Asian NICs a crisis for the previous growth path brought about a turn to industrialization based on manufacture for export. In the mid-fifties in Taiwan and the late fifties in South Korea a set of chronic problems normally associated with import substitution set in: market saturation, increased competition, low levels of manufactured exports, high levels of dependence on imports, and wide gaps in the balance of payments. As the Americans sought to cut their longer-term aid commitments, both countries faced the task of earning foreign exchange. Their limited internal markets foreclosed the course pursued in Mexico and Brazil; reliance on a second phase of import substitution in capital and intermediate goods as the major source of growth. Significant economic reforms, primarily in the exchange rate and import-control systems, altered the structure of incentives in a more outward-looking, though by no means a laissez-faire, direction. In Taiwan this policy shift began in 1958 and extended to 1962; South Korea inaugurated major reforms in 1964 and 1965.

Hong Kong faced an entrepôt crisis after the Chinese Revolution and UN embargo and over the fifties was gradually forced to replace reexports with exports of locally manufactured goods. This shift entailed no change in Hong Kong's laissez-faire policies, however. Resting initially on the activities of Shanghai capitalists and foreign buyers, the "new industrialists" gradually became linked to the city's commercial and banking establishment (Wu, 1973).

Singapore is a hybrid case. The short-lived attempt to institute an ISI strategy based on integration with Malaya had exhibited characteristic eco-

8. This motivation is confirmed by studies of Australian, British, Japanese, and American investment in Singapore (Hughes, 1969; Yoshihara, 1979:20–22).

9. Oil refining remains the single largest industry in Singapore. Accounting for 26 percent of total manufacturing output and 26 percent of total exports in 1970, it accounted for 36 percent of total output and 40 percent of exports in 1975 and 35 percent of total output and 41 percent of exports in 1979 (*Far Eastern Economic Review*, 10 October 1982).

nomic weaknesses, particularly in the balance of payments and the generation of employment, after only two years. Indonesian and Malayan development plans anticipated a greater degree of direct management of foreign
trade and financial relations, calling into question Singapore's return to the
entrepôt model. Although the entrepôt crisis was in fact slow to materialize,
development choices of the state leadership were influenced by perceived
limitations on entrepôt growth.

The role of foreign capital

In all cases except Hong Kong, which was already open to direct investment, the new emphasis on exports went hand in hand with an opening to
foreign direct investment and new relations with foreign buyers. Foreign
investment and subcontracting would ease balance-of-payments difficulties,
supply technology and expertise, and open the market channels required by
outward-looking development. From the firms' perspective, open trade policies, generous incentives, cheap labor, and political stability made the East
Asian NICs natural sites for investment.

A commonly accepted caricature portrays the East Asian NICs as little
more than multinational-dominated export platforms; this view is held in
particular by those who associated export-led growth with a new form of
dependency (Landsberg, 1979; *AMPO*, 1977). Folker Frobel and his associates (1981:383) argue that a new international division of labor is emerging
based largely on differentiated manufacturing processes integrated globally
by the multinational corporation. They argue that this form of production is
disadvantageous for developing countries, representing a new type of enclave.

This view springs from the misguided assumption that international subcontracting was at the heart of the industrial transformation of the East Asian
NICs. But only in Singapore are manufacturing output and export almost
completely dominated by foreign firms. The point becomes clearer as we
analyze the role of the export-processing zones (EPZs) and subcontracting,
present measures of the overall role of foreign investment, and examine in
more detail its sectoral composition.

Export-processing zones have four important characteristics (Grunwald
and Flamm, 1985). First, they are industrial estates where land, utilities,
transport facilities, and even buildings are supplied by the government at
highly subsidized rates. Second, the EPZs allow the duty-free entry of goods
destined for reexport. The zones thus seek to attract 100 percent foreign-
owned subsidiaries that are vertically integrated into the investing firm's
marketing and production structure. As a corollary, the zones often have
few economic linkages with the domestic economy other than the wage bill,
though local procurement has increased over time. Third, the state plays a
direct role in controlling union organization so as to preclude labor disrup-

tion. Finally, the zones usually offer to foreign firms incentives over and above those extended to foreign or local investors outside the zones.

The first East Asian EPZ was located in Kaohsiung, Taiwan, coming into operation in 1965. Two additional zones on Taiwan followed in 1970, the same year that South Korea's first came into operation at Masan. Masan was followed by another zone and a proliferation of sector-specific Export Industrial Estates. Hong Kong and Singapore have retained most of the features of free ports. Singapore now has fourteen Industrial Zones, the largest, the Jurong Industrial Estate, dating from 1968. Because of the high cost of land in Hong Kong, the government has used industrial estates to attract both foreign and local investors.

Wholly foreign-owned subsidiaries in the EPZs did not account for all exports by multinational firms, however. Much more difficult to trace are international subcontracting relations (Keesing, 1983), which can include minority equity participation and financing, provision of specifications and plans, and long-term supply contracts. One rough measure of vertically integrated offshore production and subcontracting can be seen in U.S. imports under tariff items 806.30 and 807.00, which levy duties only on value added abroad if the inputs originated in the United States.[10] Although over 50 percent of these imports come from the developed world, Taiwan, Singapore, Hong Kong, and South Korea ranked second, fourth, fifth, and sixth as beneficiaries of the scheme in 1978, accounting for 35 percent of all such imports from developing countries.

Equally difficult to gauge is the impact of integrated multinational buying groups, such as the Japanese *sogo shosha* and the buying arms of large American and European retail chains. No data exist on the role of these groups in exports by the East Asian NICs, but in the initial stages they were probably of critical inportance, providing working capital, materials, and plans to local firms.[11] Although NIC marketing remains weak, competition among buyers, the development of national marketing capabilities, and the diversification toward Third World markets suggest the probability of more arms-length transactions than is commonly believed.

In both South Korea and Taiwan the export take-off had begun before the

10. Indigenous entrepreneurs are allowed to take advantage of these tariff items by importing American inputs and assembling them independently of the multinational corporations or buyers. It is generally believed, however, that the large majority of these imports are related to offshore processing and international subcontracting arrangements. These imports rose from $953 million in 1966 to $9.7 billion in 1978 (Sharpston, 1975; USITC, 1980; Grunwald and Flamm, 1985).

11. In 1972, Jun-guun Hsiau, director of the Export-Import Association of Taiwan, estimated that 50 percent of Taiwan's exports were channeled through foreign trading companies. Ku-Hyun Jung (1983) has estimated that U.S. buying groups, agents, and vertically integrated firms handled between 35 percent and 55 percent of South Korea's trade by the late seventies but notes that Korean general trading companies have eroded the share of the Japanese trading companies. Taiwan has attempted to imitate the Korean model, though with less success, while Hong Kong already possessed an experienced commercial establishment.

TABLE 1. *Share of foreign-invested firms' exports in total NIC exports, selected years (percentages)*

	Approximate share	Year of estimate
South Korea	31.4	1974
	18.3	1978
Taiwan	30	1975
Singapore	66.5	1970
	92.9	1980
Hong Kong	11	1974
	17.8	1984
Brazil	43	1969
Mexico	37	1977

Sources. For South Korea: Lee, 1980; Korea Exchange Bank *Monthly Review,* November 1980. For Taiwan: International Bank of China *Monthly Review,* May–June 1977. For Singapore: Singapore, Economic Development Board, 1970/71, and Dept of Statistics, 1980. For Hong Kong: Hung, 1980; Hong Kong, Industry Dept., 1984. For Brazil: Nayyar, 1978. For Mexico: World Bank, 1979. Mexican and Brazilian data are for exports of manufactures.

construction of the zones, and the significance of EPZs has undergone steady erosion. By 1975 in Taiwan the zones accounted for only 8.6 percent of exports. Taiwan's three zones accounted for 13 percent of the stock of direct investment through 1976. By the late seventies the benefits of locating in the zones had eroded, new entrants were few, and some investors were leaving (Simon, 1980:chap. 5). In South Korea the relative importance of pure EPZs was also declining by the mid-seventies; specialized zones, aiming at both exports and the development of a heavy industrial base, were constructed, mostly with extensive participation by national and state-owned firms.[12] Nor should subcontracting be overestimated. South Korea's exports to the United States falling under items 806.30 and 807.00 in 1975 were 7.3 percent of its total exports to the United States. In Taiwan the share was less than 10 percent (USITC, 1980).

In 1974 firms with at least some foreign investment accounted for 11 percent of Hong Kong's exports inclusive of reexports. A 1984 survey showed foreign-invested firms responsible for 17.8 percent of Hong Kong's "domestic" exports; this figure would no doubt be lower if entrepôt trade were included (Hong Kong, Industry Dept., 1984). In 1975, however, only 3.5 percent of Hong Kong's exports fell under tariff items 806.30 and 807.00 (USITC, 1980).

Singapore is clearly a deviant case. Here multinational corporations dominate. In 1972 wholly owned foreign subsidiaries accounted for 57 percent of manufactured exports: if we include joint ventures, the proportion jumps to 84 percent. Table 1 summarizes what few data are available on the role of

12. Exports from the Masan zone in 1974, probably the peak of its relative importance, were 4 percent of total exports (*Business Asia,* 11 July 1975).

foreign-invested firms in NIC exports, comparing the four East Asian NICs with Brazil and Mexico. Except in Singapore, the export-oriented strategy has not led to any greater dependence on foreign firms for exports of manufactures in East Asia than in Latin America; indeed, the opposite appears to be true.

Dependence on foreign investment can be seen in its role in gross domestic capital formation (see Table 2), though this measure fails to capture the role of foreign firms in transferring technology or in providing market access. Two points are striking. First, Singapore emerges once again as the deviant case, much more dependent on direct investment than the other countries. Second, overall dependence on foreign investment, and thus its contribution to growth, is remarkably low.

An important qualification is required concerning South Korea. Unlike the rest of the East Asian NICs, Korea has been a substantial borrower on international capital markets; its gross external debt was $46.8 billion by 1984.[13] Debt has played an important role in financing South Korea's development, as two sets of indicators suggest. Between 1967 and 1971 foreign savings averaged 39.5 percent of total savings, though only 3.7 percent of this was direct foreign investment. Between 1972 an 1976 the average ratio of foreign savings to total savings had dropped to 25 percent, but the role of foreign investment had increased only marginally, accounting for 7.9 percent of that year's net total inflow of foreign capital. Between 1967 and 1971, by contrast, direct investment accounted for over 30 percent of total capital inflow in Taiwan, Brazil, and Mexico, and between 1972 and 1976 accounted for 16 percent, 23 percent and 16 percent respectively (Korea Exchange Bank *Monthly Review*, August 1982; Westphal et al., 1981:23). Helen Hughes and Tom Parry (forthcoming) have calculated total capital inflows as a share of gross fixed capital formation in South Korea from 1971 through 1983. This ratio hit a peak of 48 percent in 1975, falling off in the recovery of 1977 and 1978 before rising steeply on extensive foreign borrowing in 1979 (27.6 percent of gross domestic capital formation), 1980 (30.7 percent) and 1981 (24.6 percent).

South Korea has faced periodic debt servicing problems; levels of indebtedness became a major policy and political concern in the early 1980s. But it has not faced the massive reschedulings and wrenching debt-related adjustments of the Latin American NICs. The reason lies in the nature of the export-led growth strategy itself. Export success has allowed South Korea to get terms equal to or better than those granted the large Latin American borrowers while keeping its debt service ratio substantially lower.[14]

13. Data supplied by the Economic Planning Board.
14. From 1972 to 1981 Mexico's debt service ratio averaged 36.5 percent, Brazil's 25 percent, and Argentina's 18.6 percent, while South Korea's was only 12 percent (calculated from World Bank, 1983). In the early eighties, however, the government announced its intention to slow the rate of growth of foreign borrowing.

TABLE 2. *Foreign direct investment as a share of gross domestic capital formation in the gang of four, selected years (percentages)*

	Hong Kong	Singapore	Taiwan	Korea
1960			0.5	
1965			1.6	2.7
1966		12.5	1.3	.6
1968		15.1	2.6	.9
1970		21.5	2.8	1.1
1972	4.3[a]	23.2	1.3	2.6
1974	2.3[b]	6.0	1.4	2.8
1976	1.2[c]	6.5	1.2	1.5
1978	0.8[d]		1.5	.7
1980				.4

a. average, 1971–73.
b. average, 1974–75.
c. average, 1976–77.
d. average, 1978–79.
Sources. For Hong Kong: calculated from Mun and Ho, 1979; Ho, 1979; Hong Kong, TI&CD, 1979. For Singapore: Yuan, 1972; Gish, Tan & Co., 1978; Singapore Dept. of Statistics, various issues. For Taiwan: data on foreign investment supplied by the Investment Commission, Ministry of Economic Affairs; capital formation figures from Republic of China, CEPD, various years. For South Korea: data on foreign investment supplied by the Ministry of Finance; capital formation figures from Bank of Korea, various years.

Studies done in the 1970s attested to the dominant position of foreign firms in the industrial structures of Brazil and Mexico (e.g., Evans and Gereffi, 1981; Newfarmer and Mueller, 1975). In South Korea, Taiwan, and Hong Kong, however, export-led growth favored sectors in which local firms had already gained some production experience, labor was a major factor of production, and technologies were mature. This is not to say that the multinationals failed to establish important, even dominant positions in certain sectors; until the mid-seventies the growth of exports in electronics, for instance, was almost completely dominated by multinationals. Except in Singapore, however, where foreign firms came to dominate the entire manufacturing sector, domestic firms occupied important positions in most export sectors. In South Korea and Taiwan state-owned enterprises and close government support for domestic firms acted as a check on the domination of heavy industries by foreign firms.

This sectoral pattern of direct investment can be seen in all four countries. We begin with South Korea (see Table 3). From 1962 to 1966, two projects, a fertilizer plant and a refinery, accounted for over 75 percent of total foreign investment. The period of the export take-off, 1967 to 1976, was the heyday of investment in textiles, apparel, and electronics assembly. Investment in electronics continued through the seventies but shifted away from component assembly toward consumer and industrial electronics (Korean Development Bank, 1981). Textile and apparel investment dropped off to

TABLE 3. *Sectoral shares of direct foreign investment in South Korea, 1962–82 (percentages)*

	1962–66	1967–71	1972–76	1978	1980	1982	Total
Agriculture	—	1.2	1.3	.8	.4	1.0	1.2
Mining	0	—	—	—	—	—	0.2
Services	0	15.6	18.6	31.5	28.6	8.1	21.7
Manufacturing	99	83.1	79.9	67.6	71.0	90.4	76.9
Chemicals	21.5	13	9.9	29.5	50.0	31.6	20.5
Electrical and electronics	0	11.6	15.3	11.1	0	22.4	14.2
Textiles and apparel	3.8	13.9	21.0	.2	0	3.1	10.4
Fertilizer and petrochemicals	70.5	19.4	7.7	8.5	0	0	8.2
Nonelectrical machinery	1.5	3.2	6.3	6.6	6.4	10.9	7.1
Metals	0	5.5	5.9	3.4	2.6	.7	5.0
Transport Equipment	0	.3	6.3	4.8	0	5.1	4.1
Others	1.7	15.2	7.5	3.5	12.0	16.6	7.4
Total (US$ millions)	21.2	96.3	557.0	100.4	96.6	100.5	1,307

Source. Calculated from "Status of Foreign Investment Arrival as of Dec. 1982," Republic of Korea, Ministry of Finance, mimeo.

nothing, while investments in nonelectrical machinery, transport equipment, and chemicals—all targeted as key sectors—showed large increases during the seventies. This pattern reflects the growth of investment aimed at servicing the domestic market. In 1975 multinational exports were 78 percent of total shipments in textiles and 69 percent in electronics, but only 14 percent in chemicals and petroleum and 3 percent in transport equipment (Republic of Korea, Economic Planning Board, 1980).

TABLE 4. *Role of foreign firms in South Korea's manufactured exports (1974) and total value added (1977), in percentages*

	Sectoral share of total Korean exports	MNC share of exports, by sector	Sectoral distribution of MNC exports	MNC share of total value added
Textiles and apparel	39.8	12.2	15.4	10
"Other"	16.3	12.6	• 6.5	na
Electrical and electronics	12.3	88.6	34.6	27
Chemicals	10.0	57.3	18.4	13
Wood products	7.2	2.1	18.4	na
Metal products	3.1	84.2	8.3	na
Transport equipment	3.1	.7	.1	8
Petroleum products	2.6	56.2	4.7	23
Clay products	2.1	75.0	5.1	na
Machinery	2.0	93.4	5.9	9
Food	2.0	8.6	.3	na
Total, manufacturing	100	31.4	100	na

Sources. Calculated from Lee, 1980, 1981.

TABLE 5. *Sectoral distribution of direct investment, Taiwan, 1952–81 (percentages)*

	1952–70	*1971–75*	*1976–81*
Agriculture and food processing	3.7	0.9	2.6
Electronics and electrical machinery	39.4	26.4	28.7
Textiles	7.2	6.4	2.5
Chemicals	17	14	13.7
Metals	6.1	18.3	21.4
Machinery, equipment, and instruments	—	13.6	5.2
Transport	2.4	1.3	1.3
Banking	1.9	6.3	2.5
Services and construction	12.7	9.9	18.1
Others	8.7	2.0	3.1

Source. Computed from Republic of China, CEPD, various years.

The role of multinational corporations in Korean exports in the mid-seventies can be seen in Table 4. In two leading sectors the multinationals accounted for less than 15 percent of total exports. In electronics, however, almost all exports came through foreign firms. Chung Lee (1981) has argued that the dominant position of foreign firms in South Korea's exports should not be equated with overall dominance in production, and figures on the role of foreign-invested firms in total value added back his position.

The sectoral composition of investment undergoes a comparable shift over time in Taiwan, as Table 5 demonstrates, with the importance of electronics slipping and metals, machinery, and services coming to play a more dominant role. The role of foreign-invested firms in Taiwan's exports is similarly limited to specific sectors; the MNCs have a dominant position primarily in electronics (see Table 6).

No data are available on the role of foreign investment in the development

TABLE 6. *Role of foreign-invested firms in Taiwan's total manufactured exports through 1979*

	Percentage of total exports	*Exports by foreign firms as percentage of total exports*
Other	31.9	20.8
Textiles	17.0	29.6
Electronic and electrical	16.4	78.1
Machinery	9.3	14.2
Pulp and paper	7.9	10.1
Apparel and footwear	7.2	15.2
Food	6.8	6.8
Wood products	3.5	5.9

Source. Data supplied by the Republic of China, Council for Economic Planning and Development.

of particular sectors or exports by sector for Hong Kong. In 1974 foreign-invested firms accounted for 79 percent of all manufacturing establishments but employed only 9.8 percent of the industrial workforce and accounted for 11 percent of exports (Hung, 1980; Hong Kong, TICD, 1975). Table 7 shows a somewhat similar shift in the sectoral composition of foreign investment, though the data conceal significant changes *within* the important category of electronics. Electronics assembly and other light manufactures, dependent mainly on cheap labor, have given way to investments in consumer electrical goods, clocks and watches, and even chemicals. The role of investment in textiles and apparel dropped in the 1980s.

Where the dominance of foreign investment in the other three cases is concentrated in particular sectors, in Singapore it is across the board. Indeed, there was a sharp erosion in the relative position of national business betwen 1959 and 1973, as Table 8 shows. In 1959 foreign investment played a relatively small role in Singapore's economy. Foreign firms had established dominant positions in several sectors, but domestic firms still accounted for the lion's share of investment in the important food sector and in other light industry. By 1973 domestic firms had lost their position, which continued to erode across the decade (see Table 9).

Development sequencing and choice of overall strategy created a pattern of direct investment in East Asia different from that in Latin America. Taiwan and South Korea have from the beginning invited foreign investment in import-substituting sectors, such as chemicals, but these have not been leading sectors. In Korea, Taiwan, and Hong Kong national firms established a strong presence in the export of light, labor-intensive manufac-

TABLE 7. *Sectoral distribution of foreign investment in Hong Kong industry (percentages)*

	1970	1975	1979	1984
Electronics	40.9	34.7	23.0	35.5
Textiles	17.8	14.9	15.7	9.8
Watches and clocks	1.5	11.1	7.3	
Chemicals	2.5	5.7	13.2	7.0
Electrical products	1.6	5.7	9.0	8.0
Printing and publishing	4.0	3.6	6.7	
Food	1.0	3.5	5.3	7.2
Toys	4.7	3.4	2.9	
Construction	3.9	3.1	1.5	
Metal fabrication	2.0	2.8	2.5	
Metal products	2.0	2.8	4.5	
Others	17.9	8.5	8.4	24.9
Total	100	100	100	100

Sources. Calculated from Mun and Ho, 1979; Hong Kong, TI&CD, 1979; Hong Kong, Industry Dept., 1984.

TABLE 8. *Role of foreign paid-up capital in Singapore's industry, 1959 and 1973 (percentages)*

	Sectoral share of total paid-up capital		Foreign proportion	
	1959	*1973*	*1959*	*1973*
Food	32	15	13	52
Textiles	1	11	53	89
Chemicals	3	9	19	84
Petroleum and products	0	19	0	100
Metals	11	9	54	51
Machinery	5	10	43	49
Electrical products	3	8	95	74
Scientific and photographic equipment	1	4	62	94
Others	44	15	11	83
Total	100	100	21	76

Sources. Adapted from Yoshihara, 1978; Deyo, 1981.

tures, which must be attributed in part to entrepreneurial experience gained during periods of import substitution, when national firms were protected from both import and investment competition. In Singapore, however, no sustained period of ISI took place, and no significant domestic *manufacturing* bourgeoisie ever emerged. Export-led growth based on national firms, it appears, may have as a prerequisite an earlier period of import substitution.

The auspicious timing of the shift to outward-looking growth—during a period of rapid growth in world trade and investment—allowed national firms in South Korea, Taiwan, and Hong Kong to continue to develop side by side with their foreign counterparts. In Korea and Taiwan a protective attitude toward domestic firms eliminated the threat of import competition or denationalization. Overall, the role of foreign direct investment in capital

TABLE 9. *Role of foreign-invested firms in Singapore's manufacturing, 1970 and 1978 (percentage of total manufacturing)*

	1970	*1978*
Number of establishments	25.2	32.8
Output	68.9	82.4
Value added	66.2	78.4
Employment	55.3	68.7
Labor remuneration	57.5	71.0
Direct export sales	83.5	91.8

Sources. Singapore, Dept. of Statistics, various issues. Data refer to all firms with foreign investment.

formation, exports, and therefore ultimately growth itself proved relatively small. National firms were the backbone of industrial development. Only in certain sectors, such as electronics, did foreign firms dominate.

The sectoral dynamics of export-oriented investment

The convergence on export-led growth was historically auspicious not only because of unprecedented growth in world trade, but also because of important industrial changes in the advanced states which were generating new forms of foreign direct investment. Foreign investment in import-substituting manufacture and raw materials exploration, with its longer history, has received more sustained attention than the new foreign investment in export-oriented industries (Grunwald and Flamm, 1985). Some insights may be gained, however, by looking briefly at investment in textiles and electronics. This comparison also highlights the critical differences between the two major investors in the East Asian NICs, Japan and the United States.

Numerous studies emphasize that Japanese investments in the East Asian NICs differ from American investments there (e.g., Ozawa, 1979; Yoshihara, 1978). Japanese investments tend to be smaller in size, come from smaller parent companies, and are more export-oriented. American investment, on the other hand, has been concentrated in heavier, more capital-intensive industries, such as chemicals, and comes from the largest American firms. Where it has been export-oriented, U.S. investment has been primarily a defensive response to challenges in the home market.

The sector characteristic of the Japanese pattern has been textiles and apparel. The largest share of foreign investment in textiles in each of the four East Asian NICs has come from Japan, itself a new entrant into world textile trade in the 1950s. With rising wages, a revaluation of the yen, and protectionist accords, Japan began to lose competitiveness in certain segments to Hong Kong's rapidly growing industry. As Kunio Yoshihara describes the cycle, "the first response of the Japanese garment sector was to shift the center of production to small towns in Japan . . . their investments in Hong Kong and especially South Korea may be regarded as an extension of this regional diversification" (Yoshihara, 1978:117). Hong Kong entrepreneurs would later follow a similar strategy, investing in Singapore in the late sixties (Chen, 1983).

Semiconductors and televisions show a different pattern. Offshore assembly of semiconductors by American firms starts with an investment by Fairchild in Hong Kong in 1961, aimed at reexport to the United States. Other firms, Japanese, American, and European, followed suit; investment quickly spread to South Korea in 1964, Taiwan in 1965, and Singapore in 1968. The reduction of labor costs in the most labor-intensive stages of production and the exploitation of the new 806.30 and 807.00 tariff provisions in the United States were clear motivations. In black and white televisions, on the other hand, the shift of production offshore by American firms came as a defensive response to growing competition from Japanese imports (Borrus et al., 1983; Millstein, 1983).

In short the relationship between the East Asian NICs and Japanese and American foreign investment has several unique features not associated with direct investment in Latin America (with the exception of Mexico's border industrialization program). In the case of textiles a strong complementarity existed between Japan's transnational strategy of industrial adjustment and the export orientation of the four East Asian NICs. In semiconductors and televisions, changing terms of international competition pressed American and Japanese firms to locate production in the NICs.

A unique development sequence and historical timing have been important in creating a particular pattern of foreign direct investment. This is only part of the story, however. These development choices, including policies toward foreign investors, still need to be explained.

The political bases of outward-looking growth

Despite some overall similarities in pattern of foreign investment, the regulatory regimes governing foreign investment in the four East Asian NICs have varied. South Korea's policies have been restrictive, Hong Kong's laissez-faire, with Singapore and Taiwan arrayed between these two extremes. The relative weight of foreign investment has varied in the four cases as well; Singapore's pattern is fundamentally different from that of the other three. And, of course, the choice of an export-oriented growth strategy has been the crucial difference between East Asian and the Latin American NICs. Development crises, as the previous section stressed, played an important role in pushing toward an outward-looking strategy; three political factors help explain national responses to these crises.

The first concerns the relatively insulated and strong nature of the state in East Asia and the economic-ideological orientaion of state elites (Haggard, 1986). By insulation we mean simply that the activities of autonomously organized social and political groups are limited and that these groups lack effective access to centers of decision-making power within the state structure. Where corporatist channels do exist, they tend to be state-controlled rather than societal (Schmitter, 1974).

Such an instrumental, or institutional, definition of state autonomy does not mean that the state can escape various constraints in the class structure, the international system, and the business cycle. It does mean, however, that explanations of state policy must make reference to the political, economic, and ideological interests of state elites; the state must be treated as a key actor. As the level of insulation—and coercive power—rises, the projects of state elites cast a lengthening shadow over the nature of civil society itself. This implication of state autonomy is frequently overlooked.

Strategic policy choices taken by technocrats and backed by political elites have reflected a definable economic ideology that we call developmental liberalism. The state uses a mixture of direct controls and arms-length incentives to foster industrial growth, but it looks for an industrialization oriented toward the world market (Johnson, 1980, 1981). This strategy is in sharp contrast to the deeply entrenched policies of import substitution which have characterized economic planning throughout postwar Latin America[15] but is by no means laissez-faire.

Although it emphasizes international competitiveness, developmental liberalism bears little resemblance to the free trade and investment regime championed by some development economists (Balassa, 1981). In fact this liberalism has a distinctly mercantilist cast. South Korea, Taiwan, and Singapore all have dirigist bureaucracies capable of extracting and channeling resources to targeted industries and selectively altering and sequencing the system of industrial incentives, including those to foreign investors. Hong Kong is the exception. Because the colonial administration held to a virtually pure laissez-faire orientation, few instruments of microeconomic guidance were ever developed.

The second political factor determining the position of foreign capital is the dominant coalition underlying state policy. If the relative insulation of the state is given, these coalitions must be understood as tacit political agreements initiated by the political leadership. The nature of the development possible under such coalitions has depended on the capabilities of the private sector. Tacit alliances developed between the state in South Korea and Taiwan and fledgling local firms in the name of national industrial development, with state-owned enterprises playing a complementary role. The result over time was the strengthening of national capitalist classes. In return for extensive support and protection from foreign firms in the domestic market, national firms accepted significant microeconomic controls and political quiescence. Rapid growth, in turn, provided an important pillar of legitimacy for authoritarian or one-party dominant systems. Hong Kong granted no special support to local manufacturing enterprises. The government's laissez-faire orientation favored the activities of the dominant commercial and financial establishments, however, while the historical development of Chinese manufacturing capital on the mainland and the large pool of immigrant labor ensured the success of Hong Kong manufacturing. In addition the trading companies, banks, and larger manufacturing enterprises performed some of the functions taken on by the state in the other three countries, including financing of infrastructure and investment in and pro-

15. The monetarist interludes in Chile and Argentina mark sharp exceptions.

motion of smaller enterprises. The development of national firms reduced the relative importance of foreign capital in South Korea, Taiwan, and Hong Kong.

Singapore, on the other hand, experienced no such alliance between the state and national manufacturing firms. Concentration of domestic investment in the tertiary sector prevented the political leadership from turning to an indigenous manufacturing class to act as agent of economic growth and national development. The state and foreign firms both played an enhanced role as a matter of necessity, often at the expense of domestic business.

A corollary to this pattern of business-state alliances was the weakness or repression of leftist political forces and organized labor. These political developments often preceded the turn to outward-looking growth. But they proved to be an important prerequisite for a strategy predicated on a well-educated but organizationally weak labor force.

The third and final factor influencing the turn to export-led growth and shaping the particular role to be played by foreign investment was international political relationships. In Taiwan and South Korea decolonization strengthened the economic position of the state and national firms by eliminating the presence of foreign capital. Important transnational coalitions developed as both countries fell into the U.S. security orbit. American advisers supported liberalizing economic reforms, among them an opening to direct foreign investment. In the 1970s political isolation heightened for Taiwan the importance of liberal investment and trade rules as a surrogate for political ties (Simon, 1980). For Singapore, strained relations with Indonesia and Malaysia and the withdrawal of the British military presence east of Suez contributed to the need to develope a manufacturing capability based on foreign firms. In Hong Kong the colonial administration's laissez-faire economic policy has served the interests of both London and Beijing.

In this section we explore the nature of the state and the ideologies of state elites, the business-government alliance, and the role of international political relationships in shaping each government's posture toward foreign direct investment.

Singapore

Fears were already being expressed by the mid-fifties about Singapore's viability as an entrepôt (Geiger and Geiger, 1973). In 1960, 94 percent of Singapore's exports were reexports. Large-scale trade, finance, and shipping remained in the hands of the old agency houses. Some large-scale manufacturing in printing, publishing, and food and rubber processing was in the hands of Chinese family empires, but the majority of Singapore's businesses were retail and service establishments, small and capital-poor (Deyo, 1981; Buchanan, 1972:130–131). This economy proved unable to absorb the rapidly growing number of entrants into the labor force. Unemployment rose steadily in the fifties, becoming the prime political problem of the decade.

Singapore inherited a coherent and centralized administration, but the transitional self-rule governments of 1955–59 were preoccupied with de-colonizaton to the neglect of economic problems. In Taiwan and South Korea the left was defeated early, but in Singapore the Communists were serious contenders for political leadership throughout the fifties. The Communist party itself was banned, but the left had developed a strong base in the trade unions and among Chinese school students and the Chinese-educated population more generally. The liberal-nationalist People's Action party (PAP) lacked similar ties to the grass roots and was split between a moderate faction around Lee Kuan Yew and the left (Bellow, 1970; Chan, 1976; Quah et al., 1985). After adopting a united front strategy to gain electoral victory in the self-rule elections in 1959, the liberal PAP leadership then outmaneuvered and finally purged its own left wing. To minimize organizational weaknesses at the grass roots, PAP leaders embarked on a strategy that was to culminate in a one-party dominant system: the reorientation of organs of government to implement economic reforms.[16] As in South Korea and Taiwan, economic development based on control of the bureaucracy became a legitimating pillar of authoritarian consolidation.

When it took office in 1959, the PAP administration launched a development plan that recognized the importance of state action in promoting industrialization and meeting the challenge of unemployment (Lee, 1973; Lim and Pang, 1982). Goh Keng Swee, Lee's most influential economic adviser, argued that pure laissez-faire offered only a developmental deadend, the entrepôt. By 1961 the split with the left had laid the political ground for the PAP's pragmatic policy of creating a favorable investment climate while providing infrastructure, social services, and housing (Goh, 1977). New ordinances that targeted pioneer industries reduced corporate taxes dramatically, and an economic development board established in 1961 was empowered to make loans and even purchase equity in private businesses.

There was still the problem of overall development strategy, however. The PAP had long argued that association with Malaya would allow Singapore to become an industrial center serving a large internal market. In political terms Singapore's Communists would lose ground in the more conservative federation, particularly as internal security would be handled by Kuala Lumpur (Fletcher, 1969; Chan, 1971). In 1961 the debate within Singapore over merger marked the virtual end of the left; a series of arrests in 1963 further weakened the left's leadership, including the unions.

The merger itself, from July 1963 to September 1965, did not provide the

16. Lee Kuan Yew's relations with the bureaucracy were initially strained. See his speech at the opening of the Civil Service Study Centre, 15 August 1959; government press statement TTS/INFS. AU 64/59.

anticipated economic benefits.[17] In addition, serious disagreements existed about the nature of the federation: Kuala Lumpur wanted balanced industrial growth; Singapore sought to purchase a privileged economic position by accepting political underrepresentation. Some foreign investors anticipated the merger, British military spending increased, and outlays for housing and infrastructure provided a major economic stimulus. The foreign-controlled refining industry took off. Nonetheless, unemployment remained a serious problem.

Separation from Malaysia, followed by tariff wars, the announcement that the British were withdrawing lucrative military facilities, and Indonesia's continuing policy confrontation created a profound crisis of confidence (Chan, 1971). Singapore was cut off from Malaysian markets and raw materials, and import substitution was rendred completely unviable. Local investment was heavily concentrated in services, real estate, and domestic trade—conservative in outlook and with little experience in manufacturing, local firms seemed unlikely to spearhead growth. Under these conditions any outward-looking strategy was bound to involve a relatively skewed triple alliance, one which the state and foreign firms would dominate (Goh, 1977:22). Three policy actions ushered in the new course over 1967 and 1968: a renewed effort to attract foreign capital, an expanded role for the state in industrial finance, and above all, an intensification of controls on the labor movement.

The investment incentives extended under the pioneer industry ordinances of 1959 already allowed 100 percent foreign ownership and full repatriation of profits. In 1967 those ordinances were replaced by an economic expansion act that extended new incentives to foreign capital. Formal incentives, however, were probably less important to investors than political stability and the extensive controls exercised over labor. Although Frederic Deyo (1981) and Hans Luther (1979) rightly associate labor controls with the shift to export-led growth, those new controls were also the culmination of fifteen years of *political* conflict with the left and the consolidation of one-party dominance. The PAP sought to split the labor movement by forming its own unions in 1961. Following a landslide electoral victory in 1968 the PAP reduced the range of issues over which a union could confront an employer and expanded the state's power of arbitration, while also drastically reducing such fringe benefits as overtime pay, retirement benefits, and maternity and sick leave. Unionism, firmly under party and state control, was henceforth to be an instrument for mobilizing labor around the PAP's political and developmental aims.[18]

17. The belatedly established Tariff Advisory Board produced some lists of goods for a common tariff, but implementation lagged and Singapore was asked to accept the preexisting tariff structure before a common market was introduced.

18. Even the PAP-controlled National Trade Union Congress suffered a decline in membership and legitimacy.

Incentives and control of labor combined to favor the growth of foreign investment in labor-intensive manufactures. Investment in petroleum still accounted for 56 percent of the total stock of foreign investment in 1970, and 48 percent in 1973, but during those same years investment in textiles, apparel, and electronics tripled.

The importance of a politically autonomous state in forging the new development strategy could be seen not only in actions to control labor but in the PAP's ability to neglect national firms as well. Investment incentives favoring large, export-oriented investments were implicitly biased against local firms (Deyo, 1981). National firms experienced a serious erosion of relative position between 1959 and 1973, as Table 8 demonstrates. The government has encouraged, but not forced, joint ventures. Local firms confront competition with foreign firms in factor markets. Until the early eighties, when government support was increased, local firms were effectively precluded from entry into higher-technology sectors.

The government also occupies an important position in the economy. Initial public-sector investment was concentrated in housing and infrastructure. Through the Development Bank of Singapore, established in 1968, of whose shares the government owns 49 percent, the PAP administration has extended its presence in tourism, shipping, transportation, and real estate. By 1973 the bank owned seven subsidiaries outright and held shares in fifty companies. The Ministry of Finance also held equity in a number of companies, owning some outright (Pillai, 1983:chap. 3), in addition to the financial power it exercised through the Central Provident Fund, a forced savings plan covering all Singapore workers.

Singapore's turn to export-led growth and an open policy toward foreign investment thus rested on several political factors. The consolidation of single-party rule and the exclusion of the left allowed Lee Kuan Yew and the economic bureaucracy to pursue a pragmatic approach to industrialization based on a primary role for the private sector and strict control of labor. The situational imperative created by the break with Malaysia made an export-oriented strategy attractive. The weakness of domestic firms in manufacturing, however, insured heavy reliance on, and generous incentives to, foreign firms.

Hong Kong

Several problems plague any effort to discuss the relationship between state and foreign and local capital in Hong Kong. First, the state there is the British colonial administration, which has taken a distinctly laissez-faire approach to the regulation of the economy. There are, for example, no manufacturing parastatals in Hong Kong. Second, the distinction between local and foreign capital is not sharp. There is a long history of British and overseas Chinese enterprises, both commercial and manufacturing, headquartered in Hong Kong: according to one account, such British investment still controls Hong Kong's banking, insurance, trade, and utilities (Lethbridge, 1980). Nonetheless, laissez-faire allowed national firms to dominate manufacturing. The particular circumstances that helped them do so include a period of disguised ISI on the mainland, the assumption of some development functions by banks, trading companies, and larger manufacturers, and an unusually weak labor movement. A vigorous domestic manufacturing sector left a relatively small role for direct investment to play in Hong Kong's development.

Hong Kong's initial industrial ventures were closely tied to shipping.[19] Of greater significance to Hong Kong's longer-term development, however, was the highly developed service sector, including localized British banking and the large trading houses that formed the heart of Hong Kong's social as well as economic establishment. This sector, with its extensive ties to world markets, later facilitated the activities of Chinese manufacturing entrepreneurs, creating a symbiosis between commercial and manufacturing sectors not seen in Singapore.

We can explain the shift in Hong Kong from an entrepôt economy to one based on manufacturing for export in terms of external shocks rather than conscious shifts of policy. At the end of the war the entrepôt trade resumed. Following the Chinese Revolution, however, the China trade was increasingly handled through state-owned firms. Private consumption was curtailed, and closer ties developed between China and the Soviet Union. Imposition of a UN strategic embargo on China in 1951 contributed to the decline of Hong Kong's entrepôt trade. In 1947, 90 percent of Hong Kong's exports were reexports. By 1952 locally manufactured exports reached 25 percent, rising to 38 percent in 1958 before reaching 70 percent and overtaking reexports for the first time in 1959 (Economic Intelligence Unit, March 1960).

That surge in manufacturing can be traced to refugees from the mainland. Revolution brought Hong Kong a huge supply of politically unorganized labor and a significant segment of the Shanghai capitalist class that had been developing since the beginning of the century (Coble, 1980). Equally important for the inflow of capital, however, was the technical know-how, skills and even machinery that refugees brought with them. Hong Kong's industrialization is virtually synonymous with the development of the textile and apparel industries, which were almost entirely in local hands. Immigrants set up the first spinning mill in 1947, the first combined spinning and weaving mill in 1948, in conjunction with British capital (Youngson, 1982).

Private banks played a leading role in reconstruction. Most merchants had

---

19. Indigenous import substitution was given some impetus by the supply disruptions of World War I, and the Ottawa Accord of 1932 provided some incentive to export within the empire (Szczepanik, 1958).

lost inventory during the Japanese occupation, and firms had no credit
standing. The Hong Kong and Shanghai Banking Company took a long-
term view of the economy, playing the role of central bank and extending
large sums of money to public utilities and key industrial firms, often
without collateral (Endacott, 1978:307–8; Jao, 1983). The trading companies were also important to development (Geiger and Geiger, 1973): when
entrepôt trade flagged, they took the initiative in developing alternative
trade in local manufactures, particularly with the United States. This trade
included not only arms-length purchases but also the provision of specifications, the guaranteeing of loans, and the supply of credit and raw materials.
Subcontracting and the putting out system provided a start for many local
firms, creating a virtuous cycle in the growth of large and small manufacturing firms not seen in Singapore. Small manufacturing enterprises continue
to contribute significantly to total manufacturing output (Sit et al., 1979).

Hong Kong seems to defy the East Asian pattern in which interventionist
states act either to promote domestic firms, as in South Korea and Taiwan,
or in concert with multinational corporations, as in Singapore (Rabushka,
1979). Although debate continues about how laissez-faire the colonial administration really is (Oliver, 1970), Hong Kong's economy is undoubtedly
the most open and its government the least interventionist in the world.
Several peculiar conditions allowed such policies to succeed. In Hong
Kong, as noted, business benefited from disguised ISI on the mainland,
large inflows of capital, and institutions, including banks and trading
houses, which assumed some development functions.

Hong Kong's labor force, moreover, has been weak, consisting largely of
immigrants, many employed in small family concerns (Turner, 1980). Periodic waves of leftist[20] labor activity, as in 1967, have been met adroitly,
with measures that include some limited legal protections for workers and
the provision of housing, social services, and education.

Finally, it should be noted that in political terms Hong Kong fits the
authoritarian, though not repressive, mold. Even one champion of the Hong
Kong model has called it a "no-party administrative state" (Rabushka,
1979:39), while a more skeptical observer calls Hong Kong "about as
democratic as the Soviet Union" (Youngson, 1982:56). Political autonomy
allowed the ideological orientation of the colonial administration, and the
dominant commerical and financial establishment with which it was inter-
twined, to be simply imposed upon the economy.[21] Petitions for protection,

20. Leftist labor unions are those associated with People's China; they are not necessarily
more militant and have even been restrained by China's broader political and economic
interests in the colony.

21. Lethbridge (1969) argues that during the immediate postwar period, colonial and
business elites were drawn much more closely together as the government sought to support
business as one component of reconstruction (cf. Miners, 1981:chaps. 11 and 17; and
especially Davies, 1977, which traces the business-government connection).

for an expanded role for the state in industrial financing, and for a Keynesian use of the budget have been resisted.

The seat of this dominant laissez-faire approach has been the immensely powerful financial secretary, particularly Sir John Cowperthwaite who held the office from 1961 to 1971. Although successors have proved less doctrinaire, the government's economic ideology is strongly consistent: nonintervention, low taxes, balanced budgets, and the completely free movement of capital and goods. This open policy was extended to direct foreign investment.

The Hong Kong government's attitude toward foreign investment is thus unique among the East Asian NICs. There are no restrictions on entry, on the import of technology, licensing, or technical assistance agreements, or on the repatriation of profits. At the same time no distinctions have been drawn between local and foreign firms, no special credit or tax incentives offered, nor even any particularly aggressive courting of foreign firms.

Foreign investment in export-oriented manufacturing, if we exclude the activities of the overseas Chinese, began in the early sixties. Despite a decade of rapid wage growth, in 1960 Hong Kong was still a desirable site for assembly operations because of peaceful labor relations, abundant labor, the stability of the government, freedom of capital movement, and very low taxes.[22] The first electronics firm was established in 1959, a subcontracting operation for Sony which proved so successful that the Japanese government sought to impose restrictions on electronics trade with the colony. Japanese investors entered Hong Kong to supply components to American radio makers, and American firms first entered in 1963 to produce transistors. By 1965 the colony was exporting televisions, by the end of the decade sound equipment and computer parts.

Textiles was another important sector for joint ventures. In 1960 the first Japanese–Hong Kong joint venture in textiles was established, and in 1963 a British–Hong Kong Chinese joint venture became the first synthetic fiber manufacturer in the colony. The Japanese were the major investors in textiles, motivated both by the circumvention of quotas and the advantages Hong Kong enjoyed as a member of the Commonwealth, but their overall role in the industry was slight. In 1973, for example, Japanese-invested firms were only 3.3 percent of all firms in spinning (Yoshihara, 1978).

In sum Hong Kong exhibits some surprising similarities to the other East Asian NIC members, as well as important differences. Economic laissez-faire and political elitism combined to create domestically based industrialization because of a specific social configuration that included a developed domestic manufacturing class and a politically and organizationally weak labor force. The shift from entrepôt to manufacturing center, as in Singapore, was propelled by external political events, but in Hong Kong the

22. These reasons were cited, in the order listed, in responses to a survey conducted by Mun and Ho (1979).

change required no particular reorientation of economic policy. Although the investment climate was attractive, the government made no particular effort to woo foreign investors. Multinationals came to occupy a small but not insignificant position in an economy largely dominated by local firms.

South Korea

The termination of World War II faced Korea and Taiwan with similar economic constraints: loss of traditional markets, persistent balance-of-payments crises, and a heavy dependence on American aid. The tasks of reconstruction dictated an import-substituting course, but East Asian ISI differed from the Latin American pattern in ways that influenced the relative power of the state and local firms.

Throughout the East Asian NICs the political defeat of the left opened the way for an open business-state alliance. In Korea leftist forces in the labor unions, urban political parties, and countryside were weakened or destroyed by the political tactics of the American occupation forces, their own organizational limitations, and the gradual consolidation of political power at the center by the right wing of the nationalist movement under Syngman Rhee (Cumings, 1981; Cole and Lyman, 1971:chap. 1). A series of land reforms, begun under the Americans and continued under Rhee, "eliminated the fundamental divisive issue in the countryside. Thereafter, the locus of serious political conflict shifted largely . . . to the urban centers. The reform similarly eliminated the last key issue on which the left could have hoped to develop substantial support" (Cole and Lyman, 1971:21).

Despite the democratic institutions imposed by the Americans, however, Rhee was able to maintain a significant degree of executive autonomy, aided by extensive resources in the hands of the bureaucracy, among them vested Japanese properties and American aid, as well as the centrally controlled, ubiquitous, and rightist police forces. The Korean War gave Rhee a reprieve from domestic political opposition, eased tensions with the increasingly skeptical Americans, and allowed him further to consolidate his political hold, in part by developing the Liberal party into a quasi-corporatist organization that tied a pliant labor movement to the government.

After the war a crucial link developed between the U.S. aid program, Rhee's Liberal party, and the bureaucracy. Aid allowed Rhee to preempt the formation of a liberal middle-class opposition by tying favored businesses to the government. Licenses were issued to firms willing to provide kickbacks: the Liberal party was said to have substantial interests in at least 50 percent of all private projects receiving U.S. aid, which was later to inspire charges of illicit accumulation of wealth (Kim, 1975). In a perceptive analysis of business-government relations Leroy Jones and Il Sakong (1980; cf. Kim, 1976) argue that the political structure was the major impediment to Korean growth in the fifties, as it encouraged speculative arbitrage. This judgment may be too harsh, however, for while growth slowed in the later years of the decade, in part as a result of an American-imposed stabilization program, privileged access to credit and commodities allowed rapid accumulation by private enterprises that later spearheaded legitimate manufacturing activities.

Declining economic performance, partly associated with the failures of ISI, and the visible corruption of the regime finally forced Rhee to resign. Despite its reformist and developmentalist ideology, the political leadership of the short-lived Second Republic proved unable to control growing political polarization among its own supporters (Han, 1974). The disintegration of the political structure left a vacuum into which the military stepped unopposed.

Institutional changes made during military rule, from 1961 to 1964, established the particularly statist orientation that has since characterized South Korean development (Haggard, 1983:chap. 5). A range of new instruments of economic control and planning were developed; an economic planning board was created, the country's first development plan was launched, and the state seized control over the banking sector. The centralization and insulation of the political structure outlived the return to democracy in 1964, allowing Park Chung Hee to dominate economic policy and to exercise influence over trade unions and farmers' associations.

The consolidation of political authority, the centralization of policy instruments, and the ideological commitment to economic development did not of themselves constitute an economic strategy. More radical junior officers favored a self-reliant though inflationary course emphasizing investment in basic industries. Under pressure from the Americans, the military junta initiated a stabilization program in late 1963 and strengthened the hand of the economic technocrats. Economic reforms in 1964 and 1965 had their origins in the Economic Planning Board, working closely with and drawing intellectual inspiration from transnational ties with AID and the IMF. These reforms included a rationalization of import controls, more stringent monetary policy, increases in taxation, greater export efforts, and significant devaluation (Hong, 1979; Frank et al., 1975).

Initially the junta had attacked the illicitly accumulated wealth of the largest firms but, as Kyoung-dong Kim (1976:470) notes, found itself in a dilemma: "the only viable economic force happened to be the target group of leading entrepreneurial talents with their singular advantage of organization, personnel, facilities and capital resources." A tacit alliance thus emerged between the Park regime and large domestic business, though it was based on a new foundation, including extensive state control over finance. By altering trade and exchange rate policies, it eliminated zero-sum sources of economic rent, and it "simulated" a free-trade system for the individual firm through a complicated system of incentives and supports. Exports far outstripped the expectations of planners, growing at an annual average of 36 percent between 1965 and 1972.

If stabilization, trade liberalization, and the promotion of exports through financial incentives made up one half of the new government's strategy, the other was an expanded reliance on foreign capital. South Korea differs from other East Asian NICs in having already experienced an explicit political fight over foreign investment. The most obvious source for foreign investment was Japan, though political relations had never been normalized following 1945. Park recognized early that successful settlement of Korean property claims would provide crucial economic resources and expand aid and investment. In late 1962 the military reached an agreement with the Japanese on a settlement to include a $300 million grant, $200 million in government-to-government credits, and $100 million in commercial financing. Tied to Japanese purchases, the credits gave ammunition to those who saw the settlement as a capitulation to Japan's long-term strategy of integrating Korea into a broader sphere of political and economic influence (Kim, 1971; Chang, 1982). Japanese statements did not allay fears of a new East Asian Coprosperity Sphere. A joint economic survey published in 1965, for example, noted that it was "natural" for developing countries to pursue a labor-intensive strategy based on the declining industries of the developed countries, a strategy that the conservative Korean Businessmen's Association accepted with open arms (Kim, 1971:chap. 3). For opponents of normalization, the treaty crisis reflected not only popular anti-Japanese sentiment, however, but also a battle over the legitimacy of the Park government itself. As Joungwan Kim (1975) argues, the primary issue throughout the political crisis was less opposition to Japan than opposition to the government. Critics feared correctly that the government would use the influx of external financial resources to further consolidate its domestic political grip.

The opposition stressed the various imbalances in the economy, including the relative neglect of agriculture and the domestic market, as well as the political disadvantages of a strategy based on a close alliance between an insulated government, big business, and foreign capital. Park's victory on the treaty issue was followed almost immediately by new statutes governing foreign investment, but it was the combination of the treaty settlement, Park's political consolidation and the stabilization measures, and credit and exchange rate reforms which dramatically increased foreign investment.

The interest rate reforms made borrowing attractive to Korean firms as well: dollar-denominated loans were less than half the cost of domestic funds. The preference for foreign borrowing also had a political motivation. Foreign loans provided the government with an additional political instrument: firms wishing to borrow had to secure the approval of the Economic Planning Board, which in turn would guarantee repayment. The state thus acted as intermediary between domestic firms and international commercial lenders.

The state intensified the strategy of attracting direct foreign investment in the late sixties, partly as a result of the problems South Korea was experiencing with overborrowing. In 1970 some additional incentives were granted to foreign investors, and rules governing labor activity in foreign-invested firms were tightened. The contruction of the first export-processing zone in 1970 was part of a quid pro quo with the Japanese, who agreed to expand financing of some large-scale infrastructure and basic industry projects.

A series of measures in the early seventies indicated, however, that the government was not going to favor foreign investors at the expense of local capital (Haggard, 1983:chap. 5). In South Korea, as in Taiwan, the processing zones had an unintended consequence: they partitioned foreign investors away from the local market. Import-substituting investments were allowed only in sectors beyond the technological capabilities of Korean firms. External demand continued to grow rapidly, and so foreign-dominated export enclaves did not pose a serious threat to Korean exporters.

Revisions of the foreign capital inducement law in 1971 and 1973 attempted to combine generous incentives in priority sectors with protection and encouragement of the interests of domestic business. Export requirements sheltered the domestic market, guaranteeing the trade orientation of foreign firms. In April 1973 projects with 50 percent local participation received priority. Sole foreign ownership was to be allowed only where production was completely for export or where proprietary considerations demanded it. Even in favored sectors sole ownership would be allowed only on condition that foreign firms gradually transferred ownership to Korean nationals. In labor-intensive activities foreign participation could not exceed 50 percent (Korea Exchange Bank, *Monthly Review*, April 1973, June 1973).

These policies add up to a consistent effort to invite foreign investment into targeted sectors while steadily tightening the criteria governing their operation, protecting domestic producers from competition in the home market, and forcing local equity participation. Backed by generous government financing in both won and dollars, they allowed Korean firms to develop significant capabilities, beginning in sectors with relatively standardized technologies. The increase in the number of large indigenous firms for the ten-year period 1966 to 1977, Chung Lee (1981) has found, was greater than the number of foreign affiliates established during the period from 1962 to 1978 in every manufacturing sector.

Several factors help explain these policies. First, the export-oriented strategy, influenced by the American aid-giving machinery, gave to South Korean firms that developed in the fifties an incentive to export. Park relied on domestic entrepreneurs for the economic performance that served as the legitimating basis of his increasingly authoritarian rule. The left had been eliminated before the Korean War. Labor was subject to significant controls. Political opposition proved ineffective even after the return to democracy in 1964, not only because of Park's power but also because of internal, organizational weaknesses. State support such as preferential finance tied business in political terms closely to the state, as it also influenced patterns of investment. The treaty crisis of the mid-sixties demonstrated a deep-seated popular concern about the penetration of Japanese capital, to which Park was not blind. Inducing export-oriented firms to operate in the zones, taking advantage of debt and aid, and forcing local participation through joint ventures allowed the government to limit the extent of direct Japanese participation in the economy.

Taiwan

Unlike Korea and Singapore, Taiwan exhibits a fundamental political continuity across the entire postwar period. Initially statist in its economic orientation, the Kuomintang underwent a gradual change in economic-ideo-logical orientation over the fifties, in large part because of American tu-telage. This change culminated in economic reforms from 1958 through 1962 which set Taiwan on the course of export-led growth. The switch from import substitution to an outward-looking strategy, as in South Korea, was accompanied by an opening to foreign capital. But support extended to domestic firms in the 1950s guaranteed that they too would be able to exploit the new incentives. A division of labor developed between the mainlander-dominated KMT and the increasingly Taiwanese private sector. This tacit alliance has sustained a political-economic system based on one-party rule, support for business, and control of labor.

Taiwan began its postwar history with the most insulated political leader-ship of any of the NICs. As Lloyd Eastman (1972:286) notes of the Kuomin-tang on the mainland, "the Nationalist regime tended . . . to be neither responsible nor responsive to political groups or institutions outside the government. It became, in effect, its own constituency." This was even more true on Taiwan, where the Kuomintang lacked connections with local social groups. In Korea many Japanese properties fell quickly into private hands; in Taiwan, by contrast, the KMT retained control of virtually all assets in the modern sector, depriving the Taiwanese of spoils that they viewed as rightfully theirs (Gold, 1986:chap. 4). Following an islandwide revolt in February 1947, Formosan nationalists and leftists were liquidated, driven into exile, or silenced. The aim of recapturing the mainland provided the Nationalists with the rationale for martial law, which remains in effect today. Labor unions, which had been important in undermining the power of the Kuomintang in mainland cities but had been banned under the Japanese, were encouraged but under strict party controls.

In the second half of 1949 American aid began to arrive in massive quantities, supporting innovative economic reforms that included real inter-est rates for depositors and monetary stabilization. (Having experienced a disastrous hyperinflation on the mainland, the KMT had a strong political interest in macroeconomic stability.) Over the fifties a strategy of import substitution emerged; it was based on a controlled strengthening of the

private sector under state guidance, a gradual reduction of the
enterprises in the economy, and significant land reforms. '
anxious to avoid the inattention to the countryside which ha
its downfall on the mainland. Land reform preempted independent p
political activity while extending KMT control into the countryside.

The economic ideology of the Kuomintang combined private ownership
of the means of production and central planning in an eclectic mixture. In
the early 1950s significant policy debates centered on the proper role for the
state in the economy (Gold, 1986:chap. 5; Haggard, 1983:chap. 6). Although divestment of state-owned enterprises proved slow, the protectionist
instruments employed by the government had the effect of driving profits
into the hands of a relatively inexperienced private sector. Some older
Taiwan capitalists willing to work closely with the Kuomintang, became the
first generation of large Taiwanese capital (Gold, 1986; Winckler, 1981).
Small Taiwanese entrepreneurs benefited from industrialization as well,
however. Owners of family factories and those previously engaged in commerce took advantage of the new incentives to move into manufacturing
(Lin, 1973).

U.S. aid teams were willing allies of Chinese reformers, pressing for land
reform, divestment of state-owned industrial properties, incentives for private investment, and greater autonomy for technocrats and planners (Jacoby, 1966; Galenson, 1979). When import substitution ran into market
limits in the late fifties, the Americans argued for a new round of policy
reform. A package launched in April 1958 simplified the multiple exchange
rate system, relaxed some import restrictions, and rationalized the allocation
system for imports. These reforms were carried further in the Nineteen Point
Program of February 1960, a package that marked a triumph of liberal
planners over more conservative, control-oriented elements of the Kuomintang and even over business itself, which seemed to favor domestic cartelization. With the reform of the exchange rate regime and liberalization of
access to needed inputs, Taiwan was integrated into the international system
on the basis of its comparative advantage in low-wage labor. A host of
additional supports buttressed market incentives to export, however, including the provision of finance to exporters, government-sponsored cartelization
of export industries, and highly disaggregated tax policies targeting
favored sectors (Wade, forthcoming).

The incentives extended to foreign investors were largely an outgrowth of
the broader, Nineteen Point reforms of investment and trade policy. Incentives extended under the 1961 Statute for the Encouragement of Investment
were applicable to foreign as well as domestic investors (unlike under
Korea's Foreign Capital Inducement Law). Freedom of profit remittance,
100 percent ownership, and the controlled work force made Taiwan a logi-
cal site for offshore investment. The reforms profoundly altered the nature
of foreign investment, as Chi Schive (1978:chap. 2) has shown. Foreign-
invested firms established before 1960 exported only 18 percent of output.

For those established between 1961 and 1966, after the exchange rate reforms but before the building of the zones, the ratio rises to 36.6 percent. Firms established between 1967 and 1971, however, exported 75 percent of their production, hitting a peak of 93 percent for those firms entering in 1973.

Despite an investment climate more liberal than that in South Korea, the Taiwan government has followed a policy toward foreign firms which has not been laissez-faire (Huang, 1978; Wade, forthcoming). Incentives for foreign investors are governed by the Statute for the Encouragement of Investment, a key instrument of Taiwan's industrial policy. As with Singapore's pioneer industries those sectors targeted by the government are almost guaranteed entry; others must make a special case. The Investment Commission retains wide discretion, negotiating all investments on a case-by-case basis. In 1970 criteria on entry were already being tightened to limit foreign equity participation in certain industries and to restrict investment in last-stage assembly and those industries facing protection.

The Investment Commission has also sought to promote joint ventures. Although 100 percent foreign ownership is allowed in principle, in practice some investments aimed at servicing the local market face equity conditions: the greater the local sales, in general, the higher is the local equity requirement. Local content requirements and import controls have been used to force linkages with domestic firms. The Investment Commission often suggests that certain inputs for a foreign-invested project be purchased locally even where local manufacturers operate at low quality or do not even yet exist. Export requirements, meanwhile, are used to protect domestic producers from foreign competition in the local market.

There are some basic similarities between Taiwan and South Korea. Taiwanese planners have manipulated fiscal incentives to support local firms while protecting the domestic market. An opening to foreign investment accompanied the policy reforms pressed by American planners and liberals in the Taiwanese bureaucracy. New incentives favored domestic firms as well, however, cementing a tacit political alliance between the Kuomintang and the private sector. Many heavy industries, such as petroleum refining, aluminum production, and fertilizers, remained in state hands, limiting the penetration of foreign firms.

Conclusion

In all cases except Hong Kong, in sum, the opening to foreign investment was part of a more general shift in development strategy. This shift was engineered by politically insulated leaderships committed to rapid capitalist industrialization, acting with, and influenced by, liberally inclined economic technocrats. In no case did the change of policy have its origin in the consciously expressed political and economic interests of any social classes outside the state. In Singapore the change in policy was openly biased against local manufacturers; in Taiwan and South Korea it forced entrepreneurs to abandon lucrative arbitrage for a then uncertain future in the risky export business.

This liberalism demands qualification, however. In South Korea, Taiwan, and Singapore the state played a central role, supporting the activities of business, targeting particular sectors for investment, and engaging in production in heavy industries such as steel. Singapore and Taiwan, beginning with liberal incentives to foreign firms, gradually tightened controls. South Korea liberalized incentives after 1970 but never abandoned its discretionary control over investment and maintained the strictest demands for local participation.

The state formed tacit alliances with business in all cases, but those alliances took differernt forms. In Taiwan and Korea the state supported local manufacturing firms through a period of ISI, which strengthened their capabilities until they could spearhead the export drive of the 1960s. Foreign investment came relatively late, playing an important but not dominant role in exports. Laissez-faire in Hong Kong reflected not only the ideological predilections and political insulation of the colonial administration but also the interests of the dominant commercial and financial establishment. Periodic efforts by manufacturers to secure protection and support were resisted.

Leftist, populist, and labor forces were in all cases organizationally weak, or politically circumscribed, or repressed. In Taiwan the state's early consolidation of political power eliminated serious political challengers. In South Korea the Marxist left was eliminated early; the military coup of 1961 only furthered the trend toward highly centralized political control, despite the return to democracy in 1964. In Singapore the battle against the Communists was more protracted. As the left had a foothold in the labor unions, it is not surprising that a primary goal of the PAP administration was control of labor. Hong Kong's leftist forces, those oriented toward the PRC, have never sought to challenge the colony's economic system.

Finally, international political alliances and external political shocks influenced policies toward direct investment. South Korea and Taiwan were integrated into the American sphere of influence through aid, which gave the Americans leverage to push for favored liberal policies. For Singapore, the failed merger with Malaysia forced a new strategy; so did the Chinese Revolution for Hong Kong, which remains under direct colonial rule to this day.

The East Asian NICs in the 1970s and 1980s: competitive challenge and state response

By the late sixties and early seventies the East Asian NICs were beginning to face competitive challenges that were to lead to expanded state intervention in industrial development and a changed role for foreign firms. By 1970 the evidence of a new protectionism was clear, with the NICs the major targets of orderly marketing agreements and "voluntary" export restraints (Yoffie, 1983). But the growth strategy based on the export of labor-intensive manufactures faced economic as well as political problems. The income elasticity of demand for light manufactures was low, and the long-run prospects of such manufactures as engines of growth appeared limited. In addition the advanced industrial states were entering a period of slowed growth. High levels of trade dependence required the four to find new niches based on higher productivity and higher value added. Markets needed to be diversified.

Additional pressure was coming from a second tier of newly industrializing countries. By the early seventies the International Monetary Fund and the World Bank were urging a development strategy that replicated the pattern of leading sectors which characterized growth in the East Asian NICs. Over the decade manufactured exports from countries such as Colombia, Sri Lanka, and Malaysia grew rapidly. A new generation of export-processing zones in Malaysia, India, Pakistan, Sri Lanka, Bangladesh, and even People's China increased the competition to attract direct investment in offshore processing industries. In addition, of course, the four East Asian NICs faced stiff competition from one another. All four had followed similar growth strategies, and by the early seventies the composition of their exports was remarkably similar.

Underneath these competitive challenges lay the peril of success: rising real wages. Export-led growth was predicated on inexpensive labor and, in South Korea and Taiwan, surplus rural labor. Despite various controls on the organization and political activity of labor, wages could not be held below market levels. By 1970 all of the NICs began to experience rising real wages, and Singapore also faced acute labor shortages.

This combination of internal and external pressures produced a new stage in export-led growth: the effort to diversify the export basket and upgrade the industrial structure. The response across the four to this crisis of export-led growth varied in revealing ways. South Korea proved aggressive in pushing into heavy, capital-intensive industries; Hong Kong's laissez-faire tradition kept government action to a minimum. In all cases, however, we can see two important changes. First, the state played an expanded role in seeking to organize and support production in new sectors. Industrial targeting, the effort to pick winning industries, became a more pronounced aspect of strategy. Second, targeting was in all cases accompanied by a reassessment of the role of foreign firms and renewed efforts to attract foreign investment in desired sectors. Technology-intensive firms, particularly those willing to locate R&D and engineering facilities abroad, received new incentives. The dependence of the East Asian NICs on foreign direct investment, in short, increases.

Contrasts in the city-state response

It is ironic that Singapore, given its relatively late entry into the export game, was among the first of the East Asian NICs to develop a policy of industrial restructuring. By 1970 Singapore had solved the problem of unemployment, but labor shortages developed which were to lead to an inflow of guest workers in the late seventies. The tripartite National Wages Council was formed in 1972 to steer future wage increases. In 1973 wages were allowed to rise at an accelerated pace, to force firms to create more skilled positions and adopt more capital- and technology-intensive processes in order to raise productivity. This experiment in industrial restructuring was interrupted by the world recession of 1974, and from 1975 through 1978 wage restraint was reinstituted. In June 1979, as part of a policy that came to be called the Second Industrial Revolution, the National Wages Council recommended an average 20 percent increase in wages (Lim, 1984).

This wage policy naturally discouraged further foreign investments in labor-intensive industries. In 1980 clothing, textile, and footwear investments dropped (*Asian Business*, December 1981). More explicit measures were also employed to restructure relationships with foreign firms. As early as 1970 pioneer status had been withdrawn from pure assembly operations in electronics, with the effect that by 1975 consumer electronics was more important than components production in the industry (Pang and Lim, 1977). In 1975 an amendment to the act governing pioneer status passed, reducing minimum capital expenditure and extending generous new fiscal incentives. After the announcement of the Second Industrial Revolution twelve sectors were singled out for special promotion, among them computer software, specialized chemicals, pharmaceuticals, precision engineering, and electronic instruments. Despite the onset of world recession in 1980 investments in electronics and machine tools and industrial machinery increased substantially. In late 1980 special incentives came into effect to encourage the establishment of local R&D facilities, including plans for a science and technology park.

The bulk of foreign investment remained heavily concentrated in petroleum refining and petrochemicals. The region's surplus capacity in basic refining pushed the Majors to diversify, however, the bulk of new investments coming in 1980 and 1981. Forty-three percent of new foreign investment in Singapore was in the petroleum sector in 1980, but by 1982 this investment was slowing.

The Second Industrial Revolution appeared to continue Singapore's development bias against local business. The emphasis on technology and capital-intensive sectors itself favored foreign firms, which provided 86 percent of total investment commitments in 1980. Accelerated wage increases weighed more heavily on small, local firms. Though the government informally promotes joint ventures, there are no statutory controls regarding equity participation. In the early 1980s this bias against local firms surfaced as a political issue, and two new financing programs, the Small Industries Finance Scheme and the Capital Assistance Scheme, were targeted to help local enterprises while a product development assistance scheme provided support for the technological upgrading of local firms. In 1986, under pressure from declining economic performance, some features of the Second Industrial Revolution were reversed, including the high wage policy (Singapore, MTI, 1986).

In many ways the dilemmas confronting Hong Kong were more serious than those facing Singapore. Hong Kong was particularly vulnerable to the steady tightening of the Multifiber Agreement during the 1970s. Exports of textiles and apparel, electronics and plastics, on which Hong Kong became even more dependent in the seventies, will not continue to grow at earlier rates. Moreover, its ideological propensity toward laissez-faire and the lack of government instruments to promote industry at the level of the firm made Hong Kong the last of the four East Asian NICs to respond. Nonetheless, the late 1970s saw a subtle change of policy. The political pressure for a more active government role in supporting industry has come from the domestic manufacturing sector itself. Although policy includes a more aggressive wooing of foreign investors, it does not exhibit the open bias in favor of foreign firms seen in Singapore; the effort at diversification has involved if anything closer institutional relations with domestic business.

Since the early 1960s the Legislative Council had periodically debated the proper role for government in the colony's economic development (Hong Kong, 1979). Over the 1970s calls were heard for more activism in planning, the establishment of an economic advisory committee and an industrial development board, greater direct participation in industry through an industrial development bank, and particularly for control over land prices. Most appeals were resisted, on the odd grounds "either that a case had not been made out or that their acceptance would put at risk the Government's belief in minimum intervention in the economy" (ibid., p. 6). The colony's relatively poor performance when faced with world recession and, above all, protectionism led to the creation of an advisory committee on diversification in 1977.[23] Committee recommendations have served to expand the government's role in industrial development and in courting foreign investors.

In 1977 the government formed the Hong Kong Industrial Estates Corporation to develop unused properties and supply infrastructure to investing businesses that met certain criteria, particularly in land intensity of production. The result has been to lure some foreign firms that would otherwise have located elsewhere, though local industrialists have complained that the

---

23. The advisory committee had subcommittees on land, education and training, industrial development, financial facilities, shipping, and commercial relations with China.

criteria for granting leases are overly restrictive and have sought to widen the range of industries that qualify (*Asian Business*, October 1982).

Most of the incentives that have been granted, and the institutional innovations, however, do not discriminate between local and foreign investors. In fact they may be biased toward local firms. The establishment of the Hong Kong Productivity Centre in 1967, for example, was designed to supply a "one-stop" service for both local and foreign investors. Over the 1970s the center launched a drive to attract high-technology investment to Hong Kong by opening investment offices in Japan, Britain, West Germany, and the United States. At the same time it has developed plans to diversify the capabilities of domestic producers, for example, by identifying growth segments, providing technical back-up services, and evaluating the feasibility of particular undertakings. A new vocational training center has been established at industry's urging.

In response to the need to diversify, new policy machinery has been put in place. In 1980 an industrial development board was formed to coordinate industrial policies; chaired by the powerful financial secretary, it includes academics and representatives of the major peak business organizations. A web of subcommittees is designed to tackle particular problems, and the government has solicited "techno-economic and marketing research studies" that dramatically increase information on particular industries.

It is too early to weigh the success of these measures. Because of Hong Kong's historical predilection for laissez-faire, the government's promotion of industrial upgrading was late and hesitant. The major policy changes have come in general support to the private sector rather than in sectoral targeting or direct participation. This has entailed a more aggressive courting of foreign direct investment, but it has also brought more extensive supports to domestic producers and closer institutional relations between the private sector and the colonial administration.

While the governments of both city-states have pursued industrial upgrading and specialization, they have also sought to expand their roles as offshore financial centers, resulting in the creation of the regional Asian Dollar Market. The gross liabilities of the Hong Kong and Singapore markets increased dramatically over the seventies, as Table 10 shows. By the end of the decade Asian countries accounted for 88 percent of deposits and 83 percent of loans to nonbank customers. The number of foreign banks operating in Hong Kong jumped from fifty-four in 1976 to ninety-four in 1979, and the number of foreign commercial and merchant banks operating in Singapore has grown steadily from nine in 1969 to one hundred and three at the beginning of 1980 (Lee, 1983).

The drive to establish Singapore as a financial center began at the same time as the move to a more outward-oriented growth strategy. In 1968 the government's decision to waive withholding tax on interest earned from offshore currency deposits launched the Asian Dollar Market. Licenses to

TABLE 10. *Hong Kong and Singapore Euromarket liabilities (US$ billions) and share of gross Eurocurrency market, 1976–83*

	1976	1977	1978	1979	1980	1981	1982	June 1983
Hong Kong								
gross liabilities	6	8	16	21	32	43	53	54
% of gross Eurocurrency mkt	1%	1.08%	1.68%	1.7%	2.09%	2.31%	2.57%	2.62%
Singapore								
gross liabilities	17	21	27	38	54	86	103	105
% of gross Eurocurrency mkt	2.86%	2.84%	2.85%	3.08%	3.54%	4.62%	5.07%	5.1%

Source. Morgan Guaranty Trust, *World Financial Markets*, January 1984, p. 9.

operate in this market (known as Asian Currency Unit accounts, or ACUs) were granted to merchant as well as commercial banks, and foreign exchange controls were gradually liberalized. Full liberalization came in June 1978, and the Monetary Authority of Singapore took actions to develop both forward currency and short-term money markets. But although these changes in policy were important, the most significant change was the liberal policy adopted toward the offshore operations of foreign banks. Foreign banks outnumber local banks by five to one, though the government has restricted the domestic lending activities of foreign branches.

Until the 1970s Hong Kong's banking industry had primarily been concerned with the financing of trade and domestic economic activities (Jao, 1979). The evolution of Hong Kong into a regional banking center was facilitated by its laissez-faire policies: as there is no exchange control of any kind, access to offshore money markets, including Singapore, is totally unimpeded. Hong Kong was not a tax haven in the seventies, but in March 1982 it took the critical step of abolishing interest tax on foreign currency deposits, placing it in direct competition with Singapore for predominance in the Asian Dollar Market. Foreign banks have led financial development in Hong Kong as in Singapore. Since the banking crisis of 1965 the banking sector has seen a steady trend toward greater concentration, mainly through the foreign acquisition of local Chinese banks, though a significant number of joint ventures exist.

These developments in banking are part of an interesting convergence in the development of the two city-states. The Hong Kong Advisory Committee may have found that the growth of the tertiary sector would not be adequate to maintain historic growth rates, but it is clear that diversification into finance and other producer services is increasingly important to development.

South Korea and Taiwan: the lure of heavy industry

By the end of the 1970s South Korea and Taiwan were also pursuing industrialization strategies that emphasized an upgrading of the industrial structure. Larger internal markets, however, gave Korean and Taiwanese planners another option: they could pursue a second round, or deepening, of import substitution through the development of intermediate and capital goods industries. Developing these heavy industries entailed both an expanded role for the state and an attempt to lure new types of foreign investment. Motivated in part by military concerns, Korea went further along this path, attempting a big push in heavy and chemical industries which resulted in a further concentration of domestic industry (Haggard and Moon, 1983). Taiwan was more cautious. Government policy over the mid-to-late seventies emphasized the provision of large-scale infrastructure, but new state-owned enterprises were formed in petrochemicals, shipbuilding, and steel as well. The state's role also grew over the seventies in the development of technology-intensive industries.

By the late 1960s economic problems and Park's centralized style of rule had produced a vigorous political opposition, with Kim Dae Jung making a strong showing in the presidential election of 1971. Park used the authoritarian Yushin Constitution of October 1972 and a wave of new controls on labor and political activity to manage and preempt political dissent. The end of democracy was accompanied by a new economic initiative, centered on a state-led effort to build a heavy and chemical industry base.[24]

In the Second Five-Year Plan (1967–71) the government had initiated feasibility studies for a petrochemical complex and an integrated steel mill, both of them with direct state participation and assistance from the Japanese. The Third Five-Year Plan (1971–76) marked a critical turn toward a deepening strategy, even over the opposition of technocrats on the Economic Planning Board. In 1973 the Heavy and Chemical Industry Development Plan was launched.[25] The plan was a direct result of executive initiative. Prepared by a tightly insulated group around Park and involving the largest firms and the industry-oriented Ministry of Commerce and Industry, the plan openly bypassed the liberal economic technocrats in the formal machinery for planning. Although the oil shock resulted in some elements of the plan being scrapped, it actually realized some of the fears on which the strategy had been based. The plan notes, for example, that "considering the problems of advanced countries . . . and also the prospective participation of less developed countries in light industries, the promotion of heavy and

24. A debate has emerged in South Korea on the applicability of O'Donnell's model of bureaucratic authoritarianism to the Yushin period (Han, 1985).

25. These industries were defined to include iron and steel, nonferrous metals, shipbuilding, machinery, electronics, fertilizers, chemicals, oil refining, and cement (Republic of Korea, 1973).

chemical industries is justified on the principle of the international division of labor" (Republic of Korea, 1973:intro.). The United States introduced the first bilateral textile quota against South Korea in 1971. To Korean leaders, their country heavily dependent on imports of machinery, chemicals, and transport equipment, opportunities appeared to exist for an import substitution that would result in industrial self-sufficiency. In addition, upgrading has an important military motivation. The development of an independent military industrial complex would ease fears associated with the apparent increase in the political unreliability of the Americans.

The 1973 plan, continued in the Fourth Five-Year Plan (1977–81), introduced new tax and financial incentives while designating specific projects for direct state involvement. The form of participation varied by sector. Direct state ownership was the model in petrochemicals and steel; other designated projects were negotiated with large industrial groups, usually acting with minority foreign equity partners or under technology license. The government exercised control over all large projects through the banking system, occasionally taking equity positions through the Korean Development Bank.

Plans depended heavily on the inflow of foreign capital and technology but reflected a continuing preference for debt and the development of local firms. During the Fourth Five-Year Plan foreign savings provided 45 percent of the financing of heavy and chemical industry investment, but 85 percent of this was in the form of loans. The composition of foreign direct investment shifted as foreign investment in light industries was discouraged (as Table 3 indicates). The complexity of the new projects increased reliance on technology licensing agreements: sixty-seven such agreements were concluded in 1973 and royalty payments totaled $11.4 million, but in 1978, 297 agreements were concluded and royalty payments had jumped to over $85 million.[26] In its effort to link heavy and chemical industries to smaller suppliers, the state also exerted new pressures on foreign and domestic investors to expand local purchases.

Although there were major successes, such as the state-owned Pohang Iron and Steel Company, the plan was plagued with both macro- and micro-level problems (Haggard and Moon, 1983; Korean Exchange Bank, *Monthly Review*, December 1980). The rapidity of investment during 1977–79 contributed to other inflationary pressures in the economy. From the beginning the plans confused industrial deepening through import substitution with the upgrading of industrial exports. The plan reflected the belief that South Korea could do both at the same time, by moving into an emerging niche in the world market for standardized capital and intermediate goods. The strategy demanded that economies of scale be supported by an expansion of export markets, but the plan paid inadequate attention to questions of

26. Data supplied by the Korean Institute for Science and Technology.

marketing and the servicing of such exports. In some cases, such as heavy power-generating equipment, the state's desire for expanded exports conflicted directly with the strategies of the foreign firms investing and licensing in the sector. Foreign partners seeking access to guaranteed government purchases had little interest in developing South Korea's abilities to compete in exports directly with what they produced in other locations.

Technology proved a particular problem. High royalty payments, particularly in the machinery sector, raised production costs. In electronics, for example, domestic firms had difficulties gaining access to needed technologies or found them too expensive. State targeting of specific segments could guarantee neither technological and commerical feasibility nor profitability. Nor was adequate attention given to the development of local scientific and technological capabilities; almost all government lending was channeled to fixed capital investment. Finally, generous financial incentives to firms invited overborrowing, a weakening of corporate finances, duplicative investments, and surplus capacity.

In part as a result of the negative effects of the Heavy and Chemical Industry Plan itself, the Korean economy began to experience serious difficulties in 1979. Export growth slowed dramatically, business failures rose, and the second oil shock led to balance-of-payments problems. Within the government, and particularly within the Economic Planning Board, economists had begun to formulate an extensive critique of Park's economic management, including the dirigist effort at industrial targeting in heavy industries and its inflationary consequences. These economists blamed departure from comparative advantage for the economy's ills. Their vision triumphed in the April 1979 stabilization plan, though its full implementation was interrupted by the assassination of President Park in October.

With Chun Doo Hwan's consolidation of political power in May of the following year, South Korea once again shifted economic course. Liberalization became the watchword among Korean planners; it has entailed several discrete policy actions, including an attempt to liberalize imports and control over the banking sector by returning banks to private hands (Haggard and Cheng, 1987). Although the state has continued to designate favored industrial sectors, it has paid renewed attention to upgrading *within* sectors where Korea has already displayed export competence, such as footwear and shipbuilding. Duplicative investments in the heavy and chemical industries have been extensively restructured, with the government parceling out particular projects among specific firms—including, in some cases, foreign rather than domestic producers.

The new strategy, constituting a second outward turn, was also based on an attempt to upgrade the industrial structure as a whole by moving into more technology- and skill-intensive niches. A key component of this technological upgrading was the liberalization of foreign investment rules. As one report noted, "the excessive emphasis on retaining control in the hands of Korean enterprises has served as a disincentive for foreign investors to utilize their most up-to-date processes'' (Korean Exchange Bank, *Monthly Review*, December 1980). The new rules permitted 100 percent ownership in a large range of product categories, including those projects in which ''it is normal practice to invest more than 50 percent in overseas ventures'' (ibid.). In July 1981, after lengthy internal fights about which sectors to open, the discretionary control of foreign investment was eased by the new opening of 427 types of industry to foreign ownership, about 50 percent of all products in the Korean standard classification. In addition the minimum investment was lowered significantly, from $500,000 to $100,000, a move that met strong opposition from small and medium-sized firms and paved the way for greater Japanese participation in the economy. Nonetheless, further liberalization followed, in new inducements to foreign capital introduced in 1984. A negative list system increased the share of manufacturing subsections open to foreign investment from 69 percent to 85 percent. Pressure from the United States has resulted in additional liberalization in services as well (*Business Korea*, December 1985).

The political isolation of Taiwan grew across the 1970s, though the ultimate effect on foreign investment flows proved slight and short-run. Taiwan's political problems if anything intensified the quest for surrogate political ties: direct investors would come to have a stake in the island's political future. Wooing new foreign investors, particularly from Europe, became a strategy of high politics. Policy toward foreign investment during the seventies tended toward increasing discrimination by type of project with simultaneously expanding incentives.

Taiwan recognized the problem of industrial upgrading as early as the late sixties. As the Fifth Four-Year Plan noted in 1969, the next stage was the ''transformation of the current simple labor-intensive processing industry into one that is more demanding of skills and capital, such as electronics, petrochemical intermediates and finished products, precision equipment and instruments, heavy electrical machinery and shipbuilding'' (Republic of China, CIECD, 1969). Taiwan's move into heavy industries proved more judicious than South Korea's, however. The state played a direct role in organizing production in upstream petrochemicals, steel, shipbuilding, and heavy machinery, avoiding some of the duplicative investments seen in Korea. Four new parastatals were formed in the 1970s, and the state made substantial investments in infrastructure, including highways, railroad extensions, and port facilities, as well as nuclear power plants. The government's role in the economy as measured by share of gross national product grew significantly over the seventies, particularly during the recession years of 1974 and 1975.

Taiwan has expanded the incentives it offers foreign firms in the 1970s and 1980s. The government can now make direct contributions to aid technically advanced industries through loans and equity participation; ceilings on capital and profit repatriation have been relaxed; and the eighties have seen efforts to encourage foreign investment through the stock market. The new Statute for the Encouragement of Investment, passed in 1980, extended a series of benefits to both local and foreign firms in a nondiscriminatory manner. A more liberal posture emerged in 1984 and 1985 as a result of flagging domestic investment, though Taiwan's macroeconomic policy, strong domestic savings, and large trade surpluses had turned Taiwan into a large capital *exporter*. Lists of favored industries, long the preferred tool of industrial policy, went through continual revisions and broadening.

The state has also tried more direct methods to establish linkages between local research institutes, local firms, and foreign firms in high-technology industries. In the Hsinchu Science Based Industrial Park, for example, one criterion of entry is that a firm engage in some development and engineering work in the park. Some foreign firms already present on the island have expanded their activities, but the response of new investors has not been great. Nonetheless, a ten-year development plan drafted in 1979 emphasized the need to continue to move into specialized, high-value-added sectors, such as computers, many of these sectors will demand foreign participation.

It is too early to assess fully the efforts of the move by the East Asian NICs into higher-technology industries. Exports from the NICs are still concentrated in light manufactures, and indeed, upgrading at the margin within existing sectors may prove more important than the effort to shift production between sectors. The success of the broad effort to move into new, high-value-added sectors will rest on two sets of developments. Upgrading in most cases has meant an expanded reliance on foreign firms and licensing arrangements. The next phase of development will depend on the willingness of firms with new technologies to locate abroad, to transfer or license technologies, and, perhaps above all, to open market channels for the new products. As the absorptive capabilities and technological sophistication of producers in South Korea, Taiwan, and Hong Kong approaches that of producers in the advanced industrial states, firms with new technologies are likely to become increasingly reluctant to foster effective competitors. Circumstantial evidence of this problem can already be found in the complaints of Korean and Taiwanese firms about the unwillingness of the Japanese to engage in "real" technology transfer. The luring of foreign investors will demand new incentives, including access to growing domestic markets, the opening of previously closed sectors such as services, and sophisticated bargaining to insure the maximum transfer of technology. This brief summary suggests the possibility of increasing competition among the East Asian NICs for the same pool of investment, placing foreign firms in an improved position to extract concessions.

More important in deciding the fate of the four NICs over the longer run, however, will be the development of an indigenous capacity for science and technology. This has received attention particularly in Taiwan and South

Korea, where the government has funded sector-specific research institutes. There are still significant problems of technology transfer between state-sponsored institutes and local firms. So important is R&D in new industries, however that the trend toward state involvement in production is likely to continue, if in changing forms (Haggard and Cheng, 1987).

Conclusion

The most important debate in development studies over the last decade has concerned the appropriateness of market-oriented policies in solving the problems of backwardness. The four East Asian NICs are frequently cited as models of the benefits of liberalization, development miracles that might be replicated elsewhere. There is significant debate about how liberal Singapore, Taiwan, and South Korea have been (Wade, forthcoming). But there is a further issue. Development models are not simple packages of policies; they are configurations of political, institutional, and historical events. Although there are certainly economic lessons to be drawn from East Asia, we must keep firmly in mind the peculiarities of development there.

Sequencing and timing matter. All four East Asian NICs have fairly long development trajectories. The city-states have been evolving as commercial and financial centers since the 19th century. In South Korea and Taiwan import substitution, a *withdrawal* from the international system, seems to have been an important prerequisite to later export success, though in neither Korea nor Taiwan did "self-conscious" ISI last longer than ten years. As Mexico's reluctance to join the General Agreement on Tariffs and Trade demonstrates, long periods of ISI can create political barriers to the achievement of internationally competitive industry. Above all, the four countries entered the world trade system at an auspicious moment. A more protectionist and slow-growing world economy may well limit membership in the club of semiperipheral countries capable of or interested in pursuing export-led growth, even for countries that might profit from policy liberalization. It is important to remember that Latin America's turn to import substitution dates to the world depression of the 1930s.

The political conditions, both internal and external, underlying East Asian growth also appear to be unique. Insulated, developmentalist states forged business-state alliances in Hong Kong, South Korea, Taiwan, and Singapore which varied with the prior historical development of domestic entrepreneurial and commercial capabilities. In all cases the weakness or elimination of organized leftist, populist, or independent labor groupings resulted in a degree of policy freedom not found elsewhere in the developing world. Whether these combinations are replicable, or even politically stable in the long run (Haggard and Cheng, 1987), is an open question.

The uniqueness of the external political conditions of East Asian development needs little comment. External political shocks, including war, played a key role in forcing ISI in Korea and Taiwan and in reorienting entrepôt trade in Hong Kong and Singapore. The importance of American aid to South Korea and Taiwan, a function of the Cold War, is incalculable. All of the East Asian NICs have profited economically from the reconstruction of Japan and the forging of a regional economy, now complicated by economic reforms in China. China poses both problems and opportunities. Despite fears of a new competitor, all four countries have deepened their economic relations with the PRC, though indirectly in the cases of Taiwan and South Korea. Hong Kong's precise political future remains uncertain, despite the Anglo-Chinese agreement that will terminate British rule in 1997, but the economic reorientation of the city-state has been extremely rapid. Much speculation now centers on the political limits to further regional integration and the management of economic conflict and complementarity between Japan, the United States, the East Asian NICs, China, and the second-tier ASEAN states.

The growth strategies of East Asian NICs have entailed a particular form of dependence, one that differs from dependence in other regions. Dependence on foreign direct investment has been relatively low in Hong Kong, Taiwan, and South Korea, though Korea has been one of the largest Third World borrowers. More important have been the competitive pressures transmitted to the gang of four through their extensive trade. Trade dependence has forced all four countries to adopt new industrial strategies that depend on technological capabilities. The result is a pragmatic policy toward foreign investors, one likely to continue as the four East Asian NICs seek to upgrade their industrial structures.

References

AMPO: Japan Quarterly Review. 1977. Special issue, "Free Trade Zones and Industrialization of Asia." Vol. 8, no. 4, and vol. 9, nos. 1–2.

Balassa, Bela. 1981. *The Newly Industrializating Countries in the World Economy.* New York: Pergamon.

Bank of Korea. Various years. *Economic Statistics Yearbook.* Seoul.

Bellow, Thomas. 1970. *The People's Action Party of Singapore: Emergence of a Dominant Party System.* New Haven: Yale University, Southeast Asian Studies, Monograph 14.

Borrus, Michael, et al. 1983. "Trade and Development in the Semiconductor Industry: Japanese Challenge and American Response." In Zysman and Laura Tyson, eds. *American Industry in International Competition.* Ithaca: Cornell University Press.

Brown, E. H. Phelps. 1971. "The Hong Kong Economy: Achievements and Prospects." In Keith Hopkins, ed. *Hong Kong: Industrial Economy.* Hong Kong: Oxford University Press.

Buchanan, Iain. 1972. *Singapore in Southeast Asia*. London: Bell.
Callis, Helmut G. 1978. *Foreign Capital in Southeast Asia*. 1948; rpt. New York: AMS.
Cardoso, Fernando Henrique. 1973. "Associated Dependent Development: Theoretical and Practical Implications." In Alfred Stepan ed. *Authoritarian Brazil*. New Haven: Yale University Press.
Central Intelligence Agency. 1980. *Handbook of Economic Statistics, 1979*. Washington, D.C.: National Assessment Center.
Chan, Heng Chee. 1971. *The Politics of Survival, 1965–1967*. Kuala Lumpur: Oxford University Press.
Chan, Heng Chee. 1976. *The Dynamics of One Party Dominance: The PAP and the Grass Roots*. Singapore: Singapore University Press.
Chang, Dal-Joong. 1982. "Japanese Corporations and the Political Economy of South Korea–Japan Relations, 1965–1979." Ph.D. diss. University of California, Berkeley.
Chen, Edward K. Y. 1979. *Hypergrowth in Asian Economics*. London: Macmillan.
Chen, Edward K. Y. 1983. *Multinational Corporations, Technology and Employment*. London: Macmillan.
Coble, Parks. 1980. *The Shanghai Capitalists and the Nationalist Government*. Cambridge: Harvard University Press.
Cole, David C. 1980. "Foreign Assistance and Korean Development." In Cole, Yongil Lim, and Paul W. Kuznets. *The Korean Economy: Issues of Development*. Berkeley: University of California, Institute of East Asian Studies.
Cole, David C., and Princeton Lyman. 1971. *Korean Development: The Interplay of Politics and Economics*. Cambridge: Harvard University Press.
Cumings, Bruce. 1981. *The Origins of the Korean War, 1945–1947: The Emergence of Separate Regimes*. Princeton: Princeton University Press.
Davies, S. N. G. 1977. "One Brand of Politics Rekindled." *Hong Kong Law Journal* 7:44–89.
Deyo, Frederic C. 1981. *Dependent Development and Industrial Order: An Asian Case Study*. New York: Praeger.
Eastman, Lloyd. 1972. *The Abortive Revolution: China under Nationalist Rule, 1927–1937*. Stanford: Stanford University Press.
Economic Intelligence Unit. Various issues. *Three Monthly Economic Review: China, North Korea, and Hong Kong*. London.
Endacott, G. B. 1978. *Hong Kong: Economic Growth and Policy*. Hong Kong: Oxford University Press.
Evans, Peter. 1979. *Dependent Development: The Alliance of Multinational, State and Local Capital in Brazil*. Princeton: Princeton University Press.
Evans, Peter. 1981. "Collectivized Capitalism: Integrated Petrochemical Complexes and Capital Accumulation in Brazil." In Thomas C. Bruneau and Philippe Faucher, eds. *Authoritarian Brazil*. Boulder: Westview.
Evans, Peter, and Gary Gereffi. 1981. "Transnational Corporations, Dependent Development, and State Policy in the Semiperiphery: A Comparison of Brazil and Mexico." *Latin American Research Review* 16:31–64.
Fletcher, Nancy M. 1969. *The Separation of Singapore from Malaysia*. Ithaca: Cornell University, Dept. of Asian Studies, Data Paper 73.
Frank, Charles R., et al. 1975. *Foreign Trade Regimes and Economic Development: South Korea*. New York: National Bureau of Economic Research.

Frobel, Folker, et al. 1981. *The New International Division of Labour: Structural Unemployment in Industrialised Countries and Industrialisation in Developing Countries*. Cambridge: Cambridge University Press.

Galenson, Walter, ed. 1979. *Economic Growth and Structural Change in Taiwan*. Ithaca: Cornell University Press.

Geiger, Theodore, and Frances M. Geiger. 1973. *Tales of Two City-States: The Development Progress of Hong Kong and Singapore*. Washington, D.C.: National Planning Association.

Gish, Tan, & Co. 1978. *Singapore: An Economic Profile, 1978*. Singapore.

Goh, Keng Swee. 1977. *The Practice of Economic Development*. Singapore: Federal.

Gold, Thomas. 1981. "Dependent Development in Taiwan." Ph.D. diss. Harvard University.

Gold, Thomas. 1986. *State and Society in the Taiwan Miracle*. Armonk, N.Y.: Sharpe.

Grunwald, Joseph, and Kenneth Flamm. 1985. *The Global Factory: Foreign Assembly in International Trade*. Washington, D.C.: Brookings.

Haggard, Stephan. 1983. "Pathways from the Periphery: The Newly Industrializing Countries in the International System." Ph.D. diss. University of California, Berkeley.

Haggard, Stephan. 1986. "The Newly Industrializing Countries in the International System." *World Politics* 38:343–370.

Haggard, Stephan, and Tun-jen Cheng, 1987. *Economic Adjustment in the East Asian Newly Industrializing Countries*. Berkeley: Institute of International Studies, University of California.

Haggard, Stephan, and Chung-in Moon. 1983. "Liberal, Dependent or Mercantile? The South Korean State in the International System." In John Ruggie, ed. *The Antinomies of Interdependence*. New York: Columbia University Press.

Hamilton, Nora. 1982. *The Limits of State Autonomy*. Princeton: Princeton University Press.

Han Sang-jin. 1985. "Bureaucratic Authoritarianism and Economic Development in Korea during the Yushin Period." Paper presented at the International Conference on Dependency Theory, Seoul, 6–8 June.

Han, Sunjoo. 1974. *The Failure of Democracy in South Korea*. Berkeley: University of California Press.

Ho, H. C. Y. 1979. *The Fiscal Systems of Hong Kong*. London: Croom Helm.

Ho, Samuel P. S. 1978. *The Economic Development of Taiwan, 1860–1970*. New Haven: Yale University Press.

Hong, Wontack. 1979. *Trade Distortions and Employment Growth in Korea*. Seoul: Korean Development Institute.

Hong Kong, Government Secretariat. 1979. *Report of the Advisory Committee on Divestification 1979*. Hong Kong: Government Printer.

Hong Kong, Industry Dept. 1984. *Report on the Survey of Overseas Investment in Hong Kong's Manufacturing Industry, 1984*. Hong Kong.

Hong Kong, TI&CD (Trade Industry and Customs Dept.). 1975. *Overseas Investment in Hong Kong Manufacturing Industry: Industrial Survey Report*. Hong Kong.

Hong Kong, TI&CD (Trade Industry and Customs Dept). Various years. *Annual Statistical Review*.

Hsiau, Jun-guun. 1973. "Strengthening the Capacity of Private Trading Companies." In Economic Daily, ed. *Creating New Economic Prospects through Self-reliance*. Taipei. In Chinese.

Huang, Ching-yuan. 1978. *Multinationals in the Republic of China—Laws and Policies*. Taipei: Asia and the World Forum Series, 10.

Hughes, Helen. 1969. "From Entrepôt to Manufacturing." In Hughes and You Poh Seng, eds. *Foreign Investment and Industrialization in Singapore*. Madison: University of Wisconsin Press.

Hughes, Helen, and Tom Parry. Forthcoming. "The Role of Foreign Capital in East Asian Industrialization, Growth and Development." In Hughes, ed. *Explaining the Success of East Asian Industrialization*.

Hung, C. L. 1980. "Foreign Investments." In David Lethbridge, ed. *The Business Environment of Hong Kong*. Hong Kong: Oxford University Press.

Jacoby, Neil H. 1966. *U.S. Aid to Taiwan: A Study of Aid, Self-help and Development*. New York: Praeger.

Jao, Y. C. 1983. "Financing Hong Kong's Early Postwar Industrialisation: The Role of the Hong Kong and Shanghai Banking Corporation." In Frank H. H. King, ed. *Eastern Banking*. London: Athlone.

Johnson, Chalmers. 1980. "Introduction: The Taiwan Model." In James Hsiung, ed. *The Taiwan Experience, 1950–1980*. New York: Praeger.

Johnson, Chalmers. 1981. *MITI and the Japanese Miracle*. Stanford: Stanford University Press.

Jones, Leroy, and Il Sakong. 1980. *Government Business and Entrepreneurship in Economic Development: The Korean Case*. Cambridge: Harvard University Press.

Jung, Ku-Hyun. 1983. "Environmental Changes and the Channel Evolution in Korea-US Trade." Paper delivered at a conference on US-Korea Business and Economic Relations, Harvard University.

Keesing, Donald B. 1983. "Linking up to Distant Markets: South to North Exports of Manufactured Consumer Goods." *American Economic Review* 73:338–342.

Kim, Joungwon A. 1975. *Divided Korea: The Politics of Development, 1945–1982*. Cambridge: Harvard University Press.

Kim, Kwan Bok. 1971. *The Korean-Japan Treaty Crisis and the Instability of the Korean Political System*. New York: Praeger.

Kim, Kyong-dong. 1976. "Political Factors in the Formation of the Entrepreneurial Elite in South Korea." *Asian Survey* 16:465–477.

Koo, Shou-Eng. 1968. "The Role of Export Expansion in Hong Kong's Economic Growth." *Asian Survey* 8:499–515.

Korean Development Bank. 1981. *Industry in Korea, 1980*. Seoul.

Krasner, Stephen. 1978. *Defending the National Interest*. Princeton: Princeton University Press.

Landsberg, Martin. 1979. "Export-led Industrialization in the Third World: Manufacturing Imperialism." *Review of Radical Political Economics* 11:50–63.

Lee, Chung. 1980. "U.S. and Japanese Investment in Korea: A Comparative Study." *Hitotsubashi Journal of Economics* 20:26–41.

Lee, Chung. 1981. "United States and Japanese Direct Investment in Korea and the Extent of their Dominance: Some Evidence from Korean Manufacturing Industries." Mimeo. University of Hawaii.

Lee, Sheng-yi. 1983. "The Role of Singapore as a Financial Centre." Mimeo. Singapore: National University, Dept. of Business Administration.

Lee, Soo Ann. 1973. *Industrialization in Singapore*. Camberwell, Australia: Longman.

Lethbridge, David. 1980. "The Business Environment and Employment." In Lethbridge, ed. *The Business Environment of Hong Kong*. Hong Kong: Oxford University Press.

Lethbridge, Henry J. 1969. "Hong Kong under Japanese Occupation." In I. C. Jarvie, ed. *Hong Kong: A Society in Transition*. London: Routledge & Kegan Paul.

Lim, Chung-yah. 1984. *Economic Restructuring in Singapore*. Singapore: Federal.

Lim, Joo-Jack. 1977. "Some Wider Political and Social Ramifications of Foreign Investment." In Lim et al. *Foreign Investment in Singapore: Some Broader Economic and Sociopolitical Ramifications*. Singapore: University of Singapore, Institute of Southeast Asian Studies.

Lim, Linda, and Pang Eng Fong. 1982. *Trade, Employment and Industry in Singapore*. Geneva: International Labor Organization, World Employment Program, Working Paper.

Lin, Ching-yuan. 1973. *Industrialization in Taiwan, 1946–1972: Trade and Import-Substitution Policies for Developing Countries*. New York: Praeger.

Luther, Hans. 1979. "The Repression of Labour Protest in Singapore: Unique Case or Future Model?" *Development and Change* 10:287–299.

Millstein, James. 1983. "Decline in an Expanding Industry: Japanese Competition in Color TV." In John Zysman and Laura Tyson, eds. *American Industry in International Competition*. Ithaca: Cornell University Press.

Miners, N. J. 1981. *The Government and Politics of Hong Kong*. Hong Kong: Oxford University Press.

Mun, Kin-chok, and Suk-ching Ho. 1979. "Foreign Investment in Hong Kong." In Tzong-Biau Lin, Rance P. L. Lee, and Udo-Ernst Simonis. *Hong Kong: Economic, Social and Political Studies in Development*. White Plains, N.Y.: Sharpe.

Nayyar, Deepak. 1978. "Transnational Corporations and Manufactured Exports from Poor Countries." *Economic Journal* 88:59–84.

Newfarmer, Richard, and Richard Mueller. 1975. *Multinational Corporations in Brazil and Mexico: Structural Sources of Economic and Noneconomic Power*. Report to the U.S. Senate Subcommittee on Multinational Corporations. Washington, D.C.: USGPO.

Nordlinger, Eric. 1981. *On the Autonomy of the Democratic State*. Cambridge: Harvard University Press.

Oliver, A. B. 1970. "A Keynesian Ghost?" *Far Eastern Economic Review*. 19 March.

Ozawa, Terutomo. 1979. *Multinationalism Japanese Style: The Political Economy of Outward Dependency*. Princeton: Princeton University Press.

Pang, Eng Fong, and Linda Lim. 1977. *The Electronics Industry in Singapore*. Singapore: Chopman.

Pillai, Philip Nalliah. 1983. *State Enterprise in Singapore: Legal Importation and Development*. Singapore: Singapore University Press.

Puthucheary, James. 1960. *Ownership and Control in the Malayan Economy*. Singapore: Eastern University Press.

Quah, John S. T., et al. 1985. *The Government and Politics of Singapore*. Singapore: Oxford University Press.

Rabushka, Alan. 1979. *Hong Kong: A Study in Economic Freedom*. Chicago: University of Chicago Press.

Republic of China, CEPD (Council for Economic Planning and Development). Various years. *Taiwan Statistical Databook*. Taipei.

Republic of China, CIECD (Council of International Economic Cooperation and Development). 1969. *Fifth Four Year Plan for Economic Development of Taiwan, 1969–1972*. Taipei.

Republic of Korea. 1973. *Heavy and Chemical Industry Plan*. Seoul: n.p.

Republic of Korea, Economic Planning Board. 1980. "Foreign Direct Investment Special Survey, 1979." Mimeo. Seoul.

Schive, Chi. 1978. "Direct Foreign Investment and Linkage Effects: A Case Study of Taiwan." Ph.D. diss. Case Western Reserve University.

Schmitter, Philippe C. 1974. "Still the Century of Corporatism?" *Review of Politics* 36:85–131.

Sharpston, Michael. 1975. "International Sub-contracting." *Oxford Economic Papers*, March:94–135.

Siddayo, Corazon M. 1977. "Singapore's Petroleum Sector: A Case Study of the Country's Investment Growth." In Lim Joo-Jock, ed. *Foreign Investment in Singapore: Some Broader Economic and Sociopolitical Ramificantions*. Singapore: University of Singapore, Institute of Southeast Asian Studies.

Simon, Dennis. 1980. "Taiwan, Technology Transfer and Transnationalism: The Political Management of Dependency." Ph.D. diss. University of California, Berkeley.

Singapore, Dept. of Statistics. Various years. *Report of the Census of Industrial Production*. Singapore.

Singapore, Economic Development Board. Various years. *Annual Report*. Singapore.

Singapore. 1986. *The Singapore Economy: New Directions*. Singapore: Ministry of Trade and Industry.

Singapore, MTI (Ministry of Trade and Industry). Various years. *Economic Survey of Singapore*. Singapore.

Sit, V. F. S., et al. 1979. *Small Scale Industry in a Laissez-Faire Economy*. Hong Kong: University of Hong Kong.

Skocpol, Theda. 1979. *States and Social Revolutions*. New York: Cambridge University Press.

Szczpanik, Edward F. 1958. *The Economic Growth of Hong Kong*. London: Oxford University Press.

Turner, H. A. 1980. *The Last Colony: But Whose? A Study of the Labour Movement, Labour Market and Labour Relations in Hong Kong*. Cambridge: Cambridge University Press.

USITC (United States, International Trade Commission). 1980. *Import Trends in TSUS Items 806.30 and 807.00*. Washington: USGPO.

Wade, Robert. Forthcoming. *Sweet and Sour Capitalism: Industrial Policy Taiwan Style*.

Westphal, Larry, et al. 1981. *Korean Industrial Competence: Where It Came From*. Washington, D.C.: World Bank Staff Working Paper 469.

White, Gordon, and Robert Wade, eds. 1985. *Developmental States in East Asia*. Brighton: Institute of Development Studies, Research Report 16.

Winckler, Edwin. 1981. "National, Regional and Local Politics." In Emily Ahern and Hill Gates, eds. *The Anthropology of Taiwanese Society*. Stanford: Stanford University Press.

Wong, Po S. 1958. *The Influx of Chinese Capital into Hong Kong since 1937*. Hong Kong: Kai Ming.

World Bank. 1983. *World Debt Tables, 1981–1982*. Washington, D.C.

Wu, Chung-tong. 1973. "Societal Guidance and Development: A Case Study of Hong Kong." Ph.D. diss. University of Southern California.

Yoffie, David. 1983. *Power and Protectionism: Strategies of the Newly Industrializing Countries*. New York: Columbia University Press.

Yoshihara, Kunio. 1978. *Japanese Investment in Southeast Asia*. Honolulu: University Press of Hawaii.

Youngson, A. J. 1982. *Hong Kong: Economic Growth and Policy*. Hong Kong: Oxford University Press.

Yuan, Huang Peng. 1972. "Foreign Investment in Singapore." In Wong Kum Poh and Maureen Tan, eds. *Singapore in the International Economy*. Singapore: Singapore University Press.

Political institutions and economic performance: the government-business relationship in Japan, South Korea, and Taiwan Chalmers Johnson

The facts are not in serious dispute, even if their explanation and interpretation are among the most controversial issues in the field of comparative political economy today. In 1950, measured in 1974 U.S. dollars, South Korea had a per capita income of $146; equivalent figures were $150 for Nigeria, $129 for Kenya, and $203 for Egypt. Taiwan was then slightly ahead of Korea at $224 but lagged far behind Brazil at $373, let alone Mexico at $562 or Argentina at $907. Thirty years later the per capita GNP of the Republic of Korea (ROK) had risen to $1,553; Nigeria's was $670 (even with oil), Kenya's $380, and Egypt's $480. In 1980 the per capita income of the Republic of China (ROC) was $2,720; Brazil's was $1,780, Mexico's $1,640, and Argentina's $2,230.[1] To take only the two decades of high-speed growth in Korea (1962–80), GNP (expressed in 1980 prices) increased 452 percent, from $12.7 billion to $57.4 billion, achieving an average growth rate of 8.5 percent per year.[2] With regard to Taiwan, during 1983 the London *Economist* noted ruefully: "The 130 million Brazilians export only about as much as the 18 million people of Taiwan, and (outside oil) the 75 million Mexicans—though they sit on America's doorstep—export only a quarter as much as the Taiwanese."[3] And Taiwan and Korea were only the fourth and fifth richest countries in East Asia; the leaders were Japan, with a 1980 per capita GNP of $8,870, Hong Kong with $4,432, and Singapore with $4,298.[4]

Such figures are commonplaces of contemporary Asian economic journalism. The hidden issues behind them are the roles the governments of South Korea and Taiwan played in contributing to their economies' extraordinary growth rates and the relevance of these recent economic "miracles"

1. G. L. Hicks and S. G. Redding, "Industrial East Asia and the Post-Confucian Hypothesis: A Challenge to Economics" (University of Hong Kong, December 1982), pp. 3–4.
2. Citibank, *Executive Guide: Korea* (Seoul, 1982), p. 7.
3. *The Economist*, April 30, 1983, p. 7.
4. Keizai Koho Center, *Japan 1982: An International Comparison* (Tokyo, 1982), pp. 6, 8.

to the earlier and widely acknowledged one achieved by Japan. But why should the issue of governmental activities come up at all? There are several reasons, each of them highly controversial and even ideological. One is what might be called "Taira's enigma." Writing in 1982, Professor Taira Koji observed: "Japan's modern economic growth is believed to have begun in the late 1880s, curiously coinciding with the preparation and promulgation of the Meiji Constitution which defined the character of the Japanese state. . . . The combination of an absolutist state with a capitalist economy from 1889 to 1947 has been an enigma, far from fully unraveled, among scholars interested in Japanese economic history."[5]

Since 1947, despite its adoption of a formally democratic constitution and the subsequent development of a genuinely open political culture, Japan seems to have retained many "soft authoritarian" features in its governmental institutions: an extremely strong and comparatively unsupervised state administration, single-party rule for more than three decades, and a set of economic priorities that seems unattainable under true political pluralism during such a long period.[6] Because the post-1947 period also witnessed even greater rates of Japanese economic growth, it has seemed to some that the coincidence of soft authoritarianism in politics and capitalism in economics had something to do with economic performance.

Japan's achievement of the status of the second most productive economy that ever existed is no longer simply an enigma; it is a challenge to the main political and economic doctrines that currently dominate global thinking about human social organization. Japan's performance challenges the Leninist command economies because it calls into question their theory that capitalism leads to class antagonisms and political instability, and it also suggests that their resort to explicit absolutism without capitalism is misplaced and doomed to failure. Japan's performance also challenges the Anglo-American "free enterprise" economies because it calls into question their theory that governmental intervention in the economy is inevitably inefficient and distorting, and it also suggests that their faith in the market mechanism without explicit political direction is misplaced.

Needless to say, these implications of the Japanese challenge are nowhere fully accepted and are only recently even being debated in either the Communist or the English-speaking capitalist worlds. Most foreign observers, whether Communist or Western capitalist, seem to prefer theories of Japan's economic achievements that deflect attention from the connection between soft authoritarian politics and capitalist economics; and the Japanese themselves, for their own good and sufficient reasons, are among the leading

5. Koji Taira, "Japan's Modern Economic Growth: Capitalist Development under Absolutism," in Harry Wray and Hilary Conroy, eds., *Japan Examined: Perspectives on Modern Japanese History* (Honolulu: University of Hawaii Press, 1983), p. 34.

6. See Chalmers Johnson, *MITI and the Japanese Miracle* (Stanford: Stanford University Press, 1982).

creators and purveyors of such conceptual alternatives to a political theory of their achievements. The most common theme in the alternative view is that Japan's economic achievements are to be explained by Japan's unique culture, often traced back to sociological changes during the Kamakura military government of the 13th century or even earlier. Of course, if that were true then the culture is also responsible for the two-and-a-half centuries of *sakoku* (closed country) during the Tokugawa era, for the militarism and imperialism of the 1930s, and for the defeat of 1945. But no matter. The cases of the ROK and the ROC inevitably draw the analyst's attention back to the political nexus.

If postwar Japan has arguably displayed a degree of soft authoritarianism in its political system, and if this has had something to do with its economic performance, then Korea and Taiwan are "hard states" (in the words of Leroy Jones and Il SaKong) and in economic affairs, "Government, at least in Korea, is the senior partner."[7] These new cases of absolutist states and capitalist economics suggest that there may indeed be a Japanese "model" that the Koreans and Taiwanese have been refining and perfecting. In fact, the study of the new cases may reveal to us what is intrinsic and what is superficial in the older, Japanese example, particularly because the Japanese always prefer to stress the superficial in their own case, shielding the intrinsic from foreign gaze. Thus, for example, it may turn out that the real Japanese contribution lies in the method of operating the soft authoritarian side of the capitalist developmental state—the Japanese have been much more effective on this score than either the Koreans or the Taiwanese— whereas Japan's "unique" labor relations and innovative managerial techniques, staples of Western journalism on the Japanese economy, may actually be insignificant and even counterproductive because they are missing from Korea and Taiwan with no noticeable effect on economic performance.

Writing for the World Bank, Parvez Hasan notes "the apparent paradox that the Korean economy depends in large measure on private enterprise operating under highly centralized government guidance. In Korea the government's role is considerably more direct than that of merely setting the broad rules of the game and influencing the economy indirectly through market forces. In fact, the government seems to be a participant and often the determing influence in nearly all business decisions."[8] Hasan suggests that part of the solution to this paradox is the existence of mass nationalism in Korea and a widespread public-private agreement on economic goals,

7. Leroy P. Jones and Il SaKong, *Government, Business, and Entrepreneurship in Economic Development: The Korean Case* (Cambridge, Mass.: Council on East Asian Studies, Harvard University, 1980), pp. 132ff; and Edward S. Mason, Mahn Je Kim, Dwight H. Perkins, Kwang Suk Kim, and David C. Cole, *The Economic and Social Modernization of the Republic of Korea* (Cambridge, Mass.: Harvard University Press, 1980), p. 255.

8. Parvez Hasan, *Korea: Problems and Issues in a Rapidly Growing Economy* (Baltimore: Johns Hopkins University Press, 1976), p. 29.

thus eclipsing the class or pluralist pressures on governments that are commonly encountered in less mobilized societies. I agree, and I also believe that the issue of the national mobilization of a united people for economic goals is an important challenge to economic theories based on class analysis, which have proved to be particularly sterile in postwar East Asia when used as a guide to policy formulation (notably in mainland China). But what is the "apparent paradox" that Hasan sees in an intrusive government and high-speed economic growth?

Here we encounter the first serious challenge to the authoritarianism-capitalism nexus—namely, the thought that although the high-growth Asian economies are strongly influenced by their governents, their successes are to be explained not because of this influence but in spite of it. The poorly informed simply ignore the role of government in the capitalist developmental cases. Thus, for example, Milton and Rose Friedman: "Malaysia, Singapore, Korea, Taiwan, Hong Kong, and Japan—all relying extensively on private markets—are thriving. . . . By contrast, India, Indonesia, and Communist China, all relying heavily on central planning, have experienced economic stagnation."[9] That is all very well, but it ignores President Park Chung Hee's intent to attain economic self-sufficiency for Korea through the "establishment of a planned economy," Taiwan's repeated justification of its policies in terms of Sun Yat-sen's semisocialist principle of "people's livelihood," and Singapore's single-party "socialism that works."[10]

The tendency (or the desire) to downplay the role of government has been most pronounced in the Japanese case, particularly after the onset of so-called economic liberalization in the late 1970s.[11] In Japan today it is commonly argued that, even if the government once performed important roles in the economy, it no longer does so (thereby dichotomizing the issue of governmental intervention instead of stressing the government's changing role in light of new economic challenges). Many wish passionately to argue that Japanese entrepreneurship always was more important to economic growth than any policies or practices of the government. The *Economist's*

9. Milton and Rose Friedman, *Free to Choose* (New York: Harcourt Brace Jovanovich, 1980), p. 57.

10. Park Chung Hee, *People's Path to the Fulfillment of Revolutionary Tasks* (Seoul: ROK Ministry of Public Information [c. 1962]), quoted by John P. Lovell, "The Military and Politics in Postwar Korea," in Edward R. Wright, ed., *Korean Politics in Transition* (Seattle: University of Washington Press, 1975), p. 177. On Taiwan see Tillman Durdin, "Chiang Ching-kuo's Taiwan," *Pacific Community* (October 1975), pp. 92–117. Durdin's is the best available source on Chiang Ching-kuo's twelve years spent in the USSR, a subject taboo in the Taiwanese press. On Singapore, and on the American tendency generally to interpret Southeast Asian economic growth in American terms, see Donald K. Emmerson, "Pacific Optimism, Part I: America after Vietnam: Confidence Regained," and "Part II: Explaining Economic Growth: How Magic Is the Marketplace?" *UFSI Reports*, nos. 4 and 5 (1982).

11. On Japanese economic liberalization and the extent to which it has been carried out see Chalmers Johnson, "The 'Internationalization' of the Japanese Economy," *California Management Review* 25 (Spring 1983), pp. 5–26.

survey of Japan for 1983 is typical: "Foreign competitors exaggerate the importance of MITI [Ministry of International Trade and Industry] in shaping Japan's industrial future. . . . Japan's major manufacturers are laws largely unto themselves—especially when it comes to investment. . . . It is this, rather than any carefully aimed 'industrial targeting' policy on MITI's part, that has been largely responsible for the surge in Japanese exports that has been sweeping across America and Europe lately."[12] Ever since the catchphrase "Japan, Inc." was invented to refer to the Japanese government-business relationship, writers on the subject have found it *de rigueur* to misinterpret it to mean Japanese government domination of the economy and then to demolish it. But Taira's enigma, with regard to Japan or the role of government in Korea and Taiwan, does not imply domination; it refers explicitly to the *coexistence* of authoritarianism and capitalism—and that must be explained.

For the sake of discussion, the logic of the capitalist developmental state can best be understood if it is approached from the point of view of socialist theory. If one posits the existence of a developmentally oriented political elite for whom economic growth is a fundamental goal, such an elite must then develop a concrete strategy for attempting to reach that goal. If one further posits two more points, that such an elite is not committed first and foremost to the enhancement and perpetuation of its own elite privileges (something that cannot be assumed in Leninist systems or, for that matter, in the Philippines) and that the elite appreciates that the socialist displacement of the market threatens its goals by generating bureaucratism, corruption, loss of incentives, and an inefficient allocation of resources, then its primary leadership task is to discover how, organizationally, to make its own developmental goals compatible with the market mechanism (that is, with such things as prices that are real measures of value, private property in theory and in practice, and decentralized decision making).

Developmental elites are generated and come to the fore because of the desire to break out of the stagnation of dependency and underdevelopment; the truly successful ones understand that they need the market to maintain efficiency, motivate the people over the long term, and serve as a check on institutionalized corruption while they are battling against underdevelopment. The Republic of Korea is an excellent example:

> The rapid economic growth that began in South Korea in the early 1960s
> and has accelerated since then has been a government-directed development in

12. "What Makes Yoshio Run?" *The Economist*, July 9, 1983, p. 18. For an unambiguous example of contemporary industrial targeting and nurturing by MITI, see Edward A. Feigenbaum and Pamela McCorduck, *The Fifth Generation: Artificial Intelligence and Japan's Computer Challenge to the World* (Reading, Mass.: Addison-Wesley, 1983). For a study of the role of government in Japanese and Korean growth, see Miyohei Shinohara, Toru Yanagihara, and Kwang Suk Kim. *The Japanese and Korean Experiences in Managing Development*, World Bank Staff Working Paper no. 574 (Washington, D.C., 1983).

which the principal engine has been private enterprise. The relationship between a government committed to a central direction of economic development and a highly dynamic private sector that confronts the planning
machinery with a continually changing structure of economic activities presents a set of interconnections difficult to penetrate and describe. Planning in
South Korea, if it is interpreted to include not only policy formulation but also
the techniques of policy implementation, is substantially more than "indicative." The hand of government reaches down rather far into the activities of
individual firms with its manipulation of incentives and disincentives. At the
same time, the situation can in no sense be described in terms of a command
economy.[13]

In previous writing on the Japanese and Taiwanese examples, I have
listed as an indispensable element in any model of the capitalist developmental state the commitment by the political elite to "market-conforming"
methods of intervention in the economy.[14] Lim Youngil is even more explicit with regard to Korea. He argues that Korean government planning,
target setting, and incentive measures have been "market sustaining rather
than market repressing" and that it is necessary to distinguish "between
market-augmenting planning (reducing risks and uncertainties) and market-
repressing planning (increasing fragmentation of the market or rent-seeking
opportunities). The former accelerates development while the latter hinders
it." Lim further makes the point that markets do not necessarily come into
being naturally, that "one of the most common characteristics of underdeveloped countries is underdevelopment of the market system." One of the
things a state committed to development must do is develop a market system, and it does this to the extent that its policies reduce the uncertainties or
risks faced by entrepreneurs, generate and disseminate information about
investment and sales opportunities, and instill an expansionist psychology in
the people.[15] Once a market system has begun to function, the state must
then be prepared to be surprised by the opportunities that open up to it, ones
that it never imagined but that entrepreneurs have discovered. The East
Asian wig export industry is the classic example; no state bureaucrat ever
thought of it or imagined the profits to be made by switching from human to
synthetic hair. East Asia had a comparative advantage in the wig trade, but it
was never seen or seized upon until the state had set up the capitalist
development system.[16]

The logic of such a system derives from the *interaction* of two sub-

13. Mason et al., *Economic and Social Modernization*, p. 254.

14. Cf. Johnson, *MITI*, pp. 315–20; and Johnson, "The Taiwan Model," in James C.
Hsiung, ed., *The Taiwan Experience, 1950–1980* (New York: Praeger, 1981), pp. 9–18.

15. Youngil Lim, *Government Policy and Private Enterprise: Korean Experience in
Industrialization*, Korea Research Monograph no. 6 (Berkeley: Institute of East Asian Studies, University of California, 1981), pp. 4, 8.

16. B. Balassa, *The Newly Industrializing Countries in the World Economy* (New York:
Pergamon, 1981), cited in Hicks and Redding, "Industrial East Asia," p. 10.

systems, one public and geared to developmental goals and the other private and geared to profit maximization. The interaction between the two affects the nature of the decisions made in both systems.[17] The intent of the public system is to manipulate the inputs into the decision-making processes of privately owned and managed enterprises in order to achieve developmental goals, but the content of its inputs is continuously affected by feedback on profit-and-loss conditions, export prospects, raw materials costs, and tax receipts. The intent of the private system is to maximize profits, limit risks, and achieve stable growth given the political-economical environment in which it must operate, but its decisions on products, markets, and investments are continuously affected by changing costs and availability of capital, export incentives, licensing requirements, and all the other things the government manipulates.

Governmental planning in such a context is thus not merely indicative, nor is it part of a state-command allocation system. Planning has indicative functions—to lay out clearly what the elite's fixed-term goals are so that private enterprises and households can adjust to them with precision and over a definite period—but planning also sets criteria through which the operational state bureaucracy can change incentives and disincentives, or intervene directly at the enterprise level, as required. Precise fulfillment of an indicative plan is not necessarily a good measure of its effectiveness. Normally the plan should be overfulfilled, indicating that the synergisms of the system are carrying it toward unanticipated growth. Plans should be underfulfilled when changed circumstances require shakeouts and reorganization—as after the oil crisis of 1973. Korea and Taiwan both have employed explicit planning: five five-year plans (1962–86) in Korea, the first three overfulfilled, the fourth underfulfilled; and six four-year plans (1953–75), one six-year plan (1976–81), and one ten-year plan (1980–89) in Taiwan, four overfulfilled, two underfulfilled, and one without a target.[18]

A developmental elite creates political stability over the long term, maintains sufficient equality in distribution to prevent class or sectoral exploitation (land reform is critical), sets national goals and standards that are internationally oriented and based on nonideological external referents, creates (or at least recognizes) a bureaucratic elite capable of administering the system, and insulates its bureaucrats from direct political influence so that they can function technocratically. It does *not* monopolize economic management or decision making, guarantee full employment, allow ideology to confuse its thinking, permit the development of political pluralism that might challenge its goals, or waste valuable resources by suppressing

17. Cf. Ian Inkster, " 'Modelling Japan' for the Third World," in *East Asia: International Review of Economic, Political, and Social Development* (Frankfurt: Campus, 1983), 1:180.
18. For the plans and their results, see Citibank, *Executive Guide*, pp. 13–14; and K. T. Li and W. A. Yeh, "Economic Planning in the Republic of China," *Industry of Free China* (February 1982), p. 5.

noncritical sectors (it discriminates against them with disincentives and then ignores them).

Why are such political systems normally authoritarian? The first and most obvious reason is to achieve political stability and long-term predictability of the system. Continuity of the government may be achieved by explicit authoritarianism or by a rigged system that nonetheless achieves a monopolization of political power. Such quasi-authoritarian political monopolies are disappointing to liberals, but it should be understood that they are ultimately legitimated not by their ideological pretensions, as in Leninist systems, but by their results. Also, the criterion here is stability, for which authoritarianism is only a means. "Assured political stability [in Korea]," write Edward Mason and his associates, "tended to lengthen time horizons and made manufacturing a much more feasible alternative to commerce as a field of entrepreneurial activity."[19]

Authoritarianism can carry with it exceedingly damaging side effects, such as the suppression of human rights. (It should at the same time not be forgotten that authoritarianism is the most common form of political regime on earth but one that is only rarely accompanied by the trade-off of very high-speed, equitably distributed economic growth.) For Japan since 1955 we must drop the term and substitute for it one of the common Japanese euphemisms—the distinction between *tatemae* (formal principles) and *honne* (actual social reality). For purposes of this discussion, I use the shorthand term "soft authoritarianism," meaning in Japan's case the prewar authoritarianism of the Meiji and early Shōwa eras and the postwar pattern of the monopolization of political power by a single party. The issue under analysis here is not primarily the nature of the Japanese political system but rather the significance for economic management of Japan's having inhibited the coming into being of an effective two-party system, regardless of the possibilities inherent in the constitution of 1947.

In general, the Japanese have been masters at using the least amount of political authoritarianism needed to achieve stability for economic growth; but even they during the 1930s and 1940s, succumbed to the potential trap of all authoritarianism: assumption by the elite of all powers, ideologization, and the displacement of developmental goals. Normally the Japanese disguise and ameliorate their soft authoritarian system through many common, as well as some unusual, political devices: monarchical or democratic constitutions; formal and informal institutional barriers against dictatorship, such as indirect elections, party factionalism, and an implicit balance of power among political, bureaucratic, and economic elites (Japan was the only belligerent power during World War II to change its head of state in a processual manner); gerontological supervision of reigning politicians (*genrō, sempai-kōhai* relationships); a marked separation between reigning

---

19. Mason et al., *Economic and Social Modernization*, p. 267.

and ruling in the Japanese system; and the systematic nurturing of a mer-
itocratic elite. Japan has been beset by serious political instability on many
occasions since the Meiji era, including assassinations, corruption scandals,
and massive protest demonstrations, but it has avoided the particular in-
stabilities associated with mass-based political parties and their platforms.[20]

South Korea is ostensibly a democratic country but actually a militarily
dominated single-party regime—close in form, if not in ideology, to Japan
during the 1930s and 1940s. It would be irrelevant here to either attack or
defend the regimes of generals Park Chung Hee or Chun Doo Hwan. My
point is that, although the military coup of May 16, 1961, brought to power
the kind of developmental elite and political stability necessary for economic development, the personal rule of President Park, particularly after
promulgation of the Yushin constitution, made the system more vulnerable
to political disruption than it need have been. This was demonstrated by the
turmoil and incoherence following the assassination of Park on October 26,
1979. Had Park, in the early 1970s, retired to Taegu and assumed the role of
senior statesman supervising his carefully chosen successors (that is, had he
become a Korean *genrō*, not on the Meiji model but on that of Yoshida
Shigeru in Ōiso), he would be hailed today as the greatest Korean Leader of
modern times—and would probably still be alive (he was only forty-four at
the time of the coup in 1961).

Taiwan differs from both Japan and Korea in that Taiwan does not even
claim to be a democracy. Publicly, Taiwan justifies the single-party rule of
the Kuomintang in terms of the sixty-to-seventy-year-old theories of Sun
Yat-sen. Privately, it justifies single-party rule in terms of the threat from
Communist China, the political crisis caused by its international isolation,
and the need to maintain stability on the island so long as mainlander
carpetbagging (that is, rule by exiles) is still tolerated. These private justifi-
cations have been acknowledged and even to a growing degree accepted by
the Taiwanese for several reasons. First, the threat from mainland China is
real, just as the threat from North Korea is real and gives added legitimacy
to a military government in Seoul. Second, the high-growth, equitable-
distribution economy legitimates the Taiwanese government, just as economic performance has built support for the Japanese and South Korean
governments. Third, the Chinese mainland government is more authoritarian and less capable in either policy or execution than the Taiwan government, and comparison is an inherent element in legitimacy. Fourth, the
actual administration of single-party rule in Taiwan has been ameliorative
over time, and moderating trends continue in large Taiwanese membership

20. For an insightful discussion of the Japanese political system during wartime, see Ben-
Ami Shillony, *Politics and Culture in Wartime Japan* (Oxford: Clarendon Press, 1981), p. 67
and passim.

in the Kuomintang, multiple centers of power in the party, and weakening of martial law.

Nonetheless, Taiwan is the most explicitly authoritarian of the three countries and has relied for its one instance (through 1986) of leadership succession not on an electoral struggle or assassination but on the most ancient method of all, lineal descent from father to son. It would be easy to say that Taiwan and Korea would have done better with less authoritarianism, but there are no examples to support such a view. It seems more likely that they would have done better with more of the Japanese style of authoritarianism. Here the *deshi* have not yet equaled the *sensei*, even if on some other measures they have improved on their teacher.

I shall return to the topic of soft authoritarianism and other political features of the capitalist development state. First, however, I would like to summarize the discussion thus far in terms of a brief, fourfold structural model of the East Asian high-growth systems. The model's elements are stable rule by a political-bureaucratic elite not acceding to political demands that would undermine economic growth; cooperation between public and private sectors under the overall guidance of a pilot planning agency; heavy and continuing investment in education for everyone, combined with policies to ensure the equitable distribution of the wealth created by high-speed growth; and a government that understands the need to use and respect methods of economic intervention based on the price mechanism.

Each of these elements exists in the Japanese, Korean, and Taiwanese systems, although with differing weights, patterns of historical evolution, and trade-offs that arise from stressing one more than the others. Moreover, each case is a moving target: the model itself remains constant, but the actual degree of bureaucratic autonomy from politics, of public-private cooperation, of investment in education and equality, and of emphasis on incentives rather than commands varies over time. It varies in response to how far down the learning curve of the capitalist developmental state a people is and in response to exogenous and endogenous shocks to the system.

In general, the role of the government and its degrees of reliance on authoritarian intervention are enlarged by actual or anticipated crisis conditions in the environment. By crisis conditions I mean not just obvious crises, such as the oil-price hikes of 1973 and 1979, but also such events as succession struggles, ruptured alliances (for example, between Taiwan and the United States), rising economic protectionism, shifts of industrial structure from labor-intensive to capital-intensive or knowledge-intensive industries, balance-of-payments squeezes, serious exchange-rate fluctuations, and so forth. When crisis conditions abate, the balance of initiatives in the systems may once again shift from the public sector toward the private sector, as we saw in Japan during the late 1970s and early 1980s. Sometimes such a shift toward greater private initiative will reflect a governmental *policy* to forestall foreign criticism or quiet domestic unrest or shift responsibility, and it will be understood by insiders as cosmetic. The changing relations between the public and private sectors are, in my view, cyclical and not linear; the *logic* of the systems remains unaltered even though their particular structures have considerable flexibility. It is possible that all three systems under discussion here will evolve from capitalist development states into capitalist regulatory states, but the evidence is equally strong that instead many regulatory states are evolving toward greater developmental and industrial-policy commitments.[21]

I am aware that models of this sort—or even questions such as "To what extent was the government of Park Chung Hee in some sense 'responsible' for the decade-and-a-half of 10 percent real growth in Korea?"—are not, in the words of Leroy Jones and Il SaKong, "the sort of questions with which economists are comfortable."[22] And the economists are not alone. There are serious methodological problems with any theory or model that posits intentional government intervention as an independent variable. These include a historical problem (there may be causal factors other than policy intervention), a span-of-time problem (the failure to recognize long-term trends inherent in the data), the problem of perspective (mistaking random fluctuations for intentional results), and so forth.[23] There are, however, also serious problems with theories, often highly quantified, that filter out the factors of politics, strategy, and leadership.

In a short presentation it is impossible to discuss all the influences that have affected the growth of three different economies in some thirty years (for example, cheap energy until 1973, U.S. aid until the mid-1960s, a stable system of international commerce until the mid-1970s, land reform in all three countries). It seems to me, however, that sufficient time has passed, sufficient comparative data are in, and a sufficient number of alternative theories have been explored in depth to reject the views that the high-speed growth of the Japanese, Korean, and Taiwanese economies was a purely contingent phenomenon, or one dependent primarily on a favorable international environment, or one in which the role of government has been exaggerated. Most factors cited in nonpolitical theories as favoring the growth of the three East Asian economies have been equally or even more favorable for numerous other economies, with great differences in results

21. For the distinction between regulatory and developmental states, see Johnson, *MITI*, pp. 19–23. For evidence that mature regulatory states may be tending in a developmental direction, see John Zysman and Stephen S. Cohen, "Double or Nothing: Open Trade and Competitive Industry," *Foreign Affairs* 61 (Summer 1983), pp. 1113–39.

22. Jones and Il Sakong, *Government, Business, and Entrepreneurship*, p. 286.

23. For a quantitative analysis of industrial policy that is aimed at overcoming these kinds of objections, see Yakushiji Taizo, "Government in Spiral Dilemma: Dynamic Policy Interventions vis-à-vis Japanese Auto Firms, c. 1900–c. 1960," in Aoki Masahiko, ed., *An Economic Analysis of Japanese Firms* (Amsterdam: North Holland, 1984).

(for example, Mexico with its own oil, or NATO members such as Greece or Portugal or Italy).

My contention is that the Japanese, Koreans, and Taiwanese have put together the political economy of capitalism in ways unprecedented in the West and with quite different trade-offs (greater performance but less political participation). To give further substance to this proposition, I shall explore some of the similarities and differences among the three cases in terms of seven major issues of the theory of the capitalist developmental state: (1) financial control over the economy; (2) labor relations; (3) the degree of autonomy of the economic bureaucracy; (4) the degree to which the state has been captured by its main economic clients; (5) the balance between incentive and command in economic guidance; (6) special private-sector organizations, particularly general trading companies and governmentally favored industrial conglomerates, known in Japanese pejoratively as *zaibatsu* (financial cliques) and more accurately as *keiretsu* (industrial groups) or in Korean as *chaebol* or in Chinese as *caifa*; and (7) the role of foreign capital.

Financial control

In no area have the East Asian high-growth economies shown more creativity than on the front of ingenious, utterly nonideological, easily manipulated public incentives for private savings and investment. Examples range from Japan's banana-import link system of the 1950s to Taiwan's annual gold-medal awards for companies whose exports exceed U.S. $100 million a year.[24] It would be impossible to discuss here all the different kinds of incentives—Lim alone lists some thirty-eight different "export promotion policy tools" used in South Korea down to 1976—or to take fully into account how new incentives are invented when old ones must be abandoned for various reasons (negative side effects, international agreements against nontariff trade barriers, and so on).[25]

However, one enduring characteristic of all three economies is government reliance on financial and monetary means to guide and control private activities. These financial measures are often unorthodox by Anglo-American standards, particularly in their emphasis on the supply of capital to industry primarily through the banking system. In Korea, for example:

> Around 80 percent, on the average, of assets comes from loans from the
> banking system and other money markets, including the curb market,
> [whereas] the Korean stock market is just beginning to serve as a means of

24. For the banana-link system, see Johnson, *MITI*, p. 232; for Taiwan's gold medals, see *Free China Weekly* (June 5, 1983), p. 1.
25. Lim, *Government Policy*, pp. 19–20.

raising substantial capital. The remaining 20 percent comes from an internal source (equity); this compares with more than 50 percent internal financing among firms in the United States.[26]

The corollaries of such debt-based industrial financing are powerful governmental incentives for householders to save through the banking system (or through a governmental "bank," such as a postal savings system), restrictions to prevent easy foreign acquisitions of very highly leveraged firms, freedom of entrepreneurs from the influence of stockholders or securities analysts, governmental underwriting of the "overloans" of designated national banks, governmental ability to ration capital by manipulating its cost, and utter dependence of private managers on their banks in order to operate at all.[27] In South Korea, "The most potent instruments for implementing economic policy have undoubtedly been control of bank credit and access to foreign borrowers."[28]

Japan today might be thought to fit this pattern no longer, because most of its growth-promoting incentives and controls have had to be or are in the process of being dismantled following protests from foreign competitors. However, although some measures of financial "internationalization" have taken place, the government's postal savings system and its unconsolidated "investment budget" (the Fiscal Investment and Loan Plan, *zaisei tōyūshi keikaku*) are still intact and functioning as two of Japan's most important institutional inventions. During 1982 the Japanese postal savings system controlled assets about four times those of the then world's largest commercial bank, the Bank of America, and that is a very considerable financial institution to be totally in the hands of the bureaucracy for public investment and which is generally beyond the influence of pork-barrel politics. Deposits in postal savings and postal life-insurance accounts in February 1982 amounted to Y86,290 billion, or $359.5 billion at 240 yen to the dollar; deposits of the Bank of America on December 31, 1981, were $96 billion.[29] (Of course the Japanese save so heavily in postal savings accounts because, by law, these accounts offer the highest rate of interest available to small savers.)

Equally important, bank-based financing is still one of the most distinctive features of the Japanese system. The sources of funds for large Japanese companies showed almost no change during the period 1972–81: in 1972 companies obtained 75 percent of their funds through loans from banks and only 19 percent from shares, and the figures for 1981 were 68 percent and 21 percent.[30] Indirect financing remains an intrinsic feature not just of new

26. Ibid., p. 26.
27. The classic work on this subject is Suzuki Yukio, *Money and Banking in Contemporary Japan* (New Haven: Yale University Press, 1980).
28. Mason et al., *Economic and Social Modernization*, p. 267.
29. Keizai Koho Center, *Japan 1982*, p. 21.
30. "Survey of International Banking," *The Economist*, March 26, 1983, p. 76.

developmental states such as Taiwan and Korea but also of mature developmental states such as Japan. Although such a system undoubtedly restricts international capital flows, it remains in place because of the power, combined with low political visibility, it gives to Ministry of Finance bureaucrats. With regard to Korea, for example:

> The Korean government has viewed control over the allocation of credit, both domestic and foreign, as an important element of economic and political policy. It has resisted repeated advice (mainly foreign) to let interest rates and competition among independent financial institutions determine the allocation of credit. (Few Korean businessmen have ever advocated such a policy.) Instead, the government has kept loan interest rates below equilibrium levels and has intervened pervasively—although generally unofficially—in allocation decisions. The reasons for this appear to have been both economic and political: the credit instruments could be used to mobilize businessmen for major economic programs such as export promotion or development of the machinery and petrochemical industries, while on the political side they served to maintain control over, and cooperation from, the business community. All Korean businessmen, including the most powerful, have been aware of the need to stay on good terms with the government to assure continuing access to credit and to avoid harassment from the tax officials.[31]

In Taiwan, financial control and loan allocation have been as real and as crucial to economic growth as in Korea, but the form is different. The government in Taiwan tends to rely on monetary rather than fiscal policies—tax breaks and high-depreciation allowances rather than outright loans to encourage investment in particular sectors. Moreover, most Taiwanese loans go to state-owned enterprises rather than to big businesses. The state sector is much bigger in Taiwan than in Korea. In 1976 public enterprises accounted for 22 percent of Taiwan's gross domestic product but for only 9 percent in Korea.

Labor relations

Foreign analysts have often credited Japan's "unique" labor relations with being the key to Japan's economic success. The virtual absence of economically significant strikes in Japan (except in the public enterprises), a labor force that does not object to technological changes even of a labor-saving type (for example, robotics), and federations of unions devoid of all but token political power are real comparative advantages in international economic competition. It has also often been supposed that the institutions that give Japan these advantages—enterprise unionism, semilifetime employment, and seniority wage scales—rest to a significant extent on Japanese

---

31. Mason et al., *Economic and Social Modernization*, pp. 336–37.

cultural predispositions. However, the causes of the exceptional weakness of Japan's trade-union movement may lie as much in social engineering by government and management as in cultural factors.

South Korea and Taiwan resemble Japan in their tranquil labor relations, but they have achieved this goal through more directly authoritarian means. "In Korea," writes Lim, "the practice of permanent employment or company loyalty does not exist."[32] There are no Korean minimum-wage standards, and strikes and closed shops are outlawed. Of an industrialized work force estimated at eight million in Korea, only 850,000 are members of a union, a unionization rate of 10.6 percent compared with Japan's 30.8 percent, the United State's 23.6 percent, Germany's 41.5 percent, and Great Britain's 59.4 percent.[33]

Taiwan resembles South Korea: it still applies the basic labor legislation enacted by the Kuomintang on the mainland from the 1920s to the 1940s, and although the Legislative Yuan has discussed a new labor-standards law for a decade, it has yet to pass it. Strikes and collective bargaining are prohibited under martial law; the unions that do exist are under strong Kuomintang supervision, including party controls over the selection of union leaders and all union activities.[34]

Taiwan and Korea have much higher labor turnover rates than Japan, but these have not posed a serious obstacle to high-speed growth. End-of-year bonuses in Taiwan and in Korea two or four bonuses a year, each equal to a month's salary, are part of standard wage packages, just as semiannual bonuses are in Japan; but these are more important to household savings than to labor peace. Large lump-sum severance payments at retirement are more common in all three countries than genuine pensions. It seems that through a combination of authoritarianism, free labor markets, and paternalism, Korea and Taiwan achieve labor relations roughly similar to Japan's, but without Japan's sacrifice of a labor market external to the firm or the rigidities of the semilifetime employment system.

There is, however, more soft authoritarianism in Japan's labor-relations system than is commonly appreciated abroad. According to Totsuka Hideo, during the period 1955–70, "Japanese management developed a sophisticated labor management style which encouraged workers' loyalty to their supervisors and competition among the workers themselves."[35] Management's two main achievements during this period were, first, a very hard

32. Lim, *Government Policy*, p. 56.

33. Citibank, *Executive Guide*, pp. 31–34; Keizai Koho Center, *Japan 1982*, p. 64.

34. "Taiwan's Workforce Stirs," *Far Eastern Economic Review*, February 26, 1982, pp. 78–79, and A. P. Coldrick and Philip Jones, eds., *The International Directory of the Trade Union Movement* (New York: Facts on File, 1979), pp. 449–51.

35. Totsuka Hideo, "Japanese Trade Union Attitudes toward Rationalization," in *East Asia: International Review of Economic, Political, and Social Development* (Frankfurt: Campus, 1983), 1:29.

line against militant unions leading to the Mitsui Miike coal-mine dispute of 1960, when militants were fired and when the more radical federation, Sōhyō (General Council of Trade Unions of Japan), began to lose ground in the private sector to the more moderate Dōmei (the Japan Confederation of Labor); and, second, the setting up of the Japan Productivity Center in 1955, opposed by Sōhyō but supported by Dōmei, which institutionalized Japan's system of consultations (*jizen kyōgikai*) between management and labor, the zero defect (ZD) movement, and the quality circles (QC) movement.[36] During the 1970s Japanese management was able to hold the annual average rate of real wage increases to less than 2 percent; it had been 5 percent during the 1960s.

"The 'success' of Japanese management in the 1970s," Totsuka writes, "has very much depended on the full-scale cooperation of the enterprise unions which have followed the Dōmei line."[37] This is not to say that this achievement was negligible or that foreigners have nothing to learn from Japan's labor relations, where wages must be "reconciled with the national economy."[38] It is, rather, to stress that Japan's labor relations are neither as mysterious nor as culture-bound as some Anglo-American writers allege. It would also seem that all three East Asian high-growth economies inhibit political influence by the trade-union movement because developmentally oriented forces have preempted the political scene—but Japan has to be more creative than the other two because it is less authoritarian. All three nations compensate labor for its decreased political role through policies of comparatively equitable distribution and automatic wage increases tied to increases in productivity.

Bureaucratic autonomy

Serious industrial policy must be long-run in focus, consistent in its various aspects (monetary, regulatory, environmental, and so forth), and operated through mutually supportive policy instruments. It must also be externally oriented (based on cost and price competitiveness in world markets, not just the domestic market); and because it will direct some resources to high-priority sectors cheaply, it must have the power to require these high-priority sectors to meet performance goals.[39] Each of these things is difficult to do politically. Politicians tend to seek popular support in the short run;

---

36. On the Japan Productivity Center see Chalmers Johnson, *Japan's Public Policy Companies* (Washington, D.C.: American Enterprise Institute, 1978), pp. 52–53.
37. Totsuka, "Japanese Trade Union Attitudes," p. 37.
38. Ibid., p. 33.
39. Hugh Patrick, "Japanese Industrial Policy and Its Relevance for United States Industrial Policy," testimony before the U.S. Congress, Joint Economic Committee, July 13, 1983.

and there will never be a shortage of private claimants on the government, regardless of their economic performances and prospects.

Political leaders attempting to implement a long-term industrial policy must therefore have the capacity to depoliticize in part their key economic decisions. This is normally done by entrusting such decisions to a "nonpolitical elite," sheltered to some degree from direct political pressures and able to justify its decisions in terms of the good of all (for example, the Federal Reserve Board and its control of monetary policy in the United States). In the capitalist developmental states this depoliticization is achieved through a covert separation between reigning and ruling: the politicians set broad goals, protect the technocratic bureaucracy from political pressures, perform "safety valve" functions when the bureaucracy makes mistakes, and take the heat when corruption scandals are uncovered (such scandals are unavoidable when government plays *any* role in economic affairs); the official bureaucracy does the actual planning, intervening, and guiding of the economy.

Where does such a bureaucracy come from? It must first of all be created and recruited from among the technically most highly qualified people in the system. And this is why the commitment to education up to the highest levels is so important in Japan, South Korea, and Taiwan. Perhaps the greatest contrast between these three nations and the Communist states of Asia lies in the emphasis on and nurturing of a rigorously educated elite.[40]

Once the bureaucracy is in place, the greater issue becomes achieving bureaucratic independence from the political leadership. Politicians do not want to give up any of their powers, and bureaucrats usually believe that they themselves should have greater powers. The relationship between the two is *always* unstable, and the greatest task of political leadership in such systems is to maintain a balance between the main wings of the elite. Reigning and ruling are never perfectly separated, but they must be to some degree in order to impose long-term strategic goals on a society that may have strong authoritarian elements but that also has a strong private sector. All three East Asian systems have achieved a workable degree of bureaucratic expertise and independence in their state structures through a combination of historical accident, learning, and astute leadership at the top.

Japan's economic bureaucracy began its rise to power during the 1930s and 1940s in response to the crises of the Depression, the war in China, and World War II. It achieved its greatest power during the Allied Occupation and the early 1950s when its chief rivals, the military and the prewar zaibatsu, were weakened or destroyed and when the issues of economic recovery and independence commanded universal attention. Since the creation of the Liberal Democratic party in 1955 (and in light of the democratic constitution of 1947), the bureaucracy has had to share its power with a

40. Cf. "China's Educated Class Struggles for End to Harassment," *Christian Science Monitor*, July 21, 1983.

political elite. From 1955 to about 1972, the end of the Satō era, a stable pattern of tacit separation between reigning and ruling prevailed in Japan. This was also the period of Japan's unprecedentedly high-speed growth. Since 1972 the politicians have been gaining in strength. The process has been slowed by new crises that again called for nonpolitical policies (for example, energy conservation, trade liberalization), and it has been mitigated by an extensive cross-penetration of political and administrative elites. But the Japanese economic bureaucracy had considerably less independence in the early 1980s than it did in the 1950s and 1960s. Nonetheless, as long as the Liberal Democratic party continues to control the Diet, the bureaucracy of Japan will enjoy more power and more autonomy than state officials in any other advanced industrial democracy.

The Korean case was decisively altered by the military coup d'état of 1961. In a broad, sociological sense the coup was caused by extensive military influence on Korean society during the previous decade (somewhat anaologous to the case of Japan during the 1930s). The Korean military had become an intrinsic elite, and the coup merely served to make it an extrinsic, socially recognized one. "It is difficult fully to comprehend and impossible fully to document," writes John Lovell, "the cumulative impact of the process by which millions of Koreans have been exposed to military institutions and military ideas. One may safely suggest, however, that quite apart from the institutional changes effected by the 1961 coup, the social, economic, and political changes stimulated directly or indirectly by the military have been more far-reaching and significant than those generated by any other single group within the society."[41] Concretely, Cho Suk-choon argues, "especially since the advent of the military rule in 1961, advanced techniques of military management have been extensively adopted in the civil bureaucracy."[42] And Lee Hahn-been adds, "The most general contribution of the military to the development of administration in Korea was its introduction and vigorous application of a 'managerial approach.' "[43] Needless to add, many military officers transferred to and directly managed new civilian enterprises, particularly the public corporations set up in high-risk, strategic sectors (for example, Korean Oil, which in 1980 was headed by Yu Chae-hung, a graduate of the Japanese military academy and the U.S. Army's General Staff College and a former head of the ROK Joint Chiefs of Staff).[44]

The problem in Korea, then, was not a rising political elite challenging an already installed bureaucratic elite, as in Japan. Rather, it was the problem

41. Lovell, "Military and Politics in Postwar Korea," p. 189.
42. Cho Suk-choon, "The Bureaucracy," in Wright, *Korean Politics*, p. 79.
43. Lee Hahn-been, *Korea: Time, Change, and Public Administration* (Honolulu: University of Hawaii Press, 1968), p. 23.
44. Inoue Ryūichirō, "Daehan Sukyu Gongsa," *Ekonomisuto* 58 (June 17, 1980), pp. 96–97.

of a military-bureaucratic elite—President Park's Blue House—assuming political powers and then sharing its bureaucratic functions with an educated, nonpolitical elite capable of working with civilian entrepreneurs. President Park's first economic problem was the decision by the United States to end foreign aid to Korea (the ROK has been the third-highest per capita recipient of United States aid in the postwar period; first and second are South Vietnam and Israel).[45] Park solved this crisis by concentrating all Korean governmental economic powers in a newly created agency, the Economic Planning Board (EPB). The EPB, placed under a deputy prime minister, took over all planning responsibilities from the Ministry of Reconstruction and absorbed the Bureau of the Budget from the Ministry of Finance and the Bureau of Statistics from the Ministry of Home Affairs. The EPB in turn set up the Korean Development Institute, manned by a cadre of professional economists who held advanced degrees from domestic and foreign universities.

The EPB quickly gained some autonomy from the Blue House, but not primarily because Park intended for it to do so. As Lim explains:

> The First Five-Year Economic Plan (1962–1966) document reveals that the government initially did not clearly envisage adopting export-led growth based on unskilled, labor-intensive manufactures. The primary concern then was to improve the chronic balance of payments deficits that foreign aid had permitted. . . . However, this is not what occurred. The composition of actual exports differed drastically from the government's projections, or targets. It was the private exporters who played a major role in identifying and taking risks, exporting unskilled-labor-intensive products in which Korea had a comparative advantage.[46]

The EPB gained its independence as it assumed responsibilities for managing the civilian sector—rewarding the clever and aggressive, penalizing the costly and slow.

Even so, the Korean economic bureaucracy never gained the kind of autonomy from Blue House politics that its Japanese equivalent once enjoyed. This was reflected most obviously in the chaotic state of the Korean economy during 1981, when a new military leader came to power and tried to dictate economic policy to the government and private sectors. However, General Chun was soon forced to recognize that he needed the EPB's expertise even more than the EPB needed his political authority, particularly since foreign investors in the Korean economy made it clear they did not intend to finance a military leader who took very long to learn the same lessons that President Park had learned in the mid-1960s.

45. David C. Cole, "Foreign Assistance and Korean Development," in Cole, Lim Youngil, and Paul W. Kuznets, *The Korean Economy: Issues of Development*, Korea Research Monograph no. 1 (Berkeley: Institute of East Asian Studies, University of California, 1980), p. 1.

46. Lim, *Government Policy*, pp. 16–17.

Taiwan's case is similar to South Korea's in the pervasive influence of the military—China Air Lines, for example, is a direct descendant of the ROC Air Force—and in the existence of an even more firmly entrenched political elite, the Kuomintang, that had a long history of concentrating all power in ideological and political hands.[47] In breaking this monopoly, the influence of the United States was decisive,even though at the time it did not have a comprehensive understanding of what it was doing. Taiwan's economic pilot agency, the Council on International Economic Cooperation and Development (CIECD), founded in 1963, traces its ancestry back to the Council on United States Aid (CUSA), which was set up in 1948 under the U.S. China Aid Act as an interministerial council to supervise aid expenditures. As Neil Jacoby explains:

> Although [CUSA's] chairman was the president of the Executive Yuan and it contained other ministries of the Chinese government, financially the Council was semi-autonomous in nature and functioned outside of the regular ministries. . . . Being free of the need to obtain legislative approval of its expenditures, the Council was able to act speedily on developmental projects. Not being subject to all Chinese civil service regulations, it was also able to pay higher salaries that enabled it to recruit and retain a highly competent staff.[48]

With the 1963 announcement that American aid would end in 1965, CUSA became CIECD and took on developmental planning and coordination functions.

General Chen Cheng, who had been responsible (together with C. Y. Yin) for Taiwan's successful land reform and import-substitution policies of the late 1950s, was the leader, until his death in 1965, of the group concentrated in the CIECD. His main factional rival in the Kuomintang was Chiang Ching-kuo, whose chief experience until the 1960s had been in the secret police and in eliminating subversive influences on the island. With the ending of American aid, President Chiang Kai-shek quietly shifted his priorities from a military campaign against the mainland to the economic indepenence of Taiwan—and he also began to shift his son into the groups Chen had fostered (by 1969 Chiang Ching-kuo was deputy premier and chairman of CIECD). The two Chiangs also appear to have been influenced by the Korean model and by its EPB. With political support and sanction for the work of the economic bureaucracy finally secured at the top, the Kuomintang slowly began to lose some of its ideological rigidity. Somewhat surprisingly, Chiang Ching-kuo proved to be the most capable political sponsor of economic development the ROC has yet seen. The degree of autonomy permitted to expert elites by Chiang Kai-shek rested on personal factors—Chiang's full trust in Chen Cheng and C. Y. Yin; Chiang Ching-kuo enlarged and institutionalized it. Nonetheless, without the initial Ameri-

---

47. "China Air Lines," *Ekonomisuto* 59 (March 1981), pp. 100–101.
48. Neil H. Jacoby, *U.S. Aid to Taiwan* (New York: Praeger, 1966), pp. 60–61.

can pressure and Chiang Ching-kuo's adroit use of his own authority, it is hard to see how the Kuomintang would ever have invented the capitalist developmental state on its own.

Autonomy of the state

Any particular political arrangement generates its own special political problems—for example, the powers and influence of the U.S. Congress generate the extensive lobbying and political action committees that surround it, things unknown to the Japanese Diet. However, one problem of the capitalist developmental state is for the political elite to avoid becoming the captive of its major clients, who are the representatives of big, privately owned businesses. Some, particularly the Marxists, would answer that the problem is unavoidable. The whole theory of "state monopoly capitalism" in Japan is devoted to this proposition. But there is clearly a distinction between systems of public-private cooperation in which the state independently develops national goals (the East Asian capitalist cases) and systems of public-private cooperation in which the state's goals are reducible to private interests (Mexico and the so-called bureaucratic authoritarian regimes of the cone of South America). It may be true that even in the Asian cases the state cannot directly contradict the interests of big business, but it is also true that the politicians have maintained their independence to a greater degree than in other quasi-authoritarian capitalist nations. How do they do it?

In Taiwan the politicians appear to rely on authoritarian means: the ideological pretensions of the Kuomintang justify ultimate reliance on military-police powers to put down any challenges to KMT authority. The party itself also owns and manages numerous enterprises and thus is independent of big business for its own funds. Thanks to land reform, moreover, the party's electoral strength in the rural areas remains solid. At the same time it must be said that so little is known about the latter-day Kuomintang (an extremely difficult subject on which to do political research) that it would be best to pass over this case. In Japan and South Korea, however, election contests and the maintenance of large, expensive political parties require that the reigning politicians raise enormous sums of money, and this certainly makes them vulnerable to private interests.

Big business in Japan supplies money to the Liberal Democratic party (LDP) to keep it in power, but it does not thereby gain a dominant influence over government policy. The LDP supports big business, but it also relies on an electorally over-represented farming population to remain in power. The party does pay off the farmers, even though it does not give them a political voice on any subject other than agricultural affairs. In 1983, for example, when the Japanese government was imposing cuts of 5 to 10 percent on all budgetary requests (with the exceptions of defense, foreign aid, salaries, and science and technology) and had frozen public works expenditures for the previous four years, it nonetheless agreed to raise the governmental purchase price of rice by 1.75 percent over the previous year's level.

This Japanese pattern of relying on a powerful but uninfluential agricultural sector while accepting support from an influential but not all-powerful industrial sector is a creative solution to a major problem of the capitalist developmental system. It also suggests the consequences that are likely to follow from any determined foreign or domestic effort to break up the protected and privileged position of Japan's admittedly inefficient agricultural sector. Either the LDP would lose its majority in Parliament and with it the single-party rule on which capitalist developmentalism is predicated, or the LDP would remain in power but only as the captive of big-business interests, with an attendant rise in corruption and loss of national direction.

In South Korea, with its more authoritarian government, the pattern has included support for agriculture, but more with the intent of equalizing incomes among sectors than as a basis of political support. More important, the government has developed sources of income for the political system other than contributions from big business. Korean politicians have had some big expenses. Park's first and perhaps most important (although for him personally, an ultimately fatal) act was to create, by decree of June 10, 1961, the Korean Central Intelligence Agency (KCIA) as an independent political support apparatus. Originally built on a 3,000-man cadre from the existing Army Counter-Intelligence Corps, the KCIA expanded to some 370,000 employees by 1964 and became, without question, the most cohesive political organization in South Korean society. The problem was how to finance it.

Park obtained funds in two ways. First was the ratification on August 14, 1965, of the treaty normalizing relations with Japan, and second was the authorization on August 18, 1965, of the dispatch of some twenty thousand troops to South Vietnam. Both of these decisions had wide popular support in principle but were heatedly and sometimes violently opposed in context because they supplied the funds with which the military government could consolidate its rule. Joungwon Kim explains:

> The Japan-Korea Treaty and the commitment of troops to Vietnam were to provide important new resources to the Park government, both directly and indirectly. The new financial resources would provide funds not only for the carrying out of the government's economic plans, but new resources for political funding as well. During the period from 1965 to 1967, in addition to the claims payments from Japan ($12.08 million in grants and $14.07 million in loans in 1966, the first year of payment, $37 million in grants and $25 million in loans in 1967), the treaty agreement with Japan opened the way to commercial loans from that country. During 1966 and 1967, South Korea received a total of $108.5 million in private loans from Japan. Since private loans re-

quired government approval and repayment guarantees, the Korean party receiving foreign loans was required to pay a percentage (popularly believed to be 10–15 percent and sometimes as much as 20 percent of the loan amount) in payoffs to obtain the necessary government guarantees. The system, of course, applied to foreign loans from other nations as well. The decision to send troops to Vietnam in 1965 and 1966 bolstered confidence abroad in the American willingness to defend South Korea, and helped to induce commercial loans from other nations. During 1966 and 1967, South Korea received $19.9 million in commercial loans from the United States, $53.1 million from West Germany, $30.9 million from Italy and France, $2.5 million from Great Britain, and $41.2 million from other nations, making a total of $256.1 million in private commercial loans during those two years alone. Assuming a kickback-ratio as low as 10 percent, this would mean political fund resources of $25.6 million from this source.[49]

Needless to say, the money received in this manner was not used exclusively to fund the regime and the KCIA; some of it also helped replace American aid and finance the first five-year plan. But the monies also made the regime independent of domestic financial backers, which further meant that the regime's needs were not a drain on the investment funds of enterprises. A pattern similar to that of President Park's first few years emerged in the period 1981–83 under the so-called Fifth Republic of President Chun Doo Hwan, when South Korea sought some $6 billion in aid from Japan and, after a year-and-a-half fight, punctuated by the school textbook controversy, received some $4 billion.

The principle that emerges from this analysis is that the political independence of the ''economic general staff'' is not easily achieved but that, without it, the setting of long-term economic goals and industrial policy is unlikely to produce the results envisaged by theorists of public policy. If, of course, the politicians and their economic bureaucrats are themselves hopelessly corrupt (viz., innumerable African states) then no amount of foreign aid or independent funding will free them from their business sector: the money will simply be siphoned off or otherwise misspent.

Administrative guidance

All democratic governments have general, macrolevel economic policies designed to influence private economic decisions in ways that these govern-

49. Joungwon Alexander Kim, *Divided Korea: The Politics of Development, 1945–1972* (Cambridge: Harvard University Press, 1975), pp. 263–64. On the Korean party system, KCIA, Vietnam, and political funding, also see Hahn Bae-ho and Kim Ha-ryong, ''Party Bureaucrats and Party Development,'' in Suh Dae-sook and Lee Chae-jin, eds., *Political Leadership in Korea* (Seattle: University of Washington Press, 1976), pp. 67–88; Hahn Ki-shik, ''Underlying Factors in Political Party Organization and Elections,'' in Wright, *Korean Politics*, pp. 85–103; and Lovell, ''Military and Politics in Postwar Korea,'' p. 191.

ments deem desirable. One of the characteristics that distinguishes industrial policy from general economic policy is its penetration to the microlevel, meaning government attempts to influcence economic sectors (agriculture, high technology), whole industries (advanced electronics), and individual enterprises within industries (Lockheed, Chrysler). Many democratic governments also implement industrial policies in this sense, such as the American government's long-standing policy of supporting agriculture and the defense industries. But general Western theory and practice concerning either macro or micro interventions hold that they should take the form of incentives, equitably applied and available and not specific commands directed at individual firms. The Western emphasis is on the rule of law and the use of nondiscretionary controls to the maximum extent possible.

One lesson from the East Asian capitalist developmental states is that this concern for nondiscretion may be misplaced. The Japanese economic bureaucracy has long found that its most effective powers are tailor-made, verbal, ad hoc agreements implemented through "administrative guidance." And the Korean case is even clearer:

> A firm that does not respond as expected to particular incentives may find that its tax returns are subject to careful examination, or that its application for bank credit is studiously ignored, or that its outstanding bank loans are not renewed. If incentive procedures do not work, government agencies show no hesitation in resorting to command backed by compulsion. In general, it does not take a Korean firm long to learn that it will "get along" best by "going along." Obviously, such a system of implementation requires not only cooperation among the various government agencies that administer compliance procedures but continuous consultation between firms and public officials.
> Such a system could well be subject to corruption, and there is some evidence that payments are, in fact, made and received for services rendered, but again it must be emphasized that there is very little evidence that such corruption as exists interferes in any serious way with production processes.[50]

Evidence on the balance between incentives and commands in Taiwan is lacking and must await further research.

The relative importance of incentives and commands in industrial policy pinpoints an often unnoticed trade-off. It is true that, in terms of economic theory, the nondiscretionary manipulation of incentives is to be preferred because it retains to the maximum extent the motives of and information provided by the market. But it is often overlooked that such a system also inevitably increases reliance on laws, lawyers, litigation, and excessively codified procedures. Administrative guidance (a euphemism for governmental orders) is obviously open to abuse and has been abused on occasion, but it is also much faster than the rule of law and avoids the unpredictable impact of new legislation and court decisions on sectors that do not require

---

50. Mason et al., *Economic and Social Modernization*, p. 265.

adjustment but that are affected anyway because of the universal scope of laws. One of the marked differences between the regulatory and the developmental capitalist states is the pervasive influence of lawyers in the former and their minimal role in the latter. This is not simply a cultural difference but above all a result of having different political economies.

Zaibatsu

Just as the public sectors of the capitalist developmental states have contributed several institutional innovations that are unusual from the point of view of Western capitalist theory, the private sectors have been no less creative. Perhaps the best known private innovations are the general-trading companies—that is, enterprises that specialize in the import of raw materials for domestic industries and in the export of their manufactured goods. They also maximize cost and price margins through global intelligence networks concerning all available markets, and they perform important functions in the short-term financing of foreign trade. The effectiveness of these organizations is today so widely recognized that legislation has been enacted in the United States authorizing versions of them for the American economy and exempting them from some provisions of the American antitrust laws.[51]

Much more controversial are what are known pejoratively as "financial cliques," or, both in the Japanese language and today generically, as zaibatsu. These are vertically and horizontally integrated "industrial groups" or conglomerates, usually including their own trading company and, in Japan only, their own bank. Over the years, since their first appearance during the Meiji era, zaibatsu have been heavily criticized by both domestic and foreign writers for, among other things, putting their own interests before those of the nation, contributing to a marked "dualism" in the economy (that is, extensive, poorly paid subcontracting firms totally dependent upon and often exploited by the groups), and caving in to irresponsible national leaders (as in the Japanese military-industrial complex of the 1930s and 1940s). During the Allied Occupation of Japan, direct measures were taken to dissolve the zaibatsu—measures that had the unintended effect of modernizing rather than eliminating them.

Today, with several more decades of global experience and knowledge of intentional development programs, ranging from Stalinism to the Alliance for Progress, it seems that the zaibatsu may have been underappreciated. They function as powerful institutions for concentrating scarce capital for developmental projects in underdeveloped countries, and they constitute a

51. See Michael D. Erony, *The Export Trading Company Act of 1981: A Legislative Analysis and Review* (Los Angeles: Coro Foundation, 1981).

compromise between the inefficiencies of purely state enterprise and the indifference to developmental goals of purely private enterprise. Lim adds:

Vertical and horizontal integration allow an enterprise to alleviate risks and the uncertainties of market instability and rapid structural change. Vertical integration eliminates the need to depend on monopolistic suppliers of input materials or assures steady flows of needed inputs in adequate amounts. . . . Horizontal integration (participation in many different activities not related to input linkages) increases information flows and consequently reduces the uncertainty surrounding investment and production decisions. . . . These are some of the important reasons for the birth of the so-called general trading companies and enterprise groups, started in Japan and recently copied in Korea. . . . Such groups internalize uncertainty, information, and factor-market flows, and substitute for a perfect market as a way of coping with market imperfections in less developed countries.[52]

In addition, in advanced capitalist developmental states they still perform international competitive functions by making capital available more cheaply for companies in the group and by freeing new ventures from the need to make a profit in the short term.

The three leading Korean *chaebol* are Samsung (twenty-seven companies), which produces primarily consumer goods, Hyundai (eleven companies), which concentrates on producers' goods and automobiles (the Pony), and Daewoo (seventeen companies), which is spread among trade, finance, machinery, electronics, and engineering.[53] A fourth, the Lucky Group (the one hundred thirty-fourth largest firm in the world according to *Fortune's* 1978 ranking) includes Bando Trading Company, Honam oil refinery, Yochun petrochemicals, plus electronics, nonferrous metals, insurance, and securities.[54] These organizations are similar to Japanese zaibatsu except that in the prewar period the Japanese zaibatsu groups included their own bank and in the postwar period rebuilt around their own bank. Korean *chaebol*, on the other hand, "must rely on government-controlled credit institutions. This is a central fact in government-business relations in Korea and has an important bearing on the extent of private economic power."[55]

In Taiwan, large-scale enterprises, if not true zaibatsu, are very important, although there is some evidence that the culture of business in China resists conglomerate integration more than in either Japan or Korea.[56] The

---

52. Lim, *Government Policy*, p. 46.
53. See "Chaebol Case Studies," in Jones and Il SaKong, *Government, Business, and Entrepreneurship*, pp. 343–64.
54. "Lucky Ltd.," *Ekonomisuto* 58 (April 1980), pp. 124–25.
55. Mason et al., *Economic and Social Modernization*, p. 286.
56. See S. G. Redding and G. L. Hicks, "Culture, Causation, and Chinese Management" (University of Hong Kong, February 1983), p. 5.

Tatung Group, however, would appear to be a true zaibatsu. In 1977 it was by far the largest of some eight hundred Taiwanese home electric-appliance manufacturers, and it has since branched out into electronics, communications, construction, building materials, and publishing. The chairman of the Tatung Group, Dr. T. S. Lin, began his enterprise in 1942 under Japanese rule. A graduate of the engineering department of Taiwan Imperial University, Lin founded the Tatung High School for Engineering and the Tatung Institute of Engineering. He has allowed small amounts of outside capital into his group in order to obtain new technologies, including 8 percent from Tōshiba, and has entered into joint ventures with Nippon Electric and Fujitsū. In 1972 Lin expanded to the United States, and in 1980 his plant in Los Angeles was the largest electric-fan manufacturer in the country. Companies similar to Tatung include Formosa Plastics (headed by Wang Yung-ching, allegedly the biggest capitalist in Taiwan), Yue Loong Motors (in 1983 Yue Loong exported the first of its "Sunny" cars to the Middle East), Far Eastern Textiles, and Taiwan Cement.[57]

Are zaibatsu, of either the Japanese or the more attenuated Korean and Taiwanese type, an inherent feature of capitalist developmental states? More research on this subject is indicated, but it seems that zaibatsu are important for unleashing entrepreneurship—and it was entrepreneurship that provided the dynamic growth element in all of these economies. By permitting the growth of zaibatsu in Japan and Korea and encouraging their growth in Taiwan, the government helped reduce risks, encouraged greater investment than would have occurred without the zaibatsu, and ensured that private activities would be aimed unintentionally toward developmental goals. The reliance on zaibatsu as the locomotives of an entire economy meant that antitrust concerns were relegated to a lesser priority or, more accurately, that capitalist developmental states took as their standard for antitrust intervention the size and degree of oligopoly of their international competitors. There are undoubtedly trade-offs involved in adopting such a standard, but then there are also trade-offs in antitrust intervention that is oriented exclusively to domestic competition.

Foreign capital

One element of the Japanese model that appears to be contradicted by the Korean and Taiwanese cases is the degree to which the Japanese have

57. See the series "Ajia no biggu bijinesu," in *Ekonomisuto* 58 (February 1980), pp. 96–97, 58 (May 1980), pp. 96–97, and 58 (November 1980), pp. 96–97; and *Free China Weekly* 24 (June 19, 1983), p. 4. For a survey of the five hundred biggest firms in Taiwan, see *T'ien Hsia (Commonwealth: A Business Monthly)* (Taipei), September 1, 1982, pp. 49–61. The ten biggest firms in the country are analyzed in *T'ien Hsia*, November 1, 1981, pp. 43–48.

prevented foreign participation in their economy. Japanese bureaucrats, historically, have been close to paranoid on the subject of the dangers of an invasion of foreign capital. By contrast, the Koreans and Taiwanese have given virtuoso performances in how to use foreign and multinational capital without at the same time becoming subservient to it. This is a large and complex subject, and we can hope here only to signal its importance and some of its ramifications.

Postwar Japan did not totally exclude foreign investment or foreign borrowing; loans from the World Bank and from American commercial banks were important during the 1950s. Moreover, if Korea and Taiwan enjoyed large amounts of American aid, Japan probably profited more than either of them from American offshore procurement contracts and military expenditures. At the same time Japan was concerned to separate foreign money and technology, both of which it needed, from foreign-ownership rights and manufacturing facilities because it wanted to preserve its own large domestic market as a proving ground for its new industries. The domestic markets in Korea and Taiwan are significant, but they have not had the same magnetic power as Japan's for either foreign or domestic manufacturers. Foreign firms in Korea and Taiwan are producing primarily for export, whereas foreign firms in Japan would have liked to produce for the domestic Japanese market.

Moreover, just as the Korean and Taiwanese domestic markets are not large enough to sustain high-speed growth, their domestic savings capacities are smaller than Japan's. They had to internationalize in order to attract the needed savings. At the end of 1981 South Korea and Taiwan were the fourth and seventh most indebted non-OPEC, non-Communist, less developed countries (the leaders were Mexico, Brazil, and Argentina).[58] Even so, in 1982 South Korea enjoyed a debt-service ratio of 13.3 percent, below the international average of 15 percent, and it had prospects of increasing exports enough to lower its debt-service ratio to 11 percent during the five-year plan of 1982–86. Korea is not one of the countries whose liabilities threaten the solvency of the international banking system—and Taiwan is even less so.

But the issue of Korea's export prospects raises the question of the other side of the trading coin. North America and Western Europe are the world's largest markets, and access to them is indispensable for any manufacturing and exporting country. By the 1980s Japan, thanks to its highly nationalistic policies, had become the only advanced industrial nation in the world that, for all intents and purposes, did not import any products it manufactured and exported so successfully (for example, automobiles). This situation, combined with the sheer size of the Japanese economy, contributed powerfully

58. Based on reports of the Bank for International Settlements, Country Exposure Lending Surveys.

to the global trend toward protectionism (or, at the least, toward international cartelization) that appeared in the 1970s and 1980s. South Korea and Taiwan are not immune to these trends, but their access to the American and Western European markets is less threatened because of their longer histories of internationalization and market access. The lessons in this development seem to be that the neomercantilism practiced by Japan is not an inherent feature of the capitalist developmental system (Korea and Taiwan have not overindulged in it), but that the controls exercised by Korea and Taiwan over foreign investment are probably necessary to avoid neo-colonialism.

Many important aspects of the three capitalist developmental states discussed in this chapter have not been even touched upon in this sketch of their features—for example, the large public sectors in all three economies and the differing measures adopted by each nation to try to keep them efficient or to get rid of them. The model presented here does not aim at comprehensiveness or econometric detail. Its intent is threefold: to illustrate how economic performance is related to political arrangements, to argue for the essential rationality of the soft authoritarianism–capitalism nexus in terms of comparative development strategies, and to explore the range of subtle and specifically political problems that must be addressed and solved in implementing the strategy.

If these goals have been achieved in even a tentative manner, we may then conclude by asking what are the future prospects of the model for the three successful cases or for potential emulators? Superficially, it would be possible to argue that to the extent that the model implies export-oriented growth, its future prospects are poor because changes in the international environment have lowered the chances for dramatic expansions of exports. This is superficial, however, because it implies that the environment is the main determining factor in the model. If that were so, there should today be many successful capitalist developmental states and not just a few in East Asia. It seems instead that the particular political economies of the capitalist developmental states have managed to adapt more effectively and more rationally to any given environment than either their purely absolutist or their purely capitalist rivals. Thus, as a matter of batting averages rather than absolute growth rates, it would follow that in a world in which all economies may grow more slowly in the future, the capitalist developmental states will still outperform the others. This is because they have discovered ways to surmount the rigidities of zero-sum domestic competition without falling into the trap of authoritarian displacement of the market and private enterprise.

The interplay of state, social class, and world system in East Asian development: the cases of South Korea and Taiwan Hagen Koo

The growing literature on East Asian economic development is dominated by conventional economic analyses that stress the comparative advantages of the East Asian NICs and how they have reaped the benefits of these advantages through the workings of world market mechanisms (Westphal, 1978; Little, 1982; Balassa, 1982). Recently, however, scholars have begun to pay close attention to the role of developmental states in guiding and directing export-oriented industrialization through strategic intervention in the economy (Amsden, 1979; Hofheinz and Calder, 1982; Haggard and Moon, 1983; Wade and White, 1984). Although this statist approach reveals important dimensions of the East Asian development pattern, it tends to overstress the independent role of the developmental state, paying insufficient attention to other, equally important sociopolitical forces such as social classes and core-periphery relations in the world economic system.

Here I take a more comprehensive, albeit somewhat eclectic, approach, using an analytic framework advanced elsewhere (Koo, 1984a). This approach assumes that development in a Third World country is shaped by the interplay of state, social classes, and world system. The focus of analysis is not the individual factors but the *interaction* among these three sets of variables. If we do not examine these variables in their dynamic interaction, I believe, we cannot delineate the specific ways in which each set of variables influences the development process. Dependency mechanisms, for example, cannot be specified until we have investigated the ways in which external forces are linked to internal class structure. Similarly, class relations in a peripheral nation cannot be adequately understood unless we consider the influence of international capital and core states. Finally, the role of the state in economic development cannot be fully understood without its being situated in the contexts of class structure and world economic

I gratefully acknowledge assistance received from the Social Science Research Institute, University of Hawaii, while I was preparing this chapter.

system. Thus, a comprehensive framework of the political economy of Third World development must integrate these three sets of variables and comprehend the process of development as an outcome of their interaction.

While the development process is shaped by the interplay of these structural conditions, it also influences these conditions by generating new sociopolitical forces. Economic change often leads to a new configuration of the class structure, modifying relationships among social classes. Changing class relations affect the character of the state and its mode of intervention in the economy. Changes in state and class structure may subsequently result in modification of the ways in which a given economy is integrated into the world economy. In short, economic development is both a dependent and an independent variable.

Using this framework I investigate the nature of state, social classes, and external linkages in South Korea and Taiwan and examine how interactions among these structural forces have shaped economic growth in the two countries since the early 1960s. Discussion is organized sequentially around each set of sociopolitical factors, but my concern throughout is with interactions among these structural sectors. The focus of my analysis is on the structural sources of rapid economic growth, but I also consider the social consequences of industrialization in these countries.

World systems

The insertion of South Korea and Taiwan into the world system began with the expansion of the Japanese empire in the late 19th century. Taiwan became a Japanese colony in 1895 and remained under Japanese rule until 1945; Korea was under colonial rule from 1910 to 1945; and the economies of these two countries were integrated into a regional division of labor centered on Japan. Consequently the colonial government concentrated on increasing agricultural production while discouraging the development of industry. But what sets the colonial experience of Korea and Taiwan apart from that of Latin America or Africa is that primary production was not confined to some foreign enclave with only limited spillover into subsistence agriculture. In both societies, extraction of surplus was carried out not by large capitalists but by colonial bureaucrats; surplus was extracted, moreover, not from workers employed in a small export enclave but from individual small farmers and tenants. This pattern of surplus extraction seems to have mitigated the structural disarticulation usually associated with colonialism.

To increase the absolute amount of surplus, the Japanese introduced a scientific approach to agriculture and invested heavily in infrastructure. They introduced improved fertilizers, new seed varieties, and an advanced system of irrigation. For efficient shipment of extracted surplus and for military purposes, they built railroads and greatly improved other transportation systems. In the late 1930s Japan began to change its colonial economic policies in Korea and Taiwan, increasing production of certain war-related industrial goods. Although these late efforts did not produce significant industrialization, it is generally believed that Japanese colonialism in both countries left a substantial foundation of infrastructure on which later industrialization could build (Kuznets, 1977; Jones and Sakong, 1980; Ho, 1978; Amsden, 1979; Barrett and Whyte, 1982).

After World War II the births of the Republic of Korea in the southern half of the Korean peninsula and the Republic of China in Taiwan integrated the two countries into the world capitalist system in a new form, under the aegis of the United States. The United States became involved in Korean affairs mainly to counter Soviet expansion in the Far East. In the 1940s it had very little interest in the Korean economy, because this poor and resource-deficient country had little to offer. After independence from Japanese rule the southern part of Korea was under the control of an American military government for three years. The main achievement of this period of American tutelage was the destruction of indigenous communist and leftist forces and the establishment of a new capitalist state with an ultra-conservative, anticommunist leadership led by Syngman Rhee (Cumings, 1981). But at the same time, in response to strong popular demand and to establish at least minimal social order, the American military government pushed for a land reform that was to be completed by a newly formed government. This land reform, as noted below, was to have a profound impact on the class structure of Korea.

The United States initially had little interest in defending the Kuomintang regime that retreated to Taiwan, but the breakout of the Korean War in 1950 changed its Far Eastern strategy; Washington became more actively involved in Taiwanese affairs. Without active U.S. support, it is widely agreed, the Republic of China would not have survived (Jacoby, 1966; Ho, 1978; Amsden, 1979).

When we talk about the roles of South Korea and Taiwan in the world system, therefore, we must first consider not their positions in world capitalism but their roles in the world's political and military confrontations. These two states were more or less created by a strong U.S. military intervention to prevent the spread of communist revolution in the Far East. It was not so much immediate capitalist interest in the two economies as geopolitical confrontation between superpowers that shaped social formations within these two societies (Gold, 1986; Lim, 1985).

As bastions of the anticommunist struggle, South Korea and Taiwan both received enormous amounts of U.S. aid and military assistance. The average annual inflow of aid to Korea from 1953 through 1958 was $270 million. Roughly $12 per capita per year, this aid was nearly 15 percent of per capita Korean gross national product (Cole and Lyman, 1971:165).

Between 1951 and 1965 Taiwan received U.S. economic aid of about $1.5 billion, averaging about $100 million per year—around $6 per capita (Little, 1979). Military assistance to the two countries was about twice as much as economic aid and was far greater than what most other countries received. This strong U.S. support enabled the regimes of Syngman Rhee and Chiang Kai-shek not only to maintain basic economic and social order but also to make substantial investments in infrastructural development, especially in education.

It was only after this predominantly political integration into the world system, and after relatively unsuccessful experimentation with import-substitution industrialization in the 1950s, that South Korea and Taiwan made a dynamic entry into the capitalist world economy in the early 1960s through their adoption of the outward-looking industrialization strategy. This economic shift, however, was not unrelated to earlier economic changes. It is important to note that one of the most important goals of U.S. economic aid was to lay the foundation for a free market economy. The U.S. Agency for International Development played a crucial role. What Samuel Ho (1978: 117) observed in Taiwan is true as well for South Korea:

> AID . . . was strongly committed to the growth of the private sector and used its influences and resources to improve the climate for private enterprises. Without AID's influence and active intervention, the private sector would not have become Taiwan's foremost source of economic growth.

In both South Korea and Taiwan, AID persistently pressured the government to liberalize its control over the economy and to limit its military expenditures, using the level of aid as an instrument of this pressure (Zenger, 1977; Little, 1979). Apparent failures of import-substitution industrialization in the late 1950s and the impending curtailment of U.S. economic aid in the late 1950s forced both governments to search for an alternative. In 1958 Taiwan began major economic policy reforms that included a statute for the encouragement of investment, the conversion of the multiple exchange rate system to a single rate, the relaxation of trade and exchange controls, and the simplification of business laws and regulations. These and subsequent policy reforms greatly improved the climate for foreign investment, and with the early 1960s exports began to increase rapidly.

Internal political instability prevented South Korea from implementing similar policy reforms until 1962. Rhee's regime was toppled by student revolution in April 1960. Then, following the first democratically established Republic of Chang Myon (1960–61), which was too weak and short-lived to achieve any significant economic change, Park Chung-Hee came to power through a military coup in May 1961. Unlike his predecessors, Park showed a strong commitment to economic development, apparently perceiving good economic performance as a primary means for establishing the legitimacy of his regime. This difference between Park and Rhee was not simply a matter of personality; more likely, it reflected the sociopolitical contexts in which they held power. If the dominant issues of Rhee's time were political, centering on political consolidation and national unification, then the period immediately preceding Park's coming to power was characterized by predominantly economic issues. As David Cole and Princeton Lyman (1971:80) note, "the growth of economic awareness during the previous decade had made economic performance almost a 'must' for any regime that hoped to succeed after 1960." Upon assuming power, Park began a series of reforms, but the policy foundation for outward-looking industrialization was not sufficiently laid until 1964. As in Taiwan, so in South Korea, U.S. AID and the World Bank played active roles in devising an export-oriented strategy for industrialization (Cole and Lyman, 1971: 203–6).

The two countries embarked on export-led industrialization ahead of most other Third World countries, which joined the game only belatedly, in the 1970s. Timing was important. In the 1960s and into the early 1970s the world capitalist economy was on the upswing. Core capitalists were eager to invest, Euromoney was easy to borrow, and interest rates were relatively low; there were fewer trade barriers against Third World manufactures and little competition from other labor-rich developing countries. Finally, the Vietnam War was good for business in both countries. Reasons of timing alone make it difficult to imagine how the success stories of South Korea and Taiwan (or of Singapore and Hong Kong, for that matter) can be repeated in the rest of the Third World. Also, as André Gunder Frank (1982) argues, the very success of these countries in the zero-sum world of international trade eliminated the possibility of similar successes elsewhere.

In sum, we must distinguish between two world systems: the international state system, based on geopolitical and military competition between nation-states; and the capitalist world economy, governed by worldwide capital accumulation. The two are intimately connected, but, as Theda Skocpol (1979:22) argues, their separation is useful for the analysis of concrete socioeconomic transformations.

The dependency of South Korea and Taiwan was initially structured by the international state system and then came to be defined by the world capitalist system. These two countries gained several advantages from this sequence of integration. For one thing, because of their strategic value in containing communist influence in the Far East, both countries had received enormous amounts of economic and military aid from the United States before their economic penetration by private foreign capital. By the time foreign capital arrived, adequate economic foundations in both infrastructure and human capital had been laid, and the state was in firm control of the economy. The initial political integration of the two countries into the world state system, it can be argued, eased their subsequent economic integration into the world capitalist system (Gold, 1986; Lim, 1985).

Class structure

It would be a great oversimplification, as I have argued, to explain the pattern of development or underdevelopment in any Third World country in terms of the world system alone. The world system influences economic change only through its interactions with internal forces. This section examines the class structures of South Korea and Taiwan and their interactions with the world system and the state.

Japanese colonialists in Korea and Taiwan had a substantial impact on the existing class structures of the two societies. Their basic policy was to develop a system of surplus extraction based on bureaucratic means only, by slightly modifying the existing class structure and then subordinating it to the colonial state bureaucracy. Nonetheless, two important changes did occur during the colonial period: the great landlord class was seriously undermined, though the landlord class itself did not disappear, and state-class relationships were restructured. Before colonialism the state in both Korea and China was relatively weak vis-à-vis the agrarian upper class. But during the colonial period the state bureaucracy emerged as a force paramount over the class structure and over society as a whole. This pattern persisted into the postcolonial period.

After independence, successful land reforms further altered the class structures of the two societies. In South Korea, land reform programs were implemented between 1948 and 1950. Because the Rhee government was based on elements of the old landlord class, which actively resisted land reform efforts, land reform was not as successful in Korea as in Taiwan or in Japan. Nevertheless, there were significant achievements: about 70 percent of eligible land was redistributed, it was reported, and over one million of a total of two million rural households benefited. The government imposed a limit on paddy holdings of three *chongbo*, equivalent to about one hectare. The overall effect was to destroy the old great landlord class and to create a basic rural structure of small, owner-operated farms—also eliminating a significant source of political instability in the countryside (Cole and Lyman, 1971). The Korean War, which broke out in 1950, finally ended the old agrarian elite of the Korean class structure. With the war's end emerged a poor but a highly fluid and egalitarian society in South Korea.

In Taiwan the Kuomintang regime could carry out a much more thorough land reform, mainly because it was under no obligation to the island's rural elite (Amsden, 1979; Gold, 1986; Barrett and Whyte, 1982). Taiwanese agriculture was reformed in three stages, starting with rent reductions in 1949 and culminating in the Land-to-the-Tiller Act in 1953. By the time land reform was completed, the great landlord class had sunk into social oblivion, and Taiwan became a society of small owner-operators.

The postindependence societies of Korea and Taiwan were also characterized by the absence of any noteworthy comprador class. Many Koreans and

Taiwanese had, of course, accumulated fortunes in the colonial period by means of their close ties with the colonialists. But it is questionable whether they really constituted a viable comprador class; even if they had done, their class basis no longer existed after independence because they could not maintain their ties with metropolitan capital. Because of the political nature of U.S. involvement in Korea and China in the first decade after independence, hardly any private capital came in, providing little opportunity for the rise of a new type of comprador class. The strong U.S. support for the Rhee and Chiang governments if anything strengthened the position of the state and ensured state dominance of the economy.

So it was that when South Korea and Taiwan entered the development decade of the 1960s, both had a highly fluid class structure without an old agrarian upper class or a comprador bourgeoisie. When the two countries decided to pursue outward-looking industrialization, consequently, they encountered no effective class opposition. Dominant capital was primarily commercial by this time, and state development strategies and assistance quickly transformed it into industrial capital in the 1960s (Hamilton, 1983). With destruction of the old class system and social disruptions caused by war and massive migration, both countries were quickly transformed into predominantly petit bourgeois societies. The grip of tradition and status concerns had by and large disappeared, and society was full of small entrepreneurs who were continuously searching for new sources of income. Therefore the two societies had not only very few change-resistant residues of the old agrarian class structure to overcome but also great reserves of human potential to tap.

There is one very important difference between the early class experiences of South Korea and those of Taiwan. Unlike the South Korean government, the Kuomintang had already experienced the bitterness of peasant revolution in mainland China. Korea had also faced serious peasant problems in the 1940s, but these peasant struggles led neither to a successful revolution nor to a radical shift in the South Korean power structure (Cumings, 1981). These different experiences with class struggle had an apparently important influence on the economic development policies of the two states. Unlike the Park government in Korea, which pursued accelerated growth at almost any cost, the Chiang government was more seriously concerned with price stability and rural development (Lim, 1981; Gold, 1986).

One violent political movement that might have had an impact on the Park government's economic policies was the student revolution of 1960, which put an end to the twelve-year-old government of Syngman Rhee. It was an urban movement and primarily, though not exclusively, middle-class in character. This historical incident appears to have heightened Park's obsession with impressive growth rates, even at the cost of extraordinarily high inflation, while at the same time fostering a relative neglect of rural areas. In

Taiwan agriculture provided an important source of industrial accumulation; in Korea, by contrast, industrialization was achieved at the expense of the rural sector (Little, 1979; Moore, 1984). Overall, industrialization in South Korea has been more costly than in Taiwan, a matter to which we shall return when we examine the consequences of economic growth.

Unlike the countries of Latin America, neither South Korea nor Taiwan experienced successful populist mobilization before export-oriented industrialization began. If any such mobilization occurred at all, it was for only brief moments in the 1940s, just prior to the consolidation of power by the Rhee and Chiang regimes. The brutal suppression of mass uprisings in both countries—the autumn uprising of 1946 in Korea and the 1947 massacre in Taiwan—resulted in a depoliticization, rather than a politicization, of the masses (Cumings, 1981; Winckler, 1980). And so there was no need, as there was in Latin America, to exclude the mobilized masses from politics or to destroy oppositional populist ideologies. Such political requirements are often mentioned as structural sources of bureaucratic-authoritarian regimes in Latin American (O'Donnell, 1973; Collier, 1979), but they do not seem to apply to the two East Asian cases. Popular exclusion has a long history in both South Korea and Taiwan, and it cannot be seen as causally linked to the problems of dependent development.

The state

In South Korea and in Taiwan, world system and internal classes came together to produce a strong state structure. Massive American support to the regimes of Syngman Rhee and Chiang Kai-shek in the 1940s and 1950s, discussed earlier, along with an extensive police apparatus left by the Japanese, were crucial for the consolidation of state power in the turbulent period of state building after independence. The destruction of the great landlord class during the colonial period and the absence of a comprador class with strong ties to metropolitan capital provided the state with ample autonomy from class interference. Probably equally important was a long East Asian tradition of bureaucracy under the Confucian influence (Michell, 1984).

Political division in both countries and continuing confrontation with the Communists provided the state with a permanent excuse for violence and repression. They also led to hypermilitarization and the maintenance of an extensive security system of police and intelligence. As Jon Halliday (1980:7) comments, "Taiwan and South Korea are not merely militarized regimes, they are militarized societies." Because administrative and coercive organizations are the most important bases of state power, this hypermilitarization of society inevitably enhanced the power of the state over society.

Both the South Korean and the Taiwanese states are characterized not only by relative strength but also by active intervention in economic development. The South Korean economy is one of the capitalist world's most tightly supervised economies, with the government initiating almost every major investment by the private sector. South Korean development is thus often defined as state-led industrialization (Haggard and Moon, 1983; Wade and White, 1984).

The government regulates the flow of financial capital through its control of the banks; it controls the level and use of foreign loans, and it has the power to screen and monitor the activities of multinational corporations and other foreign investors; it even interferes with enterprise-level decisions concerning investment, production, and pricing. But what really distinguishes South Korea from other, less successful developing countries is not so much the level of the state's involvement as its ability to implement its economic policies (Jones and Sakong, 1980). In this sense the South Korean government is a hard state.

Economic planning in Taiwan has been somewhat less extreme than in South Korea, but the role of the state in economic development has been essentially the same (Amsden, 1979; Wade, 1984). The Taiwanese state brokered its economy into the world capitalist economy and has exercised great influence on the manner in which local capital is connected to international capital. Although the Taiwanese state has exercised less direct control over private firms, it intervenes in the economy through a large number of state-owned enterprises in key industrial sectors (Ho, 1978; Wade, 1984).

The key instrument of state control of the economy in South Korea has been its control over banks and access to foreign capital. As it holds discretionary power to allocate underpriced credit, the state can cut off the lifeblood of business at any time. Banks in Taiwan have not played as important a role in enhancing state power, but they are still important instruments of state economic control. The exact manner in which the government uses financial institutions has varied. For one thing, the South Korean government favored large-scale enterprises far more than did the Taiwanese government (Lim, 1981). But the state-capital relationship has been basically the same in both countries and changed but little through the 1960s and 1970s.

The governments of Park and Chiang have been described as strong and hard states. In class terms they enjoy an ample degree of relative autonomy from dominant classes. But the generally positive roles that both states have played in economic development cannot be explained solely in terms of strength or relative autonomy. The two governments are also characterized by their strong commitment to economic growth. In South Korea, Park Chung-Hee was very different from Syngman Rhee in his strong commitment to economic growth. Whereas Rhee had been preoccupied with political concerns, Park gave highest priority to economic development. In Taiwan, too, Chiang Kai-shek concentrated on economic development from the 1950s on. In large measure this strong economic commitment derived from the desire of the two heads of the state to enhance their political legitimacy. Both men apparently perceived economic development and improved welfare as the best means of demonstrating their right to rule.

Another aspect of the state to play a role in economic development is the state bureaucracy. As foreign observers frequently point out, South Korea and Taiwan possess a well-trained, efficient, and relatively uncorrupt bureaucracy (cf. Jones and Sakong, 1980; Michell, 1984). The core of this technocracy is American-educated economists, aid administrators, and foreign experts working for AID, the World Bank, the IMF, and the like. With almost unconditional support from the peak of the government hierarchy, these technocrats have worked in a highly favorable environment to devise an unhesitatingly capitalist path of accumulation. The politico-military positions of these states in the world system, and the propinquity of communist states, allow little ideological freedom to either South Korea or Taiwan. The result is an ideological homogeneity within the state bureaucracy, which facilitates efficiency.

The state's role in economic development is not restricted to economic planning or to the control of financial institutions. No less important is the control and discipline of industrial labor. Because the major comparative advantage of the two economies is low-wage labor of relatively high quality, the success of export-oriented and labor-intensive industrialization has depended on maintaining a low-wage and disciplined labor force. To guarantee this condition, both the Korean and the Taiwanese governments have combined corporate control of labor union activities with repression (Choi, 1984; Launius, 1984). In both societies, unions are weak and exist as no more than an arm of the government; strikes in foreign-invested sectors are illegal; and labor unrest has been severely punished. This, it appears, is one of the conditions that peripheral states must provide to promote a favorable investment climate for foreign capital while enhancing business confidence for domestic capital.

It is through the state's role in labor relations that we can see the class character of the two states clearly. Their strength and commanding power over the economy notwithstanding, the South Korean and Taiwanese states are unequivocally capitalist, and they represent the interest if not that of individual capitalists, then of the capitalist class as a whole. In both countries the government depends on capitalists, not so much for their political support as for their economic performance. In Taiwan, which is losing political support around the world, capitalists provide an important link with the international community. In sum, the states of South Korea and Taiwan enjoy only a relative, not an absolute, autonomy from their dominant classes. They are free from direct influence of individual capitalists or class segments, but they cannot transcend the collective interest of the capitalist class—both domestic and international. Most important, both states have been highly successful in exploiting this relative autonomy to promote capitalist interests and thereby to achieve high rates of economic growth in the periphery of the world capitalist system.

By way of summary, let us compare South Korea and Taiwan with Latin American countries in terms of several key aspects of political economy. First, the integration of the two East Asian countries into the world system in the mid-20th century had a character more political than economic. South Korea and Taiwan came into being as a result of the Cold War, and the United States has supported them politically and economically for their strategic value. Foreign private capital began to enter only after a state and a class structure emerged which could adapt dynamically and positively to new conditions in the world system. The role and power of the multinational corporation in both economics— especially in Korea's—has been much weaker than in Latin America.

Second, the two East Asian states have been much stronger than the states of most other developing countries, and they have enjoyed ample autonomy from dominant classes. This internal state strength was based both on world-system forces (U.S. military and political support, as well as the inheritance of a highly developed state apparatus from Japanese colonialists) and on a relatively weak configuration of class forces. The states of South Korea and Taiwan are distinguishable from their Latin American and Southeast Asian counterparts not only by their strength vis-à-vis internal social classes but also by their strong state commitment to economic development and the high degree of efficiency and discipline found in the state bureaucracy. Also important is ideological homogeneity among state managers and technocrats. The position of the state in South Korea and Taiwan in the triple alliance—among state, foreign capital, and domestic capital—seems to be much stronger than those of Latin American states (Gold, 1986; Lim, 1985).

Third, the class structure and class struggles in South Korea and Taiwan have differed enormously from those of Latin America. Both economies started their dependent development with a remarkably egalitarian class structure, which was at the same time characterized by a dense petit bourgeois desire for upward social mobility and a pervasive entrepreneurial spirit. The early stage of primary exports, which occurred while the two countries were under Japanese colonial rule, produced neither an entrenched agrarian dominant class nor a comprador commercial class. Instead, Japanese colonialism and political turmoil after independence effectively destroyed the old agrarian class structure, producing a very fluid stratification of society. In short the relatively favorable experiences of dependent development in South Korea and Taiwan are largely attributable to the fact that in the late 1950s the two societies possessed a class structure that was very congenial to dependent capitalist accumulation. No class posed a serious obstacle to export-oriented industrialization; rather, the dominant classes

responded constructively when the state tried to propel the economy into this
new pattern of dependent development.

Sociopolitical consequences of rapid economic growth

The rapid economic growth of the past two-and-a-half decades has brought
great social changes in South Korea and Taiwan. The political economies of
the two nations have been transformed, and future economic development
will be determined by newly emerging class forces and by new patterns of
relationship between state and society. The position of the two countries in
the world economy has changed a great deal, creating new structural constraints upon development strategy. Systematic analysis of these changes is
beyond the scope of this chapter, but I shall discuss some of the most
substantial changes.

One of the most significant consequences of rapid economic growth can
be observed in the transformation of the class structure. Industrialization in
the two countries has brought about the rise of two principal classes of a
capitalist society, the capitalist class and the industrial working class. The
economic power of capitalists has grown in direct proportion to the expansion of the national economy. In both countries the capitalist class was a
creature of the state, and it retains a subordinate political position. But some
significant changes have occurred in state-capitalist relations. In a capitalist
society the economic power of a social class cannot fail to affect its political
power, if only in the long run. In both countries, but especially in South
Korea, tensions between the state and big business have been increasing.
Large capitalists, having grown under state protection, no longer welcome
massive state intervention and have pressured the state to loosen its grip on
the economy. Partly as a result of this domestic pressure, as well as foreign
pressure, the Korean government has permitted a considerable degree of
economic liberalization since 1980. In Taiwan and South Korea business
leaders have become bold, vocally attacking bureaucratic delays and ineffi-
ciency. In both countries the class power of big business has grown too big
to be ignored in major economic policy decisions.

Yet capitalist classes of South Korea and Taiwan reveal interesting contrasts. Capital concentration has been more pronounced in South Korea than
in Taiwan. Consequently the Korean economy is now controlled by a few
giant players; Taiwan's economy allows greater space for many small
players. The core of the Korean capitalist class is thirty to fifty conglomerate
business groups (*chaebol*), each owned and run by a single family. The
position of the *chaebol* in the economy is overwhelming. In 1983, for
example, the combined net sales of the top thirty *chaebol* equaled about
three-quarters of South Korea's output of goods and services. In the 1980s
this concentration has become an acute political issue, engendering intense

popular criticism of the monopolistic growth of the *chaebol* and of state policies that have facilitated such a development. The South Korean government now seeks to curb further expansion of the *chaebol*, but so central is the place the *chaebol* occupies in the Korean economy today that it will not be easy to reshape their behavior in accordance with government wishes (see *Far Eastern Economic Review*, 12 December 1985).

Small business in Taiwan, in contrast, has found a much more favorable environment and has played a major role in Taiwan's economic growth. Taiwan's industrial structure is consequently less polarized than Korea's, and there seems to be much less anticapitalist sentiment among the populace. This difference between the two countries is to a large extent an outcome of their different developmental policies. Park in South Korea gave exclusive attention to rapid economic growth, giving excessive support to a few star players to achieve his goal. Chiang, on the other hand, was more concerned with balanced growth and social stability. This difference in orientation did not result from a simple personality difference between the two leaders but from the two societies' different experiences with previous class struggles. Of particular interest here is how the state's development policies have affected the composition of dominant social classes. Although South Korea and Taiwan have pursued broadly similar development strategies, they have diverged in specific development policies, with differing consequences for class formation.

Another significant consequence of industrialization was a rapid expansion of the industrial working class. In South Korea the proportion of production workers increased from 13.2 percent of the active labor force in 1960 to 28.2 percent in 1980. In 1980 they constituted 42.8 percent of the urban labor force (Population and Housing Census Report, 1960 and 1980). The increase in the industrial work force has been even faster in Taiwan: there production workers went from 18.5 percent in 1963 to 41.9 percent in 1980, and of the nonfarm labor force in 1980 they constituted 51.8 percent (Statistical Yearbook of ROC, 1976 and 1983). This remarkable occupational change has entailed a massive proletarianization of the working population. A large proportion of the new proletariat is composed of young female factory workers (Kung, 1976; Arrigo, 1980; Cho and Koo, 1983). In relative size and social significance the industrial working class may now be the most significant social class in Taiwan and South Korea.

To what extent has this first generation of industrial workers developed class consciousness and organizational solidarity? Has it transformed itself from a "class in itself" to a "class for itself"? There are few empirical studies, but available information does suggest that class formation has developed to a greater extent in South Korea than in Taiwan. In both countries the state has played an active role in suppressing labor movements through the corporatist control of labor unions (Deyo, 1981; Choi, 1984; Launius, 1984; Koo et al., 1986), but South Korean workers have proved less compliant. Fairly volatile throughout the 1970s, the Korean labor movement in the 1980s has become more threatening to the government: labor protests are frequently organized by independent, grass-roots labor unions and linkages are slowly being forged between radicalized students and grass-roots labor organizations. In comparison, Taiwanese labor has been relatively passive. There have been few overt manifestations of class formation, and Taiwanese capitalists have enjoyed greater industrial peace.

Systematic study alone can account for this difference between South Korea and Taiwan, but one important factor again seems to lie in state policies. The Taiwanese state has been more welfare-oriented, paying greater attention to equity problems than has the Korean state; consequently, greater inequality in income distribution has developed in South Korea than in Taiwan (Fields, 1982; Koo, 1984b). Furthermore, the Taiwanese state has promoted rural-based industries through policies of industrial decentralization, and decentralization has prevented the kind of proletarianization that has occurred in South Korea, where workers have left rural areas permanently for the cities. Another possible factor may be the nature of the middle class, especially the intelligentsia, for the Korean intelligentsia and students have been noted for their political activism and their critical stance toward the government since the days of Japanese colonialism. In the 1970s and 1980s church groups and activist students have played an important role in politicizing the Korean labor movement.

Finally, let us consider the changes that have occurred in state-society relationships because of changes in the economy and in class structure. Although the states of South Korea and Taiwan are still characterized as hard, dirigist, and developmental (Haggard and Moon, 1983; Wade and White, 1984), they now seek to manage an increasingly complex and politically sophisticated society. The continuing ability of the state to lead the process of development is now widely questioned, and big business seriously challenges it. As capitalist and working classes have become increasingly potent political forces, so the state has lost a considerable degree of the relative autonomy and institutional insulation that were essential to the major shift in development strategy of the early 1960s. The capitalist class has grown too strong to be easily dominated by the state, and workers are not as docile and quiescent as they once were. At the same time the presence in both countries of a relatively large, well-educated middle class exerts pressure on the state for political democratization. In neither country can economic growth alone legitimate the authoritarian state.

Geopolitical conditions have also changed a great deal. Taiwan has lost support from the international community, and South Korea is no longer as essential for U.S. military hegemony as it was during the Cold War. Both states can thus expect reduced political support from core states. At the same time, an extensive network of external economic linkages has affected the two states' economic policy making abilities. In South Korea an enormous foreign debt now limits the state's freedom to devise new industrial strategy, while in Taiwan substantial foreign direct investment creates a similar structural constraint.

In the 1980s, therefore, faced externally with increasingly unfavorable world markets and domestically with increasingly potent pressures from social classes, the states of South Korea and Taiwan have a substantially reduced space in which to maneuver. In all likelihood, both states will continue to play a major role in economic development in the foreseeable future. But they must find new ways to intervene in the economy and develop new patterns of relationships with a highly differentiated society.

References

Amsden, Alice. 1979. "Taiwan's Economic History: A Case of Etatisme and a Challenge to Dependency Theory." *Modern China* 5:341–380.
Arrigo, Linda. 1980. "The Industrial Work Force of Young Women in Taiwan." *Bulletin of Concerned Asian Scholars* 12:25–34.
Balassa, Bela, ed. 1982. *Development Strategies in Semi-industrial Economies*. Baltimore: Johns Hopkins University Press.
Barrett, Richard. 1982. "State Intervention in the Taiwanese Economy in the 1960–1980 Period." Mimeo. University of Illinois, Chicago Circle, Dept. of Sociology.
Barrett, Richard, and Martin K. Whyte. 1982. "Dependency Theory and Taiwan: A Deviant Case Analysis." *American Journal of Sociology* 87:1064–1089.
Cho, Uhn, and Hagen Koo. 1983. "Economic Development and Women's Work in a Newly Industrializing Country: The Case of Korea." *Development and Change* 14:515–531.
Choi, Jang-Jip. 1984. "A Corporatist Control of the Labor Union in South Korea." *Korean Social Science Journal* 11:25–55.
Cole, David, and Princeton Lyman. 1971. *Korean Development: The Interplay of Politics and Economics*. Cambridge: Harvard University Press.
Collier, David, ed. 1979. *The New Authoritarianism in Latin America*. Princeton: Princeton University Press.
Cumings, Bruce. 1981. *The Origins of the Korean War: Liberation and the Emergence of Separate Regimes, 1945–1947*. Princeton: Princeton University Press.
Deyo, Frederic C. 1981. *Dependent Development and Industrial Order: An Asian Case Study*. New York: Praeger.
Fields, Gary. 1982. *The Labor Market and Export-led Growth in Korea, Taiwan, Hong Kong, and Singapore*. Seoul: Korea Development Institute.
Frank, André Gunder. 1982. "Asia's Exclusive Models." *Far Eastern Economic Review*, 25 June, pp. 22–23.
Gold, Thomas. 1986. *State and Society in the Taiwan Miracle*. Armonk, N.Y.: Sharpe.

Haggard, Stephan, and Chung-In Moon. 1983. "The South Korean State in the International Economy: Liberal, Dependent, or Mercantile?" In John Ruggie, ed. *The Antinomies of Interdependence*. New York: Columbia University Press.

Halliday, Jon. 1980. "Capitalism and Socialism in East Asia." *New Left Review* 124:3–24.

Hamilton, Clive. 1983. "Capitalist Industrialization in East Asia's Four Little Tigers." *Journal of Contemporary Asia* 13:35–73.

Ho, Samuel P. S. 1978. *Economic Development of Taiwan, 1860–1970*. New Haven: Yale University Press.

Hofheinz, Roy, and Kent Calder. 1982. *The Eastasia Edge*. New York: Basic.

Jacoby, Neil. 1966. *U.S. Aid to Taiwan: A Study of Foreign Aid, Self-Help and Development*. New York: Praeger.

Jones, Leroy, and Il SaKong. 1980. *Government, Business, and Entrepreneurship in Economic Development: The Korean Case*. Cambridge: Harvard University, Council on East Asian Studies.

Koo, Hagen. 1984a. "World System, Class, and State in Third World Development: Toward an Integrative Framework of Political Economy." *Sociological Perspectives* 27:33–52.

Koo, Hagen. 1984b. "The Political Economy of Income Distribution in South Korea: The Impact of the State's Industrialization Policies." *World Development* 12:1029–1037.

Koo, Hagen, Stephan Haggard, and Frederic Deyo. 1986. "Labor in the Political Economy of East Asian Industrialization." *Items* 40. New York: Social Science Research Council.

Kung, Lydia. 1976. "Factory Work and Women in Taiwan: Changes in Self-image and Status." *Signs* 2:35–58.

Kuznets, Paul. 1977. *Economic Growth and Structure in the Republic of Korea*. New Haven: Yale University Press.

Launius, Michael. 1984. "The State and Industrial Labor in South Korea." *Bulletin for Concerned Asian Scholars* 16:1–21.

Lim, Hyun-Chin. 1985. *Dependent Development in Korea: 1963–1979*. Seoul: Seoul National University Press.

Lim, Youngil. 1981. "Structure and Efficiency in Manufacturing: Japan, Korea, and Taiwan." Research Report. Seoul: Korea International Economic Institute.

Little, Ian. 1979. "An Economic Reconnaissance." In Walter Galenson, ed. *Economic Growth and Structural Change in Taiwan*. Ithaca: Cornell University Press.

Little, Ian. 1982. *Economic Development: Theory, Policy, and International Relations*. New York: Basic.

Michell, Tony. 1984. "Administrative Traditions and Economic Decision-making in South Korea." In R. Wade and G. White, eds., 1984.

Moore, Mick. 1984. "Agriculture in Taiwan and South Korea: The Minimalist State?" In R. Wade and G. White, eds., 1984.

O'Donnell, Guillermo. 1973. *Modernization and Bureaucratic-Authoritarianism*. Berkeley: University of California, Institute of International Studies.

Skocpol, Theda. 1979. *States and Social Revolution: A Comparative Analysis of France, Russia, and China*. New York: Cambridge University Press.

Wade, Robert, and Gordon White, eds. 1984. *Developmental States in East Asia: Capitalist and Socialist*. Brighton, England: Institute of Development Studies, IDS Bulletin 15.

Westphal, Larry. 1978. ''The Republic of Korea's Experience with Export-led Industrial Development.'' *World Development* 6:347–382.

Winckler, Edwin. 1980. ''State Struggle and Class Conflict on Taiwan.'' Paper presented at the Taiwan Political Economy Workshop, East Asian Institute, Columbia University.

Zenger, J. P. 1977. ''Taiwan: Behind the Economic Miracle.'' *AMPO: Japan-Asia Quarterly Review* 19:79–91.

State and labor: modes of political exclusion in East Asian development Frederic C. Deyo

Strong, developmentalist states have been important in guiding and orchestrating rapid industrialization in Singapore, South Korea, and Taiwan, especially during the economic restructuring of the 1970s. These states, or more correctly the public-sector organizations that have formulated and implemented national development strategies, have been substantially insulated from the political forces that typically compromise technocratic "rationality" in other Third World countries. In part this state autonomy from social forces has been rooted in the political subordination of organized labor. What are the political sources of that subordination?

East Asia's developmentalist states have enjoyed marked political autonomy from social forces in general, but the export-oriented industrialization (EOI) they have pursued has given special prominence to the developmental role of labor. East Asian manufacturing for export has been based largely on the effective economic deployment of labor, the only significant developmental resource available to these small, resource-poor countries, and on maintenance of competitive labor costs (see Lim, 1986). Disciplined and low-cost labor, here even more than elsewhere, has been a prerequisite of development.

Labor's political weakness is, of course, of a piece with the broader political exclusion under East Asian authoritarian regimes. Under single-party systems in Singapore and Taiwan, as under military-based rule in South Korea, authoritarian regimes have contained and suppressed political opposition. Even in laissez-faire Hong Kong, autocratic colonial rule has presented few opportunities for political representation for the popular sectors.

I am grateful for helpful comments to Richard Abrams, Richard Barrett, Gary Fields, Stephan Haggard, Hagen Koo, and Janet Salaff, and for research assistance to Whasoon Lee. Support for research was provided by the State University of New York University Awards Program, the National Endowment for the Humanities, and the National Science Foundation.

But regime variation among these countries and over time suggests a more complex explanation for the successful insulation of political elites from public intrusion. The point is perhaps most evident in labor relations. The East Asian NICs vary significantly in the degree to which the state plays the dominant role in labor control. In Hong Kong and to a lesser extent Taiwan, labor discipline remains rooted in employment relations at the level of the firm. Labor controls in Singapore and South Korea, conversely, have shifted perceptibly upward to the state. Moreover, labor regimes in these dynamic industrial economies have changed over time. Politically and economically repressive regimes in Taiwan and Singapore have adopted ''softer,'' welfare-based corporatist controls, while since 1970 South Korea has grown harsher and increasingly repressive. Hong Kong's less statist industrial relations system has remained relatively permissive and increasingly supportive of labor's position in industry. The sequence in Taiwan and Singapore, it may be noted, reverses that of the Latin American NICs of the Southern cone, especially Brazil and Argentina, where in the 1960s and 1970s repressive military regimes violently displaced earlier, populist regimes based on authoritarian corporatism.

This chapter explores the varied and changing relationships between state and labor in East Asia during early and recent periods of export-oriented industrialization. In it I seek to explain cross-national variation, as well as temporal change, in the nature and effectiveness of labor regimes in the Asian NICs by reference to development strategy, class dynamics, elite structure and unity, economic structure, and external political and economic linkages.

Asian industrialization and labor exclusion: the early period

Industrialization in Latin America, oriented toward the domestic market, minimized any need to maintain internationally competitive labor costs as a basis for growth. Indeed, import-substitution industrialization (ISI) encouraged stimulation of domestic purchasing power to support industrial development, and thus it partially muted the contrary pressure from employers to restrict labor costs and justified government efforts to increase welfare expenditures by firms and the state for workers. Such a context fostered the growth of broad, developmental coalitions of the urban middle classes, industrialists, state bureaucrats, and unionized workers.

This linkage between domestic purchasing power and industrial production was weaker in the case of export-oriented development. In East Asia, export competitiveness, the key to industrialization, was highly dependent on low-cost, disciplined labor. Politically or socially guaranteed labor peace and the containment of labor costs were indispensable requirements for growth. But *how* these requirements were met varied considerably across the East Asian NICs. Where a history of labor militancy posed a threat to the emergent strategy for development, as in Singapore, the launching of EOI was accompanied by heightened labor repression (Robinson, 1979:119). In Taiwan and perhaps South Korea, on the other hand, political controls earlier established sufficed to maintain labor discipline in the early years of EOI. Finally, where a weak, internally fragmented, and politically inert labor movement—or intact and effective enterprise-level controls—guaranteed labor discipline, as in Hong Kong and perhaps Taiwan, state intervention was less pronounced or more indirect.

In Hong Kong, a tightening of state labor controls did not accompany early EOI. Although the colonial government maintained relatively restrictive ordinances regarding political demonstrations and protest, including prohibition of strikes deemed to "coerce the government" or to inflict significant social hardship on the community (in the 1949 Illegal Strikes and Lockouts Ordinance), it made little effort to intervene in industrial relations. Apparent exceptions to this pattern, such as introduction of voluntary arbitration under the 1948 Trade Disputes Ordinance and provision of minimum disability, death, and other benefits under the 1953 Workmen's Compensation Act, subsequently expanded, actually introduced little real change in employment relations. Voluntary arbitration was rarely used, and so minor were the compensation provisions that they were irrelevant to employers and workers.

On Taiwan the incoming Chinese nationalist government brought with it most of the repressive labor legislation enacted in the mainland context of a protracted civil war. This legislation effectively prohibits strikes through mandatory arbitration of disputes, restricts wage bargaining by unions, and subjects all unions to supervision by local government. Such controls, along with domination of local unions by Kuomintang cadres and a broad restriction of political rights under martial law, certainly contributed to the early suppression of labor conflict, providing a basis for labor discipline at the outset of EOI in 1959–61. But the absence of systematic local implementation of conflict management provisions suggests the law's weak connection with circumstances on Taiwan itself. There was little elaboration either of industrial relations machinery or of implementing regulations at the local level. Disputes continued to be handled largely at the enterprise level with little in the way of government intervention beyond the local organization of ad hoc mediating committees (U.S., Bureau of Labor Statistics, 1972).

More important than the direct state management of industrial conflict in Taiwan were controls over personnel practices and local unions at the enterprise level. Under the 1932 Factories Act, large enterprises were required to establish factory councils consisting of representatives from labor and management. Employers were also obligated to provide welfare, housing, and educational and other forms of employee assistance. (Such enterprise corporatism was to be substantially extended during the 1970s.) Finally, early legislation and government practice gave at least nominal support to enterprise unionism. The control function of such unions, all of which had to affiliate with the Chinese Federation of Labor (CFL), was ensured by the prominence and leadership of enterprise management and local Kuomintang cadres in union affairs. These and other controls at the level of the local enterprise have been shaped in ways that permitted them to remain vigorous and effective throughout the period of industrial transformation.

In Hong Kong the absence of substantial state intervention in labor relations may in part reflect a general commitment to laissez-faire. But a more important explanation for the lack of heightened labor repression in Hong Kong and in Taiwan is that labor posed a major threat to employers or the state in neither country. Hong Kong's labor passivity derived from many factors, including the large number of immigrant workers who feared deportation back to the mainland, political competition between mainland-oriented and Taiwan-oriented labor unions, and pressure from Beijing to minimize political disturbances in an economically important entrepôt and financial center (see Turner, 1980). In Taiwan, labor peace reflected an early imposition of a unitary, one-party political system, the lack of earlier nationalist or other political mobilization of factory workers, and a predominantly agricultural work force. In both countries these varied circumstances ensured a continued vitality for enterprise-level controls; direct state intervention in local labor affairs was not needed.

Quite different were labor circumstances at the start of EOI in South Korea and Singapore. Immediately after imposing martial law in 1961, General Park sought first to establish political control and soon thereafter to initiate EOI. Despite the state's stringent, repressive measures, however, a highly politicized labor movement with deep historical roots in the opposition to Japanese occupation threatened elites and the chosen course for development. Park's initial response to labor included a total ban on strikes, deregistration of all existing unions, and arrest of many union activists. After destroying oppositional unionism in 1961, Park sought renewed political legitimacy by establishing civilian rule and liberalizing labor and other legislation. But at the same time he ensured the emergence of politically docile trade unions by creating an umbrella labor organization, the Federation of Korean Trade Unions (FKTU), with which all reactivated unions had to affiliate. Until the mid-1970s the national industrial unions that made up the federation functioned mainly to moderate union demands, implement government policy, and discipline recalcitrant locals.

Labor activism provoked similarly drastic government intervention in Singapore. Following the politically disruptive elections of 1963, in which the People's Action party defeated the leftist Barisan Socialis, opposition union leaders were jailed, unions deregistered, and legislation passed which proscribed political activity by labor. The subsequent turn to EOI was accompanied, in 1968, by legislation that reduced permissible benefits regarding retrenchment, overtime work, bonuses, maternity leave, and fringe benefits while giving management full discretionary power in matters of promotion, transfer, recruitment, dismissal, reinstatement, assignment or allocation of duties, and termination (Deyo, 1981). In both South Korea and Singapore, political consolidation before EOI destroyed opposition parties and leftist unions; the later adoption of EOI saw heightened direct state intervention in labor relations.

The consequences of this labor repression in South Korea and Singapore can be seen in available data on unions and industrial conflict. It was not until 1966 that membership in Korean unions reached 1960 levels, and unionization has never included as large a proportion of workers as it did before Park took power. Similarly, Singapore's union membership declined from 189,000 in 1962 to 112,000 in 1970. Even more dramatic are changes in levels of industrial conflict. Korean work stoppages dropped from an average of seventy-nine per year between 1955 and 1960 to only fifteen per year during 1963–71, while those in Singapore declined from an average of sixty-two per year in 1958–62 to twenty-eight in 1963–67, and four per year between 1968 and 1980. The more stable labor regimes of Hong Kong and Taiwan have seen no such dramatic changes in levels of unionization or numbers of work stoppages.

Changing labor regimes in industrializing East Asia

State repression of labor, as we have seen, accompanied or preceded the adoption of EOI as the new development strategy in South Korea and Singapore and, less forcefully and more indirectly, in Taiwan as well. During Hong Kong's early EOI period, in the late 1950s and early 1960s, labor controls remained relatively permissive. These early cross-national differences we can in part attribute to differences in levels of labor militancy and threat to development policy and ruling elites. But how have such regimes changed in subsequent years?

Hong Kong authorities have maintained restrictive controls over political dissent and disruption throughout the postwar period. Firmly enforced public order legislation, for example, effectively contained the 1966–67 spillover of political activism from the mainland cultural revolution (England and Rear, 1975:chap. 1). Labor legislation, on the other hand, has increasingly favored workers. Under a 1961 ordinance, unions were specifically granted full freedom to strike and to picket peacefully, although other provisions under the same law encouraged weak and fragmented unionism by recognizing unions with as few as seven registered members; they also prohibited unionization across occupations, industries, or trades, and the hiring of full-time unionists not employed in the industry (Turner, 1980; Salaff, 1981). In 1968 a new employment ordinance prescribed criminal sanctions for employers refusing to pay back wages, a chronic problem in the colony, and in 1973 a labor tribunal was established to permit workers to make monetary claims against employers under existing contracts or to seek redress in cases of violation of existing labor law (Turner, 1980). In 1975 a new ordinance established the right of unions to demand arbitration or appointment of a public board of inquiry in disputes with employers. And in 1977 unions were permitted to hire full-time professionals to handle union affairs.

All in all, then, Hong Kong's labor regime remains quite liberal. Through the 1970s the colony lacked minimum wage legislation, centralized wage machinery, compulsory collective bargaining, and other conventional elements of industrial relations (Cheetham, 1980). Those limited changes which were instituted in the sixties and seventies have offered workers some support in dealings with employers. But they do not imply that the elite lacks substantial control over workers. In fact Hong Kong workers generally face repressive labor controls at the hands of employers and powerful foremen at the enterprise level (England and Rear, 1975), despite new labor law that seeks to reduce abuses of power. Although owners of large textile mills of Shanghai origin show some tolerance for employer-dominated unions, most other firms rigidly repress or control union activities. Smaller, Cantonese firms, which employ the majority of industrial workers, deal severely with any efforts by workers to unionize and normally dismiss union activists outright (Turner, 1980). To some extent government encouragement of trade unions in the mid-1970s countered such blatant antiunionism (Hong and Levin, 1983). But though unionization did increase in Hong Kong in the 1970s, organizational gains occurred not in the critical export industries but rather among public-service, utilities, and other nonmanufacturing workers.

Although they are politically far more restrictive, Taiwan's labor controls have, like those of Hong Kong, remained centered in the enterprise. In general there has been little change of substance, in labor legislation or in enforcement, since the early 1960s. Rather, state-mandated welfare programs at the enterprise level have expanded. In 1978 the Ministry of Interior called for tripartite national consultations on the expansion of union and enterprise assistance to employees in such areas as housing, dormitories, dining facilities, uniforms, education, entertainment, and consumer coops. That same year the Executive Yuan revised labor insurance legislation to improve provisions on retirement and compensation. Subsequent years saw periodic increases in the minimum wage as well as further development of existing welfare programs for workers. Such programs tend both to obviate the need for state involvement in these areas and, more important, to tie workers ever more tightly to their employers by bonds of obligation and self-interest. This latter consideration is most apparent in the direct linking of retirement pay with seniority in the firm.

With revitalization in the mid-1970s of the previously moribund CFL

(Galenson, 1979) began a renewal of support for the organization of manage-
ment- and Kuomintang-controlled unions. In the seventies this effort doubled
the unionized percentage of the labor force. The most important measures
have been organizational drives that the government has supported and
publicized. In addition, unions have been given greater responsibility for
recreation, housing, and other employee benefit programs. And, finally, the
status of unions has been elevated through expanded (albeit limited and
largely symbolic) labor representation in the Legislative Yuan and the National Assembly, as well as in government agencies. The restrictions and
controls placed on Taiwanese unions, as well as the prominent role of
management in union affairs, suggest that these recent organizational drives
should be seen largely as an extension of indirect state controls, exercised
through rather than parallel to enterprise-level structures of control. Suggestive was an effort in the early 1980s, spearheaded by Chen Hsi-chi, legislator
and CFL president, to launch a "Factory as Home and School" movement,
stressing labor-management agreement and the "positive participation" of
workers in solving industrial problems.

In part because of the continuing vitality of Taiwanese enterprise controls, the pattern of minimal direct intervention by the government in industrial disputes has continued. Walter Galenson (1979) suggests that only
about 5 percent of the work force is covered by legally binding collective
agreements; most firms continue to operate under unwritten, informal, and
usually management-imposed labor agreements. The major difference between Hong Kong's labor regime and Taiwan's is that though both operate
primarily at the enterprise level, personnel practices in Hong Kong remain
predominantly repressive while those in Taiwan, in response to state pressure and legislative regulation, have become ever more welfare-corporatist.

South Korea, following the liberalization of labor law which accompanied reestablishment of civilian rule in 1963, has gradually returned to
more repressive controls (Kim, 1978). First, following labor disturbances at
two foreign manufacturing firms in 1968 and 1969, the government issued a
new statute that required approval by the Office of Labor Affairs (OLA) to
establish unions in foreign firms, as well as discretionary OLA referral of all
labor disputes for conciliation, and possible binding arbitration, by a central
labor committee. Then, following Park's slim victory in the 1971 presidential elections, the president established emergency rule under which he
could declare any strike illegal and submit the dispute concerned to "mandatory mediation." A new, "revitalizing constitution" of 1972 prohibited
strikes altogether in the state sector, public enterprises, local government,
utilities, or any business deemed important to the national economy. That
same year labor unions were brought more directly under government control for the duration of the emergency, while a 1973 amendment to labor
legislation provided that collective bargaining could not proceed without
prior labor committee certification as to its legality. And throughout this

period the Korean Central Intelligence Agency played a prominent role in selecting leaders in the Federation of Korean Trade Unions.

In the mid-1970s the government started a new effort to reinvigorate the FKTU. Organizational drives in 1975–79 were reinforced by the devolution to union offices of medical insurance programs, pension systems, and cooperative services, along with a government crackdown on unfair labor practices, an important deterrent to union organizing (Choi, 1983). Union membership doubled, from 531,000 in 1974 to over one million by 1980 (Deyo, 1984).

This organizational drive was interrupted by the political crisis and imposition of martial law which followed the assassination of President Park in 1979. Under Park's successor, Chun Doo Hwan, a tightening of labor controls has resulted in a rapid decline in union membership. New labor legislation enacted in 1980 banned interference by third parties in local collective bargaining. This provision eliminated an important organizational role of the FKTU while simultaneously outlawing involvement by church and other activist organizations in industrial disputes. Parallel to this decentralization of collective bargaining was renewed support for nonunion labor-management councils, enhanced company welfare programs, and other efforts to encourage enterprise loyalty and work discipline. Perhaps most important of all, consolidation of the Chun regime included the dismissal or forced resignation of many union leaders who had played an oppositional role during the earlier crisis.

Singapore's experience, despite its apparent similarity at the adoption of EOI, contrasts sharply with that of South Korea. Singapore's labor controls have, like Korea's, remained state-centered and extensive. Substantive regulation to some degree increased, particularly regarding wage levels, worker compensation, and safety. But far more important has been a shift away from earlier repression toward a government-controlled corporate structure, the National Trades Union Congress (NTUC), as an instrument of development policy. This revitalization of unions after the destruction of labor opposition was accomplished, as elsewhere, by creating a wide range of benefits and services for members of NTUC affiliate unions. Most important among these were retail, transportation, insurance, and other cooperative services, along with various other direct benefits. In response to these incentives, union membership climbed rapidly during the 1970s, especially in those unions most extensively involved in the new union benefit programs. When efforts were started to introduce higher-technology industry in the late 1970s, the NTUC became a vehicle for productivity campaigns, training programs, and other efforts to enhance labor's contribution to development. But we must recognize that this expanding corporatism signaled no relaxation of labor controls. The continuation of substantial controls could be seen in the government's ability to restrain wages despite growing labor shortages across the 1970s. Growing corporatism reflected only a shift toward modes of control more effective in changing economic conditions. It should also be noted that Singapore's corporatist thrust was earlier and more successful than South Korea's, in part because the PAP had been more successful earlier in eliminating labor opposition.

The early 1980s saw an abrupt shift toward a more decentralized structure for trade unions, with a less dominant national center and greater local control over bargaining, albeit under continued strict government supervision (Lim and Pang, 1984). Accompanying this decentralization has been a partial dismantling of government welfare programs in favor of private ones (Lim, 1983). Especially important in this regard was the launching in 1982 of COWEC, a company welfare fund inspired by Japanese company practices (Chan, 1983). In addition, house unions have been strongly encouraged in recent years, beginning with their establishment in national statutory boards and other government organizations.

How will labor regimes evolve in Singapore and South Korea? Recent developments may indicate an increasing similarity among labor regimes in Singapore, South Korea, and Taiwan. Taiwan authorities have encouraged and supported management-centered labor controls and management-dominated unions, but there is some indication of increasing state intervention in the settlement of disputes. The South Korean government has emasculated the FKTU in favor not only of more autonomous locals but, significantly, of increased emphasis on factory councils and other nonunion-mediated welfare programs at the enterprise level. In Singapore the highly centralized NTUC is giving way to a decentralized union structure and house unions. In all three cases, enhanced welfare programs for workers are increasingly administered by management rather than by unions. Such changes may presage a general convergence on state-regulated enterprise corporatism and a corresponding shift away from union corporatism in Singapore and South Korea. It is noteworthy that union membership levels have declined noticeably during the early 1980s in both countries. But it is unclear whether such declines will continue, and whether they reflect a shift toward an enhanced managerial role in labor relations, declining employment in labor-intensive industry, or other factors.

Nor has the growing similarity among regimes been altogether unconscious. The governments of Taiwan, Singapore, and South Korea have continued to study and emulate Japanese industrial and labor policy, while changes in Singapore's labor policy from the late 1970s have been accompanied by study tours for high-ranking union leaders to observe Taiwanese industrial relations.

Export-oriented industrialization and changing labor regimes

Otto Kreye (1980) and others have suggested a close relationship between state repression of labor and Third World export manufacturing. This relationship, they argue, follows from the importance of cheap, disciplined labor for production for the world market, as well as from the presumed major role of foreign investment in such production. But the experience of the East Asian NICs suggests a more complex set of conclusions which offers only partial support for the thesis. Labor discipline has with few exceptions been maintained throughout the period of EOI in all four countries, and political and labor "stability" has figured prominently in the investment decisions of foreign firms; however, such discipline has had varied sources. Hong Kong, most obviously, remains an authoritarian outpost of colonial rule, but its labor regime can hardly be termed repressive, and clearly other factors have played a greater role in maintaining labor peace there. To the extent that labor discipline has followed from state repression in the other countries, moreover, repression in some cases preceded EOI and was based on political rather than economic considerations (Lim, 1986). Martial law in both South Korea and Taiwan predated EOI; similarly, Singapore's political consolidation under PAP rule destroyed significant leftist opposition before the new industrial policy was adopted.

The characterization of East Asian labor regimes as repressive fails to capture their complexity and flux and is of little assistance in understanding the shift in the mid- and late 1970s toward union- and then enterprise-based corporatism. Furthermore, the assumption that the state is the crucial source of labor control in the Third World is weakened by evidence of effective enterprise-level authority in Hong Kong and Taiwan. Although such authority may, as in Taiwan, depend crucially on state controls over political participation in the larger society, the management of local economic conflict clearly need not depend solely on direct state intervention.

Labor discipline has been an important prerequisite for a development strategy that centers on manufacturing for world markets. Whether this prerequisite is met by elite controls established earlier or newly instituted; whether such controls are predominantly repressive or corporatist; and whether their energizing source is the state or the enterprise, successful EOI development has presupposed effective and politically exclusionary labor regimes. Perhaps the clearest illustration is to be found in Singapore, in the massive wave of foreign investment in electronics and other light industry immediately following promulgation of the harsh labor legislation of 1968.

This close relationship between strategy and labor regime, it might be argued, was most evident early in EOI development, when cheap labor defined the competitive advantage of East Asian manufactured products in world markets. What of the more recent years of economic restructuring and the corresponding shift of emphasis from cheap to skilled and productive labor? Taiwan, South Korea, Singapore, and to a lesser degree Hong Kong made some effort during the 1970s to reinvigorate trade unions and enterprise authority, as noted, and such efforts were associated with and presumably were causally related to increasing union membership. In part this corporatist shift, too, may be explained by the evolving logic of EOI development. If early EOI development was based on the mobilization of cheap, disciplined, low-skilled labor for export manufacturing, then such development would eventually erode the labor supply that made it possible. By the early 1970s upward wage pressures (*Asian Labour*, March 1979; Fields, 1984) and high rates of labor turnover began to threaten EOI by encouraging investors to look beyond the East Asian NICs to Thailand, Malaysia, the Philippines, and mainland China—countries with more abundant cheap labor. In general the four have sought to meet this problem by trying to induce greater investment in heavier industry or in higher-technology, high-skill manufacturing, or both, to maintain internationally competitive labor costs. This effort to alter the position of domestic economies in world markets has necessitated heightened efforts by the state to increase worker skills through manpower training programs, vocational training schools, and incentives for private-sector training schemes (Lim and Pang, 1984). In some cases the union- and enterprise-based corporatist labor policies of the late 1970s and early 1980s responded to primarily political considerations, as in South Korea under Chun. In all cases, however, they enhanced the stability and commitment of the work force and thus encouraged productivity increases and facilitated investment in training programs. All the attempts to achieve a fuller economic mobilization of the work force by incorporating workers into enterprise and union control structures stand in marked contrast to the primarily repressive approaches of the 1960s. The recent move to encourage smaller, house unions may be seen in part as extending this regime shift. In 1983 the Republic of Singapore's Committee on Productivity justified the new emphasis on house unions in the following terms:

> In reinforcing company identification, one should generate identification with a particular company and also establish in the minds of the workers that their benefits and welfare depend on the company's future. . . . The committee believes that house unions should be promoted because it [*sic*] helps workers to identify with the company and its future (pp. 12, 14).

Political roots of regime effectiveness

The political exclusion of labor is not unique to the East Asian NICs. Far more repressive labor controls have been instituted elsewhere, as in the Southern cone of Latin America in the 1960s and 1970s. But these regimes have rarely proved as durable in the face of rapid industrialization and proletarianization as in Taiwan, Singapore, and, to a lesser degree, South Korea.

These regimes in East Asia universally excluded labor from enterprise-level decision making and national politics at the outset of export-oriented industrialization. Exclusion was seen as closely related to the requirements of development. But the functions of social phenomena do not explain their causal origins. While the economic rationale of Singapore's tough 1968 labor legislation seems clear, the *political* sources of the continuing, effective, exclusion of labor there and in South Korea and Taiwan are equally evident. These political roots are to be found in elite unity, on the one hand, and external geopolitical linkages, on the other. In the absence of strong regional or landed elites (Choi, 1983), and following consolidation of power by military groups or exclusionary political parties, elite unity discouraged the sort of oppositional mobilization that typically energizes labor movements. In addition, unlike the early industrial coalitions of Latin America, which were externally isolated, South Korea and Taiwan played a geopolitical role in U.S. Far East military policy which guaranteed substantial U.S. economic and political support for anticommunist, authoritarian regimes along with the forceful destruction of leftist trade unions. Similar external support was available to Hong Kong's colonial government, while Singapore's anticommunist regime was supported first by Britain and later under the ANZUS military alliance.

Equally important have been the consequences of subsequent industrialization for the consolidation of effective exclusionary regimes. First, EOI development has been associated with a rapid increase in the economic stakes held by core countries, further consolidating external support for domestic elites. Benjamin Cohen (1975) in fact argues that the open-door policy toward foreign capital may be rooted less in economic considerations than in a desire to maintain political-military alliances. George Fitting (1982:740) develops this argument in his discussion of Taiwan:

> In the international realm, the expansion of foreign investment in Taiwan has been a considerable bonus to the regime in Taipei. As foreign capital flows into Taiwan, international corporations develop a vested interest in the continued viability of the regime that both invites and protects their investments. Foreign investors inevitably seek to influence their government's policies in support of Taiwan's international position. For Taipei, American investment in Taiwan has meant that there are additional voices in Washington calling for the support of the regime in Taipei. The American Chamber of Commerce of the Republic of China has been most vocal in insisting that the United States continue to support Taiwan.

The emergence of an independent bourgeoisie may threaten elite unity, of course, by creating an independent economic resource base for opposition groups, and so it is important to understand the implications of EOI for domestic business. Only in South Korea did a significant ISI bourgeoisie emerge which might have been expected to oppose the liberalization of trade and foreign exchange which accompanied early EOI. Even there, however, such opposition was foreclosed by the political discrediting of a "corrupt" business elite at the collapse of the Rhee regime in 1960, by continued protectionism in key industrial sectors, and by the relative brevity of the import-substituting period itself. In general, the industrial bourgeoisie in all the East Asian NICs has flourished primarily during the period of EOI and thus has grown dependent upon that strategy, the elites that supported it, and the foreign capital and subcontracting that provided the basis for domestic participation in it.

In South Korea, and to a lesser degree Taiwan, the political subservience of the industrial bourgeoisie was further assured by a channeling of foreign loan capital to local businesses through state-owned or state-controlled banks (Launius, 1983). In Singapore massive foreign investment has substantially displaced local industry, marginalizing the local business community economically as well as politically. By 1975 foreign corporations absorbed 76 percent of manufacturing inputs, produced 71 percent of outputs, and accounted for 65 percent of manufacturing capital formation. And by 1979 wholly foreign-owned firms alone accounted for 63 percent of total industrial employment (Deyo, 1981).

The economic structural demobilization of organized labor

The economic structural consequences of industrialization for trade unions provide a further explanation for the effectiveness of East Asian labor regimes. EOI development has until recently centered on expansion of a few light export industries, such as electronics and apparel. These new industries tend to attract large numbers of young women into employment characterized by low wages, minimal job security, low skill levels, and little possibility of advancement (Elson and Pearson, 1981). Consequently turnover rates are quite high (Ogle, 1977:183), while commitment to job, employer, and coworkers is low (Ho, 1979). Workers in these sectors have been as active as other workers in industrial protest. Female textile workers have in fact played a key role in initiating labor opposition in South Korea (Lim, 1986). On the other hand, such circumstances of employment hinder independent organizational efforts (Elson and Pearson, 1981) and thus reduce the likelihood of effective labor mobilization (Deyo, 1984). Although rates of unionization may be quite high, the source of organization is more often to be found in state sponsorship than in grass-roots mobilization. Even in South Korea, where EOI workers have been most active in labor protest, Jang Jip Choi (1983) finds that workers in textiles are significantly less likely to have played the lead role in organizing their unions than their counterparts in the metal (excluding electronics) and chemical industries. In addition, employment conditions in light EOI industries hinder the development of stable proletarian communities in which labor movements might find an autonomous organizational base. Generally, protest among workers in these industries tends to be short-lived, poorly organized, largely defensive, and easily contained (Turner, 1980; Salaff, 1981).

Economic structural factors also help explain the greater effectiveness of enterprise-level controls in Hong Kong and Taiwan, and the relatively greater role of state-level controls in Singapore and South Korea. Latin American industrialization was associated with a marked concentration of the industrial work force in large, urban-based manufacturing plants. In East Asia such a characterization applies to South Korea and Singapore but not to Hong Kong or Taiwan. Hong Kong government data show a decline in the percentage of workers employed in factories of at least two hundred persons from a high of 50 percent in 1966 to 29 percent in 1980. In Taiwan 42 percent of all employees worked in factories of at least one hundred persons in 1961; the percentage rose to 64 percent in 1971, thereafter declining to 33 percent by 1980. Contrary to this pattern of smaller enterprises, South Korean workers in factories of at least one hundred employees rose from 33 percent of the work force in 1960 to 56 percent in 1968 and 74 percent in 1974. Comparable early employment data are not available for Singapore, although it may be noted that in 1975 fully 70 percent of all workers were employed in factories of over one hundred persons (Deyo, 1984). These data suggest that small-scale production has played a greater role in the industrialization of Taiwan and Hong Kong than of either South Korea or Singapore; the result has been a greater organizational dispersion of the growing industrial proletariat. In Taiwan the dispersal of the work force has been furthered by successful state encouragement of industrial decentralization to rural towns (Ho, 1979).

But what are the implications of these differences for labor regimes? The small firms and dispersed industries of Hong Kong and Taiwan have sustained a measure of continuity in localized authority structures rooted in personal networks of community, family, and enterprise (Djao, 1981; Stites, 1982) without substantial direct state intervention. Proletarian concentration in Singapore and South Korea has been associated, conversely, with a bypassing of local authority, requiring the state to play a greater role in labor discipline.

Of particular importance for our understanding of the effectiveness of East Asian labor regimes is the temporal relationship between evolving labor regimes and economic structural demobilization. EOI development necessitated, as noted, early establishment of effective exclusionary labor regimes; later development benefited from a deepening of the corporatist structures that more fully mobilized the labor force for economic restructuring. These regimes owe their exclusionary nature and their effectiveness to political factors both domestic and external. In all cases the early imposition of effective labor controls politically preempted labor movements, first through coercion and later through corporatist/organizational structures (Choi, 1983). Preemption has been enhanced by a pattern of development that, during its early phase, structurally demobilized labor and thus permitted a sustained period of regime consolidation. So the sequence of political and economic structural changes associated with EOI development has enhanced the long-term preemptive power of elite controls over East Asian labor.

Finally, though the effectiveness of East Asian labor regimes stands out sharply by contrast with that of regimes in Latin America and elsewhere, intraregional comparison makes it equally clear that South Korean elites have been less successful than their counterparts in Hong Kong, Taiwan, and Singapore in preempting and containing industrial conflict. In South Korea workers in both light and heavy industry have defied employers, legislative proscription, and police intervention with stoppages, demonstrations, and other forms of collective action. Their actions have been triggered by real wage declines, layoffs, and unacceptable working conditions, but also by opposition to government-coopted union leadership (*Business Asia*, 3 May 1985). South Korea may have known relatively higher levels of conflict because it has a somewhat more "Latin American" configuration: greater elite conflict; oppositional mobilization by students, church groups, and dissident politicians; inadequate development of preemptive political organization in urban communities; greater development of heavy industry; more uneven economic growth; and greater concentration of a relatively stable industrial proletariat in large factories and urban centers. Clearly the socioeconomic profiles of the other East Asian NICs are generally more supportive of effective labor regimes.

The question of economic inclusion

Export-oriented industrialization has had various structural consequences that have helped assure labor peace: mobilization of external core support for ruling elites; undercutting of a politically independent domestic bourgeoisie; creation of a transient, temporary proletariat; and, in Hong Kong and Taiwan, the spatial and organizational dispersal of the industrial proletariat. But a further explanation for East Asia's record of labor peace and regime effectiveness might be found in the economic consequences of continued development for public welfare. Rapid, labor-intensive industrialization in these small Asian countries has reduced earlier, high levels of unemployment while contributing to increases in real wages and material standards of living. By 1980 unemployment rates had fallen substantially from their levels at the outset of EOI, a decline attributable in part to expanding employment in the new export industries. Similarly, EOI development, unlike ISI development in Latin America, has not been associated with increased income inequality (Chen, 1979:chap. 8). Gary Fields (1984) concludes a recent review of available data on income distribution that "during the 1960s and 1970s, inequality fell in Taiwan, fell and then rose in Korea, and fell and then leveled off in Hong Kong and Singapore."

Such findings imply a substantial economic inclusion of workers
of East Asian development, particularly during early EOI. In ad
support a twofold explanation for labor peace, based first on ar
legitimation of ruling groups and strategies (Little, 1979:491) and second on
a displacement of collective action by individual market-based mobility
adopted by workers in these full-employment economies (Lim, 1986).

Economic inclusion as an explanation for East Asian labor peace is per-
suasive, but it must be tempered. It should be noted that real wage increases
started from a very low base and remain low by world standards. As recently
as 1980, and despite more rapid increases in East Asia, Latin American
industrial wages remained higher than those in Asia (see Table 1). In addition, at least through the 1970s, wage increases generally lagged behind
productivity increases, a reflection in part of the weak political status of
Asian labor. And workers in East Asian light export industries, pace setters
for economic growth through the mid-1970s, experienced greater job inse-
curity and worse working conditions than their counterparts in modern industrial sectors in Latin America. Finally, and most important, relative
income equality in Asia may be a consequence not so much of equitable
sharing in the fruits of economic growth as of very high levels of labor
extraction among low-income workers and families. The average number of
hours worked per week by Korean manufacturing employees is among the
highest in the world (ILO, 1984). In all four Asian cases employment
expansion in export industries has involved a massive entry of secondary
household earners, especially young women from low-income families, into
low-wage jobs. Among Latin America's work force in industry, by contrast,
fewer households contain multiple earners (see, for instance, Portes, 1985).
Thus income equity among Asian households in part reflects no more than
intensified labor outlays among poor families.

Nor is it clear that the state has compensated for low wages with public
welfare expenditures that might raise the effective social wage of workers.
Indeed, East Asian governments have expended a smaller portion of total

TABLE 1. *Hourly wages rates in selected countries, 1980*

	U.S.$	Increase from 1975 (percent)
Mexico	2.76	46%
Brazil	1.73	53
Hong Kong	1.51	113
Taiwan	1.25	160
South Korea	1.10	197
Singapore	1.09	42

Source. *Asia Research Bulletin* 12 (30 June 1982).

outlays for education, health, social security, and welfare than have the governments of Latin America (see Table 2).

Like money wages, these East Asian social wages have recently shown substantial growth from previously much lower levels of expenditure. Does heightened welfare spending indicate increased political vulnerability or growing state paternalism? In some cases, especially in South Korea, social expenditures have indeed been used to respond to localized labor protest. Generally, however, welfare expenditures have been justified as investments in human capital and associated with efforts to enhance the productivity and quality of labor during late EOI. In no case is there any indication that politically insulated planners and technocrats have significantly compromised their primary emphasis on "production first."

What, then, of the argument that the positive consequences of EOI development for employment, living standards, and income distribution have generated labor peace and regime effectiveness (Little, 1979:491)? This explanation fails to come to terms with indications that economic inclusion in East Asia is relatively limited. It also confronts another observation relating to the *locus* of labor protest. Latin American income inequality is partly attributable to a relatively small, protected, high-wage employment sector in modern industry and mining which has emerged alongside a very large pool of low-wage, marginalized workers engaged in household labor, self-employment, and other informal-sector activities (Portes and Benton, 1984; Evans and Timberlake, 1980). It is primarily among Latin America's economically *privileged* workers, in the modern industrial sector, that one finds strong and increasingly independent labor movements, and there despite the relative economic inclusion of such workers (Spaulding, 1977; Hewlett, 1980; Pereira, 1984; Keck, 1985). Although recession and hardship have generated protest everywhere, it is among these Latin American workers that such protest has been politically effective. Only among heavy industry workers in Korean mining and metals does one find a close parallel to the Latin America case.

It is not economic exclusion, it appears, so much as stable employment,

TABLE 2. *Percentage of total government expenditure devoted to education, health, social security, and welfare in selected countries*

Argentina (1980)	46.8%	South Korea (1982)	20.8%
Brazil (1979)	54.5	Taiwan (1982)	29.2
Mexico (1980)	36.3	Singapore (1982)	12.6
		Hong Kong (1982)	26.3

Sources. University of California at Los Angeles, Latin American Center, *Statistical Abstract of Latin America* (Los Angeles, 1984); United Nations, *Statistical Yearbook for Asia and the Pacific* (New York, 1982); and Republic of China, *Statistical Yearbook, 1983* (Taipei, 1984).

strong unions, cohesive working-class communities, and the other concomitants of economic inclusion which support strong labor movements and effective opposition and thus foster the capacity to act collectively and effectively when times are bad. East Asian labor, generally lacking such resources, could mount little more than sporadic protests in response to the layoffs that accompanied the 1974 recession.

Conclusion

Labor-intensive manufacturing for export provided the impetus for rapid East Asian industrialization during the 1960s and early 1970s. Success for this development strategy depended on a marriage of cheap, disciplined local labor with international technology, capital, and markets. Labor discipline, in turn, has required labor's political exclusion to ensure the full exploitation of this most important economic resource for national development. East Asia's trade dependency has thus played a role resembling that of Latin America's foreign investment dependency in encouraging authoritarian labor controls.

If the four East Asian NICs may be labeled New Japans in recognition of their successful emulation of Japan's export-led industrialization, then Taiwan may be the most Japanese of the four in its reliance on traditional corporatist controls at the enterprise level to assure labor peace and continuing industrial investment. This is not to say that the state has played an insignificant role in Taiwanese labor relations. Rather, the state has played an important if indirect role in promoting enterprise-level corporatism, by its encouragement both of dispersed rural industry and of company paternalism. The experience of other Asian industrializers suggests the importance of both. Lacking a viable small-enterprise sector, South Korea and Singapore have elaborated comprehensive state regulatory regimes to achieve political control and economic mobilization. Conversely, employment dispersal in conjunction with a laissez-faire state has permitted Hong Kong's autocratic employers to take full advantage of the weak position of labor.

In all cases the political autonomy of technocratic planners, which has permitted the state to ignore political claims on development policy, has been rooted in the weakness and dependency of domestic social classes, in elite unity, and in external support for authoritarian regimes. Internal unity and autonomy fostered exclusionary regimes at a very early point in industrialization, which preempted organizational efforts during the subsequent emergence of an industrial proletariat and assured that emergent trade unions were closely allied with ruling groups. The early political inclusion of Latin American industrial workers, by contrast, encouraged the development of strong labor movements that later were able partially to shelter a privileged segment of the labor force from repression.

So successful has EOI development been in reducing previously high levels of unemployment that it has encouraged a deepening and more recently a decentralization of corporatist regimes to mobilize the work force more fully to meet the demands of economic restructuring. In Hong Kong an unwillingness on the part of the colonial government to assume a greater role in industrial development or labor relations may make the transition more difficult than in the other countries. Similarly, continuing high levels of social conflict in South Korea's industrial relations, where stronger labor meets more repressive state controls, may create a chronic instability in efforts to install a union-based corporatism, as the political events of the early 1980s suggest.

The effectiveness of East Asian regimes has been enhanced by the consequences of EOI development for employment structure, elite unity, and external regime support. The massive recruitment of a new proletariat into insecure, low-wage, low-skill employment discouraged the development of either strong, independent unions or a settled, class-conscious proletariat. Local business remained economically dependent on the state for assistance and promotion, cementing together strong business-state coalitions. And growing economic linkages to core-country markets and companies deepened already substantial external support for local elites.

Can the East Asian corporatist shift endure in the context of international economic vulnerability for specialized export economies? On the one hand are corporatism-inducing pressures to elicit a deeper and more stable occupational and organizational commitment from industrial workers in order to facilitate the transition to a high-technology, high-skill economy. On the other hand, the failure of such an endeavor may induce backsliding into repression. Restrictions on world trade and market fluctuations have immediate employment effects in many export industries. Industrial retrenchment in turn produces economic dislocation and increased worker protest, as occurred throughout the region in the recessionary periods of the mid- and late 1970s. Although the disorganization of the labor force outside corporatist structures ensures that typically such protest is easily contained, increased protest does trigger elite repression, thus reversing corporatist deepening. One obvious illustration is the political crisis surrounding and following the assassination of President Park Chung Hee. Similar pressures to resume repression may result from continuing demands for real wage increases for which skill and technology cannot adequately compensate, as well as from growing unemployment and labor protest as capital moves to lower-wage areas. The Latin American experience suggests a further possibility: if economic restructuring is successful, the result is a relative expansion in stable, high-skill employment which may generate conditions for the emergence of stronger, more independent labor movements. Finally, and perhaps most important, the rapid expansion of a relatively well-educated middle class enhances opportunities for cross-class oppositional coalitions. These latter two structural factors go some distance in explaining the growing labor crisis in South Korea. At a minimum, these emergent and often conflicting forces for change in East Asian labor regimes suggest a need for much caution in extrapolating future trends from the experience of the recent past.

References

Chan, Heng Chee. 1983. "Singapore in 1982: Gradual Transition to a New Order." *Asian Survey* 23:201–207.

Cheetham, J. A. 1980. "Wages: Hong Kong." In International Labor Office, *Wage Determination in Asia and the Pacific: The Views of Employers' Organizations*. Geneva: ILO Labour-Management Relations Series 58.

Chen, Edward. 1979. *Hyper-growth in Asian Economies: A Comparative Study of Hong Kong, Japan, Korea, Singapore, and Taiwan*. New York: Holmes & Meier.

Choi, Jang Jip. 1983. "Interest Conflict and Political Control in South Korea: A Study of Labor Unions in Manufacturing Industries, 1961–1980." Ph.D. diss. University of Chicago.

Cohen, Benjamin. 1975. *Multinational Firms and Asian Exports*. New Haven: Yale University Press.

Deyo, Frederic C. 1981. *Dependent Development and Industrial Order: An Asian Case Study*. New York: Praeger.

Deyo, Frederic C. 1984. "Export-Manufacturing and Labor: The Asian Case." In Charles Bergquist, ed. *Labor in the Capitalist World-Economy*. Beverly Hills: Sage.

Djao, A. W. 1981. "Traditional Chinese Culture in the Small Factory of Hong Kong." *Journal of Contemporary Asia* 11:413–425.

Elson, Diane, and Ruth Pearson. 1981. "Nimble Fingers Make Cheap Workers: An Analysis of Women's Employment in Third World Export Manufacturing." *Feminist Review* 7:87–107.

England, Joe, and John Rear. 1975. *Chinese Labour under British Rule: A Critical Study of Labor Relations and Law in Hong Kong*. Hong Kong: Oxford University Press.

Evans, Peter, and Michael Timberlake. 1980. "Dependence, Inequality, and Growth in Less Developed Countries." *American Sociological Review* 45:531–552.

Fields, Gary S. 1984. "Employment, Income Distribution, and Economic Growth in Seven Small Open Economies." *Economic Journal* 94:74–83.

Fitting, George. 1982. "Export Processing Zones in Taiwan and the People's Republic of China." *Asian Survey* 22:732–744.

Galenson, Walter. 1979. "The Labor Force, Wages, and Living Standards." In Galenson, ed. *Economic Growth and Structural Change in Taiwan: The Postwar Experience of the Republic of China*. Ithaca: Cornell University Press.

Hewlett, Sylvia. 1980. *The Cruel Dilemmas of Development: Twentieth Century Brazil*. New York: Basic.

Ho, Samuel. 1979. "Decentralized Industrialization and Rural Development: Evidence from Taiwan." *Economic Development and Cultural Change* 28:77–96.

ILO (International Labour Office). Annual. *Yearbook of Labor Statistics*. Geneva: ILO.

Keck, Margaret E. 1985. "Labor and Politics in the Brazilian Transition." Paper presented at the annual meetings of the Latin American Studies Association, Albuquerque, N.M.

Kim, C. I. Eugene. 1978. "Emergency, Development, and Human Rights: South Korea." *Asian Survey* 18:363–378.

Kreye, Otto. 1980. "World Market Oriented Industrialisation and Labour." In Folker Froebel, Jurgen Heinrichs, and Kreye, *The New International Division of Labour*. Cambridge: Cambridge University Press, 1980.

Launius, Michael. 1983. "The State's Corporatization of Labor in South Korea." Paper presented at the annual meeting of the Association of Asian Studies, San Francisco, March.

Lim, Linda Y. C. 1983. "Singapore's Success: The Myth of the Free Market Economy." *Asian Survey* 23:752–764.

Lim, Linda Y. C. 1986. "Export-Oriented Industrialization and Asian Labor: Myths and Confusions." Paper presented at Duke University, 31 March–1 April.

Lim, Linda, and Pang Eng Fong. 1984. "Labour Strategies for Meeting the High-Tech Challenge: The Case of Singapore." *Euro-Asia Business Review*, April.

Little, Ian. 1979. "An Economic Reconnaissance." In Walter Galenson, ed. *Economic Growth and Structural Change in Taiwan*. Ithaca: Cornell University Press.

Ogle, George. 1977. "Labor Unions in Rapid Economic Development." Ph.D. diss. University of Wisconsin, Madison.

Pereira, Luiz. 1984. *Development and Crisis in Brazil, 1930–1983*. Boulder: Westview.

Portes, Alejandro, and Lauren Benton. 1984. "Industrial Development and Labor Absorption: A Re-interpretation." Paper presented at the Workshop on the Political Economy of Development in Latin America and East Asia, San Diego, Calif.

Portes, Alejandro, et al. 1985. "The Urban Informal Sector in Uruguay." Paper presented at the annual meetings of the Latin American Studies Association, Albuquerque, N.M., April.

Republic of Singapore, Singapore Committee on Productivity. 1983. *1983 Report*. Singapore.

Robinson, Joan. 1979. *Aspects of Development and Underdevelopment*. Cambridge: Cambridge University Press.

Salaff, Janet. 1981. *Working Daughters of Hong Kong: Filial Piety or Power in the Family?* Cambridge: Cambridge University Press.

Spaulding, Hobart. 1977. *Organized Labor in Latin America*. New York: Harper & Row.

Stites, Richard. 1982. "Small-Scale Industry in Yingge, Taiwan." *Modern China* 8, 2:247–279.

Turner, H. A., et al. 1980. *The Last Colony: But Whose? A Study of the Labour Movement, Labour Market and Labour Relations in Hong Kong*. Cambridge: Cambridge University Press.

United States, Bureau of Labor Statistics. 1972. *Labor Law and Practice in the Republic of China (Taiwan)*. Report no. 404. Washington, D.C.: GPO.

Class, state, and dependence in East Asia: lessons for Latin Americanists Peter Evans

Recent contributions to the analysis of East Asian development have shown a striking ambivalence toward the theoretical perspectives associated with dependency theory in Latin America. On the one hand the dependency approach is clearly considered the most interesting theoretical interlocutor, even by those who disagree with it. Several studies have effectively borrowed frameworks developed from the Latin American experience for the analysis of East Asian NICs (e.g., Lim, 1982; Gold, 1981). On the other hand most scholars of East Asia are adamant that the dependency approach "does not fit."[1]

Since I have done no primary research on East Asia, the focus here will be less on what dependency theory can tell us about East Asia and more on the potential contributions of the work of East Asianists to the development of the dependency approach. The work of East Asianists has already proved itself useful to specialists on Latin America who work within the dependency tradition. East Asianists have added fuel to the fire that is gradually consuming the simplistic, mechanical hypotheses sometimes associated with the idea of dependence. They have provided valuable new evidence and suggested reinterpretations of important propositions. They have also called attention to important factors previously slighted because they are less salient in the Latin American context.

The insights of East Asianists, if properly integrated with work on Latin America, may move us closer to an adequate general understanding of dependent capitalist development. To explore the implications of recent work on East Asia for the dependency approach, we need to look more

I thank Bruce Cumings, Gary Gereffi, Tom Gold, and Van Whiting, who provided very useful comments and criticisms on a previous version of this chapter.

1. Amsden argues (1979:342), for example, that "dependency theory is unable to come to grips with the Taiwan paradox." Gold affirms that the facts of Taiwanese development "fly in the face not only of the predictions but also of the assumptions of dependency theorists of all shades" (Gold, 1981:307). Barrett and Whyte (1982:1064) suggest that "Taiwan draws attention to the flaws in the arguments of most dependency theorists."

closely at dependence in East Asia and how it differs from dependence in Latin America. We must also examine the relations between East Asian state and domestic class, particularly agrarian elite and industrial bourgeoisie. First, however, the dependency approach must be stated clearly.

The simple hypotheses to which the dependency approach was sometimes reduced, more often by North Americans than by Latins, may have served a useful polemical purpose, but they also did violence to the sophistication of major dependency thinkers. Ten years ago Fernando Henrique Cardoso, the premier dependencista, was already attacking those who assumed that dependency meant that capitalist development was impossible on the periphery or that local bourgeoisies were no longer an important social force in dependent capitalist countries (Cardoso, 1975). Later he carefully distinguished the historical-structural method that he and Enzo Faletto had outlined in their classic introduction to the dependency approach from the mechanistic formulations of North American consumers of his ideas (Cardoso, 1977).

Over the last fifteen years the Cardosian version of the dependency approach—not simply the works of Cardoso himself but works by a variety of authors using some variant of the historical-structural approach—has clearly gained preeminence. The most widely cited review of the dependency literature (Palma, 1978) considers the historical-structural approach to be heuristically the most productive and perhaps the only viable version of the dependency approach. Recent writers on Latin American dependent development have followed Cardoso's lead, rejecting simplistic hypothesis and turning instead to more complex analyses of situations of dependence which are reminiscent of Cardoso's own pioneering work (e.g., Becker, 1983; Gereffi, 1983).

From the beginning dependencistas have insisted that an understanding of capitalist development on the periphery requires an analysis of how groups and classes in the periphery interact with groups and classes based in the metropole to transform peripheral social structures. Unlike orthodox Marxist approaches or modernization theory, the dependency approach has assumed that development in peripheral countries must follow a trajectory that is distinctive compared to that of the original industrializers, because development always entails the interaction of metropole and periphery. It has further assumed that certain contradictions exist between the interests of international capital and the full development of the economic potential of the periphery. Links with the international economy did not make development impossible, nor was foreign capital always and everywhere opposed to industrialization, but there were substantial contradictions to be overcome if a country enmeshed in the capitalist world system was to change its position in the international division of labor.

From the historical experience of Latin America, dependencistas argued that when foreign capital controlled the outward-oriented extractive sectors that were principal generators of surplus, the surplus, and therefore the dynamic impulse of these sectors, was transferred to the metropole unless or until local classes with an interest in industrialization grew politically and economically strong enough to contest the strategies of foreign capital. Central to such a change in the political balance was the growth of a stronger local state apparatus (see Evans, 1979; Evans, 1985). Even with industrialization under way, an active state apparatus was still required to counteract the tendency of international capital to centralize newer, higher-return kinds of industrial activity in the core. In the Latin American experience a "triple alliance" arose from the interaction of the more active state, local capital, and transnational companies; this alliance was exclusionary. The development it produced brought neither political democracy nor economic equality but instead authoritarian rule and the highest levels of income inequality in the world.

The dependency vision of Third World political economy is scarcely fixed. The changing reality of Latin American development continually forces reevaluation, most recently with the breakdown of the bureaucratic authoritarian regimes that many had considered the "natural" political vehicle for dependent development. But East Asia poses a challenge of a different order of magnitude. East Asia offers a completely different historical context and, therefore, an invaluable opportunity to reexamine the dependencista vision in a fresh light. Using a few recent contributions on the East Asian political economy, I focus here principally on Taiwan and South Korea, making occasional references to Hong Kong and Singapore, the city-states that fill out the East Asian NICs, and to the very important deviant case of the Philippines. Even this limited confrontation with the East Asian literature suggests some interesting lessons, both positive and negative, for dependencistas.

Dependence in East Asia

All Third World countries are dependent in the sense that they are vulnerable to the effects of economic (and political) decisions made in the core. Dependence in this vague, general sense is not an interesting concept.[2] What is of interest are specific situations of dependence, some of which constrain and shape development. The specific situations of dependence that characterize East Asian NICs are strikingly different from those that characterize the major Latin American NICs. For theory, the most important of these differences is the degree of external control over the management of

2. Some critics of dependency even use the concept as though autarky rather than diminished vulnerability were the alternative, which, of course, makes it meaningless for modern nations. See Gereffi and Evans, 1981:fn. 3 for a brief discussion of dependence and nondependence.

the internal productive apparatus—that is, the role of direct foreign investment.

Foreign direct investment

The first thing that strikes a Latin Americanist looking at the principal NICs of Northeast Asia is the restricted historical role played there by transnational capital. Industrialization in Latin America extensive by foreign capital penetration. The East Asian NICs, by contrast, experienced a dramatic decoupling of their economies from metropolitan capital before their successful industrialization and did not reestablish ties until the process was well under way.

Prior to World War II direct foreign investment in Latin America, as elsewhere in the world, concentrated primarily in extractive activities, agricultural or mineral. The principal investors, moreover, the United States and Britain, were also the principal customers for the raw materials exported by these extractive industries. The result was close ties between foreign capital and the traditional elites associated with agriculture and mining. Complementing extractive investments, and quite important in some countries, among them Brazil, were various fledgling investments in manufacturing.

Extractive investments did not disappear after World War II. In some of the Andean and Caribbean countries they remained the most important form of investment; but in the major NICs manufacturing soon attracted the bulk of investment. U.S.-owned transnational corporations were from the outset important in shaping the course of postwar industrialization. In the major NICs, as well as in the smaller countries, transnational corporations were given privileged positions as leading manufacturing sectors were created. Because the new industrialization after World War II was oriented primarily toward producing goods for local consumption, the transnationals shaped consumption patterns as well as the structure of the productive apparatus.

Latin American industrialization occurred in a context that maximized the consequences of direct foreign investment. The major investor, the United States, was in political terms the hegemonic power in the region, and the foreign capital involved had deep roots in the traditional economic and social structures of the region. In some cases, such as W. R. Grace, the companies involved in industrial projects had previously been involved in extraction. In others, the companies were building on markets they had previously developed through export. The shift to manufacturing investment, though important changes accompanied it, represented a continuity of foreign economic domination.

The involvement of transnational corporations in the major East Asian NICs has no comparable history. East Asian industrialization came later, when worldwide norms governing relations between Third World states and the transnationals were quite different. More important, the crucial transition to an industrial economy was accomplished during a hiatus in direct foreign investment. For the twenty years between the end of World War II and the mid-1960s, transnational corporations were virtually absent from the scene.

Japanese investments were confiscated at the end of World War II and did not reappear as an important force until the mid-sixties. Nor were U.S. companies important actors during this period. North American transnationals were busy taking over the fledgling consumer durables industries of Brazil and Mexico, dominating them through tightly concentrated sets of oligopolistic, wholly owned subsidiaries;[3] but they showed little comparable interest in East Asia. Not only were Taiwan and South Korea small and poor, they had no history as previous markets for U.S. exports and little familiarity with the consumer durables on which import-substituting industrialization was based in Latin America. Even more important, previously successful Communist armies sitting just north of the thirty-eighth parallel and just the other side of the Formosa Straits made Taiwan and South Korea very unattractive investment sites to political risk analysts.

As late as the 1960s foreign direct investment was still playing a minuscule role in the industrialization of the major East Asian NICs. Hyun-Chin Lim, describing Korea at the beginning of the Park regime in 1963, states flatly that "the MNCs were entirely absent from the local scene" (1982: 139). Volker Bornschier and Christopher Chase-Dunn (1985:108–9) observe that in 1967 the stock of direct foreign investment in Korea totaled only $78 million, about 2 percent of the Brazilian total. South Korea's score on their index of MNC penetration, which controls for the size of the local stock of capital and the size of the local labor force, was only 12 percent of the average for one hundred three developing countries in 1967; Brazil's score on the same index was 140 percent of the average.

The role of direct foreign investment in East Asia has, of course, increased substantially in the past twenty years, but current flows of direct investment to the major East Asian NICs are still substantially smaller than those to their Latin American counterparts. World Bank statistics on net inflows of direct private investment illustrate the point. From 1979 to 1982 net inflows to South Korea never exceeded $60 million a year and were on average negative. The major Latin American NICs, on the other hand, experienced massive inflows of direct foreign investment in the same four years. Brazil averaged $2.2 billion despite the worst industrial recession in its recorded history. Mexico averaged $1.5 billion, despite its own considerable economic difficulties. Even when we correct for the larger gross national products of the Latin American countries, these numbers are of a

---

3. The auto industry, which became the leading sector in the industrialization of the major Latin American NICs during the 1960s is the archetype of this process. See Kronish and Mericle, 1984; Bennett and Sharpe in Newfarmer, 1985; and Bennett and Sharpe, 1985.

different order of magnitude. The World Bank no longer provides data on Taiwan, but in 1978 (the last year Taiwan was included) it recorded a net inflow of just over $100 million, a level similar to that for South Korea and dramatically different from those for Brazil and Mexico.[4]

Not only are the aggregate amounts of direct investment much smaller, but the conditions under which the transnationals operate are quite different. In South Korea only 6 percent of the subsidiaries of transnationals are wholly owned, and foreign capital owns only a minority of most of the ventures in which it is involved (Lim, 1982:160). In Brazil, by contrast, over 60 percent of transnational subsidiaries are wholly owned (see Gereffi and Evans, 1981:48). Even in Mexico, which has taken a position generally more nationalist than Brazil's with regard to local ownership, 50 percent of local subsidiaries remained wholly owned.

For the major East Asian NICs, therefore, the case is clear. If transnational domination of industrialization is the core of contemporary dependency, then South Korea and Taiwan are not dependent in the same way that Latin American NICs are dependent. If developmental outcomes in these countries have differed from those in Latin America, the difference must be considered a confirmation of those lines of dependency thinking which focus on the role of foreign direct investment.

There is one East Asian case that does seem to fit the Latin American mold of investment dependence. The Philippines had the United States rather than Japan as its colonial power before World War II and has therefore experienced a continuity in direct foreign investment which is more Latin American than East Asian in character. American investments in extractive industries preceded industrialization and were linked to reliance on the U.S. market. Direct foreign investment shifted in the direction of manufacturing soon after World War II, and by 1974 the Philippines had more American direct investment in manufacturing than any Third World country other than the five Latin American leaders in manufacturing investment (Evans, 1979:295). Philippine development has also approximated Latin American experience in terms of growth rates and levels of inequality; it confirms previous thinking on investment dependence.

This is not to say that East Asia produces no anomalies for dependency thinking about the consequences of foreign investment. Singapore is a tiny city-state, and it therefore might be expected to exhibit the continuity from extractive to industrial investment that we observe in Latin America. But in

4. Bornschier and Chase-Dunn (1985:159) show the level of transnational penetration in Taiwan as higher than in South Korea but still less than half the average for their sample of 103 countries. Barrett and Chin in this volume also show levels of direct foreign investment in Taiwan similar to those in South Korea. See their Table 8. Of course, overseas Chinese are the source of about one-third of ''foreign'' investment in Taiwan. As Gold (1981, 1984) and others have been careful to point out, the overseas Chinese, in terms both of their links to the Taiwanese state and of their economic strategies, are much more like members of the local bourgeoisie than U.S. transnational corporations.

the last twenty years its rate of growth and levels of inequality have been more typical of East Asia than of Latin America. Singapore does suggest limits to the contexts in which investment dependence will have its expected effects.[5] South Korea also suggests an important qualification on how we think about investment dependence. Although South Korea is low on most measures of direct foreign investment, it is one of the largest recipients of loan capital in the Third World. According to the World Bank, in 1985 only Argentina and Mexico had higher levels of foreign debt per capita. For dependencistas who might be tempted to make the simple equation between flows of loan capital and flows of direct investment, Korea is a useful caution.

These caveats do not change the basic fact that as far as direct investment is concerned, the East Asian cases essentially confirm earlier dependency thinking. Direct foreign investment, however, is not the most important form of dependency in East Asia. We need to consider what East Asia has to say regarding dependence on aid and trade.

Aid and trade

East Asian countries are highly dependent on international trade; yet dependence on trade does not seem to have slowed down their economic growth or limited the distribution of its benefits. Aid is often assumed to have effects comparable to those of direct foreign investment, but it is hard to find such effects in South Korea even though it received more aid per capita during the 1950s than any other developing country in the world. The effects of aid and trade, like the effects of foreign capital, must be understood in the context of particular historical and social situations of dependency. The absence of "dependency-like" consequences for aid and trade in East Asia provides an opportunity to analyze the logic behind the predicted effects.

Aid, it is assumed, is associated with increased political leverage on the part of the metropole. In the context of penetration by foreign capital, aid might also reinforce the interests of foreign capital. And aid may be used to keep in power traditional elites considered less threatening to U.S. interests than possible successors. In all cases aid may restrict the changes necessary for economic growth or reinforce inegalitarian patterns of income distribution. In the East Asian NICs, however, aid had little to do with the interests of U.S. transnational corporations, which were hardly involved in the re-

5. Hong Kong, the other city-state, is ambiguous in terms of investment dependence. Its 1967 level of investment penetration was quite high according to Bornschier and Chase-Dunn (1985:158) but, according to Haggard and Cheng (this volume, Tables 1 and 2) and transnational corporations account for a small and declining share of capital formation in Hong Kong and play a much less important role in producing manufactured exports than in either Taiwan or South Korea.

gion. It was, of course, aimed at preserving the domestic political status quo, but its principal aim was to strengthen the ability of states to confront neighboring Communist regimes.

Because the interests involved seemed global, the aid was enormous. Edward Mason and his collaborators estimate that U.S. aid was equivalent to nearly 80 percent of gross domestic capital formation in Korea (cited in Lim, 1982:73) between 1953 and 1962. U.S. aid also accounted for five-sixths of Korea's imports during the 1950s. In the case of Taiwan, aid averaged over 35 percent of gross domestic investment and about the same level of imports (Amsden, 1985). Most of this aid went to the military rather than to economic development, of course, but it did mean that the burden of maintaining a massive military apparatus was borne primarily by American taxpayers, not South Korea's fledgling economy. In Taiwan the arrival of massive amounts of American goods was also useful in cutting inflation, from 3,400 percent in 1949 to 9 percent in 1953 (Amsden, 1985).

The geopolitical context of American aid, combined with an absence of previous ties to traditional elites, meant that the political leverage afforded by aid was used not on behalf of traditional rural elites but on behalf of a thorough land reform in both countries. The Americans could promote land reform only because internal social structural conditions resulted in a politically weak landlord class and a degree of separation between state apparatus and landlords. Nevertheless, aid created political leverage that was used to promote an unquestionably progressive transformation in both of these NICs.

Finally, U.S. aid in certain respects strengthened the state apparatus vis-à-vis the local bourgeoisie, especially in Taiwan in the early 1950s. Although U.S. AID was dedicated to free enterprise, private capital had to work with and through the state apparatus to get a share of the economic action created by aid flows. Thus one of the unintended consequences of early aid was to strengthen the system of bureaucratic capitalism in these states, which made the state apparatus a central arena in which the gains and losses of "private" capital were decided (see Amsden, 1979:362).

Trade, like aid, must be understood in the context of local social structures and the ways in which they are linked to international structures of political and economic power. The principal disadvantage of trade, in the eyes of dependencistas, has been that it leaves Third World countries pursuing static comparative advantage in primary products at the expense of developing their industrial potential. Economists at the Comisión Económica para America Latina have argued forcefully that long-term trends in exchange relations work against those who specialize in primary products. Even more important, continued reliance on extraction strengthens the domestic political and economic position of either foreign-owned, raw materials transnationals or traditional agrarian elites (see Cardoso and Faletto, 1979). Indeed, if Korea had stayed a Japanese colony, its reliance on trade might have implied exactly these kinds of difficulties. In practice, however, the East Asian NICs increased their reliance on trade under very different circumstances.

In the early 1950s, their colonial trade patterns disrupted by the Japanese defeat, South Korea and Taiwan embarked on what Bruce Cumings calls "remarkably similar import-substitution programs" in which key industries were "protected by and nurtured behind a wall of tariffs, overvalued exchange rates, and other obstacles to foreign entry." This early period of withdrawal from international markets was critical to the construction of an industrial base in both countries. Nor was the tendency to ignore the apparent logic of the international market simply a passing phase. An OECD study done in 1970 (cited in Amsden, 1985) found that in Taiwan, "protection given to production for sale on the home market was much higher than in Mexico." Both countries embarked on import-substituting industrialization again in the early seventies, again against the advice of American advisers, this time in heavy industries.

For the East Asian NICs, reliance on trade has meant neither a stronger traditional coalition of extractive foreign capital and agro-exporters nor the passive pursuit of comparative advantage based on natural endowments. Instead it has entailed a changing basis for comparative advantage engineered to a large degree by intervening states. This pattern of trade dependence has not carried with it the same consequences as the "outward-oriented" growth that preceded industrialization in Latin America (cf. Cardoso and Faletto, 1979).

South Korea has not completely escaped the vulnerability that comes from reliance on trade. At the beginning of the 1980s Korea's trade-dependent growth began to look like what Cumings terms an "export-led trap," as increased U.S. protectionism and declining U.S. growth left South Korea's export earnings flat while payments on its debt of $42 billion dollars continued to fall due. Nonetheless, the record of growth and transformation already noted makes it clear that the consequences of trade between poor and rich countries depend on the specific social structure in which trade takes place, not on some abstract, universal logic of unequal exchange. Clearly central to the social structure are the role, strategy, and character of the state apparatus.

The state and the triple alliance

The recent dependencista literature has consistently argued that dependent development requires that the state ally with local and multinational capital around a project of local accumulation (see O'Donnell, 1978; Evans, 1979; Canak, 1983; Evans, 1985). An active state is one of the keys to the movement from a situation of classic dependence to one of dependent development (within which industrialization can move forward). Asian NICs strongly confirm the dependent development model insofar as they reaffirm the centrality of state intervention to overcoming the negative consequences of dependence. Indeed, they allow us to explore the consequences of states that are relatively more autonomous than those of the major Latin American NICs.

In Latin America the state is a critical actor in the triple alliance, but most analysts would agree that the interests of private capital predominate.[6] Although East Asian NICs clearly cater to the interests of capital, most analysts argue that the state plays a more dominant role. Lim (1982:139) states flatly that "it is the distinctive feature of South Korea's dependent development that the state has the upper hand over both local capital and the multinationals." Thomas Gold is equally emphatic in his assertion (1981: 313) that "Taiwan's triple alliance is dominated by the state."

There are several reasons for the state's predominance. Japanese colonial rule reinforced earlier traditions of interventionist state bureaucracies and left behind strong administrative infrastructures, and concrete threats to regime survival legitimated the extraordinary powers given to the military. In the case of Taiwan the politico-military apparatus arrived on the island fully developed, while civil society was still politically disrupted by the repression of Japanese colonialism, and a cohesive vanguard party thoroughly integrated with the state apparatus enhanced the state's ability to dominate civil society. These East Asian states have a strength reflected in the nature of the state's relations with the local industrial bourgeoisie, with transnational capital, and, most of all, with local agrarian elites.

The state and the local bourgeoisie

Japanese colonialism left little space in East Asia for the emergence of even the relatively weak industrial bourgeoisies to be found in Latin America at the end of World War II. The Japanese used their colonies as sources of raw materials and showed relatively little interest in developing industry.[7] The industry that existed was controlled by the Japanese and not by locals.[8]

6. See Fitzgerald (1976,1977), Cardoso and Faletto (1979), and Evans (1979), for general arguments. See also Gereffi's study of the steroid hormone industry (1983) and Bennett and Sharpe's study of the automobile industry (1985) for examples of how transnational corporations can use the interests of local private capital successfully to oppose or at least to reshape policies that they find threatening.

7. Japanese policy did emphasize industry in Taiwan immediately before World War II, but this strategy was halted by the war and had limited impact beyond infrastructure (see Amsden, 1979:346–48). It is worth noting, nonetheless, that Taiwan was in this respect definitely not in worse shape than most of China. In fact, according to Gold (1981:232), "Taiwan's industrial foundation was superior to any other Chinese province."

8. See, for example, Kim (1983:11) on ownership of industrial enterprises in colonial Korea. See also Lim (1982:60).

In both Korea and Taiwan the abrupt removal of the colonial power left a weak bourgeoisie and a state that owned formerly Japanese assets. This was particularly important in Taiwan, where the Kuomintang state apparatus not only controlled basic industries, such as petroleum, steel, and aluminum, but also consolidated state control over the financial system (see Gold, 1981:233–34). Confiscated Japanese enterprises became the basis of a system of state-owned enterprises which was accounting for 56 percent of Taiwan's industrial production by 1952 (Amsden, 1979:367).

In South Korea the local industrial bourgeoisie was further weakened by the fact that most heavy industry was in the north, under control of the Communists. In addition, Koreans with industrial management experience had, almost by definition, been collaborators with the Japanese. What is perhaps surprising in the Korean case is not that the state played a dominant role vis-à-vis the local bourgeoisie but that the bourgeoisie managed to play an important political role until the military led by Park Chung Hee toppled the Rhee regime in 1961. In Taiwan the local (Formosan) bourgeoisie was not only underdeveloped, it was also a potential base for political opposition to the Kuomintang mainland "invaders" (see Amsden, 1979:348–51). More important, the financial capitalists who had dominated the Kuomintang regime on the mainland (e.g., T. V. Soong and H. H. Kung) were less influential on Taiwan (Gold, 1981:237). What had been a regime completely dominated by particularistic private interests became on Taiwan relatively more autonomous.[9]

With regard to the role of the state, as with foreign direct investment, one of the city-states is an exception and the Philippines comes closer to the Latin American model. Hong Kong, with its British-style laissez-faire government and its powerful Chinese bourgeoisie, is the exception.[10] The Philippines, despite more than a dozen years of authoritarian rule under Ferdinand Marcos, lacks the dominant, institutionalized bureaucratic apparatus that characterizes Taiwan and South Korea. In some ways Marcos is closer to the Latin American tradition of the caudillo than to the East Asian style of bureaucratic authoritarianism. The nature of relations between state and local bourgeoisie make it more difficult, as Robert Snow (1984) points out, for the state smoothly to impose such policy preferences as export-oriented industrialization.

---

9. It is difficult to assess the degree to which the state apparatus in either Taiwan or Korea has been penetrated by the local bourgeoisie. Some researchers (e.g., Enos, 1984) on Korea give the impression of very little penetration. Others (e.g., Amsden, 1979, on Taiwan and Cumings in this volume on Korea) give the impression of more substantial penetration. Even those more skeptical of the integrity of the state apparatus, however, still agree that the state is essentially "in the driver's seat."

10. Singapore, as both Deyo and Haggard and Cheng point out in their chapters, has an extremely dominant state.

The state and the landlords

Recent analyses of the "pact of domination" in Latin America, especially my own (see Evans, 1979, 1982), have tended to neglect rural elites.[11] The East Asian cases show that this neglect is dangerous. The degree to which the state apparatus was decoupled from landed elites is even more important to the developmental successes of the major East Asian NICs than is the relative autonomy of the state vis-à-vis the industrial bourgeoisie. Again geopolitics played a clear role, and again Taiwan is a clear-cut example.

If the landlord class central to the Kuomintang's political base on the mainland was not left behind physically in the flight to Taiwan, its class power certainly was. Land ownership in Taiwan was either in the hands of the Japanese, and therefore subject to confiscation, or in the hands of Taiwanese landlords who, as the Formosan nationalist rebellion of 1946–47 demonstrated, were just as likely to oppose the Kuomintang as to support it. At the very least the Kuomintang was in no way beholden to the local landlords. In addition, both the Kuomintang and its American advisers were well aware that the Kuomintang regime's inability to separate itself from landlord interests on the mainland had been critical to the Communists' construction of a rural base on which, eventually, the traumatic defeat of 1949 was founded.

The state on Taiwan was separated from the landlord class to a degree unparalleled in the nonrevolutionary Third World. Moreover, the only metropolitan interests in the continuation of traditional rural social structures, those of the Japanese, had been neutralized by military defeat. As a result the Kuomintang had the freedom to engage in unprecedented economic transformation, first in an extraordinarily thorough land reform followed by pervasive state support for the newly created class of "self-exploiting" small peasant proprietors, second in systematic extraction of the surplus from what became a highly productive agrarian sector to promote industrial capital formation.

Taiwan is the most dramatic case, but the disconnection of state apparatus from rural interests is a general feature of the East Asian "economic miracles." Korean landlords managed to survive World War II with considerable political power intact, but the Korean War produced revolutionary land reform during the brief North Korean occupation and then American-sponsored land reform carried out by the Rhee regime. "The rural power of the landlord class was eliminated," as Nora Hamilton (1982:39) notes. In Hong Kong and Singapore the absence of a rural sector freed the state from having to deal with a landlord class.

The Philippines, here as with direct foreign investment, presents something closer to the traditional Latin American pattern. The Philippine "sugar

11. O'Donnell's (1973) formulations of the bureaucratic authoritarian alliance might also be accused of this neglect.

bloc" survives as an agrarian elite linked to U.S. markets and U.S. firms much as Latin American elites were linked during the classical period of dependency on agrarian exports. Although this bloc is no longer the dominant fraction of the local bourgeoisie, it is still a powerful political and economic factor. As Robert Snow (1984) puts it, "Philippine land tenure and social structure have remained essentially semi-feudal."

Elsewhere in East Asia the state's separation from rural elites stands in sharp contrast to the situation of state apparatuses in even the more "modern" countries of Latin America. In Chile, for example, Maurice Zeitlin and his collaborators (1976) found the state apparatus thoroughly penetrated by families that had strong interests in traditional rural social structures. In Brazil political analysts continue to be impressed with the ability of rural powerholders to retain a central place in the political system despite industrialization (see, e.g., Flynn, 1978). In Peru it was only the 1968 military revolution that signaled a displacement of the landed oligarchy as the central political support for the state apparatus (see Stepan, 1978). In Mexico the Cárdenas reforms were followed not by the development of prosperous peasant farms along East Asian lines but by the emergence of large-scale capitalist agriculture and the development of a new agrarian elite. Overall, the absence of rural elite influence from the formation of state policy unites the East Asian cases and separates them from those of Latin America.

The state and foreign capital

The lack of relative interest by transnational corporations about investing in the East Asian NICs set the stage for a relationship between state apparatus and foreign capital very different from what is typical in Latin America. In Latin America bureaucratic authoritarian state apparatuses emerged in societies already thoroughly penetrated by direct foreign investment. In East Asia, by contrast, bureaucratic authoritarian regimes were already in command by the time foreign investors began to take a real interest. Consequently the state was from the beginning in a much better position to determine what role transnational capital would play in the industrial division of labor. The state's greater power vis-à-vis the local bourgeoisie also made the state a much more attractive partner for the transnationals once they had decided that entry was worthwhile. As Thomas Gold puts it, discussing early investments in Taiwan (1981:192), "American investments in the fifties in general were joint ventures with the only enterprises that could offer the large markets and production scale to justify the effort, the state corporations."

The role of the Kuomintang state in the development of Taiwan's petrochemical industry provides a good illustration of the character of state-transnational relations in the East Asian NICs. The China Petroleum Corporation had been established before the Kuomintang even left the mainland, specifically to take over Japanese assets in the industry and make sure that petroleum did not fall back into the hands of the Majors (Gold, 1981:269). When the time came to move downstream into fertilizers and other petrochemicals, the corporation first created a joint venture with Allied Chemical and Socony Mobil and later bought out its partners. The China Petroleum Corporation went on to organize the triple alliance in the petrochemical industry, keeping upstream activities under state control, encouraging joint ventures in intermediate products, and drawing local private capital into downstream activities.

In South Korea the pattern of interaction with the transnationals was somewhat different, but the prominence of the state, as protagonist and as ally, is clear. In discussing South Korea's petrochemical industry, John Enos (1984:26) characterizes the state as the "ever-visible protagonist." It was the state that planned the petrochemical complexes, set the terms for foreign participation in downstream ventures, pushed for increasing indigenous control over the technology, and bought out foreign partners when they became dissatisfied. Those who have studied the Korean industry argue that the state's constant attention has resulted in levels of performance clearly superior to those of similar plants in other Third World locations (Enos, 1984:30–31).

In the South Korean case, however, the state's participation in joint ventures was of minor importance compared to its role in relation to loan capital. Foreign loans, as already pointed out, constituted the principal link to transnational capital in the Korean case. But it is critical to add that reliance on loan capital has not meant simply a shift from dependence on industrial transnationals to dependence on transnational bankers. From the beginning, reliance on loan capital has strengthened the hand of the Korean state in relation to the local bourgeoisie. It appears, in fact, that South Korea derives its preference for debt rather than equity in part from the consequences of debt for state power.

In both Taiwan and South Korea, of course, the state's control of domestic financial resources in the period before foreign banks would consider lending to local companies was crucial in establishing the state's preeminence; but the shift to foreign loans extended rather than undercut the state's role. Local capitalists wanting foreign loans needed government approval and repayment guarantees. Because access to low-cost foreign loan capital was a crucial competitive advantage, the Korean state became a principal arbiter of which local capital groups could expand and in which areas they could expand, particularly as large Korean enterprises tend to operate with very high debt-equity ratios. Consequently, scholars of Korean dependent development such as Lim (1982:147) believe that "the most potent instrument for influencing local capitalists was control of bank credit and foreign borrowing."

Even in Singapore, where foreign direct investment has played an overwhelming role in industrialization, the growth of such investment was stimulated by an emergent bureaucratic state that developed an impressive, technically sophisticated bureaucratic apparatus for dealing with foreign investors (see Encarnation and Wells, 1982) and took an active role in directing foreign as well as domestic capital toward "pioneer industries." In addition, the state apparatus has become increasingly active in an entrepreneurial way as the number of state-owned enterprises grows and the state becomes a more important source of industrial financing.

In current relations between the state and foreign capital one is struck by apparent parallels, as for example in the structure of ownership in the Brazilian and Taiwanese petrochemical industries; but the difference in sequencing is crucial. In Brazil the transnationals were firmly ensconced in the leading industrial sectors on a wholly owned basis before being coaxed into joint ventures. In Taiwan wholly owned ventures in electronics and other industries followed the earlier alliance of state and transnationals in joint ventures. The important contrast with Latin America is the fact that in East Asia well-organized bureaucratic authoritarian states with an explicit project of fostering capital accumulation *preceded* the involvement of the transnationals and shaped the character of that involvement.

State domination of the history of the triple alliance in the major East Asian NICs provides a plausible explanation for the greater ability relative to Latin American NICs of these countries to construct new bases of comparative advantage and exploit new openings in international markets. It is, in short, very useful in explaining the performance of these countries in terms of accumulation. It is less obvious how the ability of the state to dominate its domestic and foreign allies might relate to the better performance of these countries in terms of distribution.

Inequality in East Asian dependent development

Its exclusionary character, both in political and in economical terms, is the most obvious negative quality of dependent development in Latin America. On the political dimension there is a grim similarity between the East Asian NICs and the major Latin American NICs.[12] On the economic side, however, there is a sharp contrast.

The performance of the Latin American NICs in distributing the benefits of their rapid industrialization is strikingly bad. Brazil is the archetype. The mass of the Brazilian population has clearly not received anything like a fair

---

12. Political pessimists could easily use this cross-regional similarity to argue for the incompatibility of democracy and industrialization. In a more optimistic vein it is nonetheless worth noting that both Latin American and East Asian NICs have experienced continual pressure toward democratization—sufficient pressure that eventually we may be able to argue once again for a connection between economic development and democracy.

share of the benefits from the country's rapid industrialization. Indicators of basic welfare, such as infant mortality rates, remain far higher than Brazil's per capita income warrants (see Knight, 1981), and its distribution of income reaches levels of inequality among the highest in the world. Although other Latin American countries exhibit slightly less dramatic discrepancies between rates of accumulation and levels of welfare, Mexico shares Brazil's exceptionally high Gini index level (circa .60), and Latin American countries generally experience high levels of inequality.

The performance of the East Asian NICs is quite different. Before I try to explain that difference, however, I must qualify their performance. First, it should be remembered that the egalitarian results attributed to East Asia apply principally to Taiwan. Taiwan started the 1960s with a Gini moderate by Third World standards. It managed not only to bring it down from .46 in 1961 to .33 in 1964 (see Jain, 1975) but also to preserve that downward trend while continuing to industrialize. The index reached a level below .30 in 1972 and held that level in the mid and late seventies (see Kim, 1983; Fields, 1984).

Other East Asian countries, while generally exhibiting lower levels of inequality than those in Latin America, are much less spectacularly successful. South Korea's Gini hit a low of .33 in the late 1960s but began to rise again in the 1970s (Kim, 1983:62–64; see also Koo, 1984). Hong Kong and Singapore have Ginis around .40 and have not experienced declines concomitant with industrialization similar to those in Taiwan (see Fields, 1984:table 4). These caveats bear on the plausibility of different explanations for the contrast between East Asia and Latin America. The contrast itself, however, remains clear-cut.

One explanation fits perfectly with the previous thinking of dependencistas. A long, unbroken historical experience of foreign direct investment produces a greater likelihood of inequality. The same holds true even if we look at current levels of direct investment, not at historical experience. So the East Asian cases tend to confirm one of the most robust of the findings of quantitative cross-national work in the dependency tradition—the relation between transnational penetration and inequality (Chase-Dunn, 1975; Evans and Timberlake, 1980; Bornschier and Chase-Dunn, 1985).

If we add the case of the Philippines, East Asia confirms the relation between transnational penetration not merely in negative terms (lack of investment and low levels of inequality) but in positive terms as well. The Philippines deviates from the East Asian model on the distributional dimension just as it does in terms of its history of transnational penetration. Its recent economic growth has been accompanied by rising inequality, and its income distribution is very similar to that in Argentina and Chile (though less inegalitarian than in Brazil and Mexico). In the Philippines, then, high (Latin American–like) levels of inequality are associated with a long, undisrupted history of high (Latin American–like) levels of foreign direct investment.

If the East Asian NICs can be said to confirm dependencista assertions regarding the relation between transnational penetration and inequality, however, they suggest some important modifications of dependency thinking regarding the relation between foreign capital, the bureaucratic authoritarian state, and inequality. In Latin American theorizing, domination by foreign capital—and the corresponding inability of the local bourgeoisie to survive in a competitive capitalist environment—is an important element in the emergence of an authoritarian polity. In East Asia this is clearly not the case. One might argue for a correspondence between authoritarian regimes and transnational domination in the sense that the emergence of authoritarian regimes makes transnational investment more likely, but even this relation does not hold up particularly well. It works nicely for Singapore but poorly for South Korea. More important, however, are the questions raised by the East Asian cases for the relation between political domination by an authoritarian state and inegalitarian income distribution.

The authoritarian state prevents labor from organizing on behalf of its economic interests, in Latin American theorizing, and thereby creates the conditions for a growing disparity of salaries between skilled and unskilled as well as a growing gap between incomes of wage earners and returns to capital. In East Asia the authoritarian state has clearly played the expected role in repressing labor's demands, but repression has not been accompanied by increasing levels of inequality.[13] This suggests that, despite the "relative autonomy" of authoritarian states and the similarities among them, such states must be analyzed in the context of the class configurations in which they operate and in light of the broadly defined development strategies that have emerged from those configurations. In concrete terms the different consequences of authoritarian regimes in East Asia and Latin America must be examined in light of the strategy of export-oriented industrialization and the prior transformation of the agrarian sector which characterized East Asia.

Taiwan is once more the crucial case, for it is there that the distributional results are most striking. In Taiwan, land reform combined with the systematic provision of uniformly distributed credit, technical assistance, and fertilizer by the state to make smallholder agriculture viable, thereby providing a more positive backdrop to industrial labor markets as they developed. In Brazil latifundia-minifundia agriculture has produced rural incomes that are half the level of urban incomes and just as unequally distributed (see Denslow and Tyler, 1983:table 6). Their greater chance not only of surviving

13. This implausible result is, of course, quite explicable in the eyes of neoclassical economists. By preventing the "market distortions" that an organized labor movement would create, the authoritarian state has kept the price of labor closer to its "marginal product" and thereby encouraged increased employment (see Fields, 1984). Unfortunately this explanation, while it works nicely for East Asian cases, does not account for the inegalitarian consequences of authoritarian repression of the labor movement in Latin American countries such as Brazil.

but of actually increasing standards of living on the farm gave the Taiwanese labor force a certain implicit bargaining power that Latin American labor lacked.

Later, as industrial employment absorbed a larger proportion of the labor force, a family employment strategy that included both farm and nonfarm work remained important to the maintenance of working-class living standards (see Amsden, 1979:359–60). Return to the countryside is rarely a viable option for a Latin American worker confronting an employer's attack on his or her real wages, but a worker whose family owns a productive agricultural smallholding is in a different position. Indeed, the rural population of Taiwan chose to remain parttime farmers as late as the early seventies, even though most of them were deriving most of their income from nonfarm work, indicating the importance of this unusually strong rural base in working-class economic strategies (see Amsden, 1979:360).

The labor-absorbing character of the assembly operations that dominate the export-oriented manufacturing sector in Taiwan has obviously complemented and extended the equalizing impetus generated by land reform. It would be a mistake, however, to assume that manufactured exports automatically provide more egalitarian industrialization. The second decade of export-oriented industrialization in Korea, as Hagen Koo (1984:1030–31) points out, aggravated income inequality rather than ameliorating it. Increased employment helped improve income distribution, but a substantial increase in inequality within manufacturing worked to worsen it. More important, it would be a gross generalization of the East Asian experience to suggest that a strategy of openness to the international economy would produce the egalitarian results seen in East Asia in the absence of the other social-structural features of the East Asian NICs. As Gary Fields (1984) has pointed out, in the small, open economies of the Caribbean the combination of a heavy reliance on trade with traditional Latin American social structures produces very high levels of inequality.

All in all, the East Asian experience is much less damaging to dependencista thinking on inequality than might be expected. It does suggest the need for a more careful assessment of the consequences of export-oriented manufacturing operations, but at the same time it confirms Latin Americanist suspicions regarding the negative welfare consequences of transnational-dominated industrialization. Most important, it suggests some useful ideas regarding the importance of agriculture and the role of the state. These are perhaps best presented as lessons.

Lessons for dependencistas

The East Asian experience clearly contradicts the caricature of dependency theory which purports to argue that stagnation and exclusion will follow in proportion to the extent of international connections; but so does Latin

American experience. If East Asianists can speed the demise of some of the simplistic and mechanical propositions with which the dependency tradition has become burdened, so much the better. If, on the other hand, we confront the East Asian experience with an historical-structural or Cardosian version of the dependency approach, we find the results for that approach more confirmatory than contradictory. Work by Latin Americanists has clear heuristic value in suggesting ways of analyzing East Asian outcomes; East Asian sequences suggest intriguing directions for dependencista thinking.

Perhaps the most important impact of the East Asian cases is to extend previous dependencista thinking on the role of the state in dependent capitalist development. In East Asia, as in Latin America, there is clearly a triple alliance behind dependent capitalist development, one in which transnational and local private capital are essential actors, but in East Asia the state is the dominant partner. Latin America produced a variety of evidence in favor of the proposition that a more active and entrepreneurial state was essential for successful capital accumulation at the local level. The major East Asian NICs increase the evidence in favor of this hypothesis by offering cases where both the relative autonomy of the state apparatus and the effectiveness of state intervention are well beyond what can be observed in Latin America—and where the success of local capital accumulation is also more pronounced.

Dependencistas should not, however, lapse into self-congratulation. If East Asian evidence is generally confirmatory of their recent thinking with regard to the role of the state, it also raises important questions with respect to the impact of state policy on inequality. Indeed, though East Asian evidence is consistent with earlier assertions about the connection between transnational penetration and inequality, the other factors that appear to be associated with relative East Asian equality suggest the need to revise current models of dependent development and inequality.

First, the East Asian experience suggests that Latin Americanists should be careful not to overprivilege industrial class relations when they analyze the exclusionary character of dependent capitalist development, even in the most industrialized NICs. The early work of such Latin American "structuralists" as Celso Furtado strongly emphasized the importance of rural class relations; more recent analyses, my own among them, have tended to stress the industrial sector, neglecting the continuing importance of rural social structures. The gains that have accrued to East Asian NICs from early, thorough transformations of the agrarian sector remind us of the extent to which the persistence of traditional class relations in rural Latin America has retarded and distorted the overall development of that region.

Even more important in theoretical terms, the distributional concomitants of bureaucratic authoritarian rule in East Asia remind us how little we understand the consequences of relatively more autonomous state machinery. In Latin America the more autonomous state has presided over increasing inequality; in East Asia it has done the reverse. In East Asia very powerful states with close ties to and sympathy for both local and foreign capital have helped produce income distributions in which the top 10 percent of the population gets one-half of what their counterparts in major Latin American NICs receive—and less than the share received by the richest 10 percent under a popularly elected government in the United States. The literature on bureaucratic authoritarian regimes in Latin America offers few insights as to how or why this should occur.

Evidence from East Asia not only suggests rethinking in some areas where the literature on Latin America is already rich; it also provides useful reminders of how parochialism can limit the scope of theoretical imagination. The point is perhaps most obvious in relation to geopolitics. In Latin America geopolitical influences might be summarized as U.S. attempts to protect the economic status quo without doing grave violence to reality. In East Asia such a summary would be ludicrous. There U.S. hegemony is again a central feature of the geopolitical environment, but the way in which the United States has defined its postwar interests had different consequences for the development strategies of the East Asian NICs. In East Asia, U.S. geopolitical concerns stimulated attacks on vested economic interests, at least in agriculture, and support for economically interventionist states. Geopolitics also has a salience for the internal politics of the East Asian NICs that goes far beyond what is normal in Latin America. State policies in Taiwan and South Korea can be understood only in light of a continual preoccupation with the fight against external Communist enemies.

One aspect of regional geopolitics in East Asia does fit rather nicely with dependency thinking. The abrupt removal of Japan as a colonial power created exactly the kind of space for the emergence of more dynamic local social structures that the dependencistas would expect, both politically and because it helped create a long hiatus in the participation of foreign capital which allowed for a restructuring of the role of the transnationals. Likewise, dependency analysts would predict that the split between Japan and the United States over which should dominate the East Asian region would be an advantage to individual states, as indeed it has been. Concretely, the powerful economic presence of Japan has helped mitigate the consequences of conflicts between the United States and its East Asian clients over economic issues, most obviously in Korea's deepening attempts during the early 1970s.

As U.S. policy in Latin America becomes increasingly dominated by geopolitical concerns, at least in Central America and the Caribbean, so the lesson about the importance of geopolitics seems more and more à propos for Latin Americanists. The lesson is not that U.S. geopolitical concerns will have the same consequences in Central America as they have had in East Asia. On the contrary, small, open economic and political disasters are more likely than variations on the East Asian miracles. The lesson, rather, is that the boundaries of theorizing must be expanded. Any dependencista who attempts to predict American actions in Central America and the Caribbean simply on the basis of expected flows of capital, profits, or trade will sadly miss the point. Only when Central America is understood as a geopolitical battleground, like East Asia, do American excesses make sense.

This last point deserves to be reiterated in more general terms. Perhaps the most important lesson for those who would try to compare the experience of the two regions is to avoid false parallels. Extracting structural relations from the historical context of one region and using them to make predictions—or, more dangerously, policies—in the other would be a bad mistake. The newly enlightened dependencista who expects land reform in Brazil now to have the same consequences as land reform in Taiwan after World War II is in for a severe disappointment. Not only is Brazilian industrialization at a point entirely different from Taiwan's, but Brazil has never had a productive smallholder peasant agriculture on which land reform might build. Brazilian agriculture and income distribution in that country might benefit from even a belated land reform, of course, and Latin American countries in general might want to consider Taiwan a demonstration of the benefits to be attained from destroying the power of the traditional landholding class. But careful analyses of concrete historical situations must precede any expectations about results from policy.

The same is even more true for export-oriented industrialization. To suggest that Guatemala or El Salvador will be able to reproduce Taiwanese or Korean results by opening their economies and focusing on assembling light manufactures for export would be a cruel hoax. Ironically, Cuba and Nicaragua might in some respects be in a better position than America's clients in the region to follow the Taiwanese example. They have important prerequisites for the construction of new bases of comparative advantage, including highly autonomous state apparatuses and thorough land reforms. In practice, of course, the geopolitical prerequisites of successful export led growth (i.e., access to the U.S. domestic market) make this suggestion facetious, but it does serve to underline the fact that the preconditions of export-led growth along Taiwanese lines go beyond currency devaluation and lower tariffs.

If scholars working in the dependency tradition can avoid false lessons from East Asia while using the East Asian experience to expand their theoretical imagination, the result will be a more robust general understanding of dependent capitalist development. Whether we call the resulting approach an historical-structural analysis of the political economy of Third World capitalist development or dependency does not matter as long as the useful insights of dependencistas are effectively used to construct future theoretical models.

References

Amsden, Alice. 1979. "Taiwan's Economic History: A Case of Etatisme and a Challenge to Dependency Theory." *Modern China* 5, 3:341–380.

Amsden, Alice. 1985. "The State and Taiwan's Economic Development." In Peter Evans, Dietrich Rueschemeyer, and Theda Skocpol, eds. *Bringing the State Back In*. New York: Cambridge University Press.

Barrett, Richard, and Martin K. Whyte. 1982. "Dependency Theory and Taiwan: Analysis of a Deviant Case." *American Journal of Sociology* 87, 5:1064–1089.

Becker, David G. 1983. *The New Bourgeoisie and the Limits of Dependency: Mining, Class and Power in Revolutionary Peru*. Princeton: Princeton University Press.

Bennett, Douglas, and Kenneth Sharpe. 1985. *Transnational Corporations vs. the State: The Political Economy of the Mexican Automobile Industry*. Princeton: Princeton University Press.

Bornschier, Volker, and Christopher Chase-Dunn. 1985. *Transnational Corporations and Underdevelopment*. New York: Praeger.

Canak, William L. 1983. "The Peripheral State Debate: Bureaucratic Authoritarianism and State Capitalism." *Latin American Research Review* 19, 1:3–36.

Cardoso, F. H. 1975. *Autoritarismo e democratização*. Rio de Janeiro: Paz e Terra.

Cardoso, F. H. 1977. "The Consumption of Dependency Theory in the United States." *Latin American Research Review* 12, 3:7–24.

Cardoso, F. H., and E. Faletto. 1979. *Dependency and Development in Latin America*. Berkeley: University of California Press.

Chase-Dunn, Christopher. 1975. "The Effects of International Economic Dependence on Development and Inequality: A Cross-National Study." *American Journal of Sociology* 40:720–738.

Denslow, David, and William Tyler. 1983. "Perspectives on Poverty and Inequality in Brazil." Paper presented at the annual meeting of the Latin American Studies Association.

Encarnation, Dennis, and Louis T. Wells, Jr. 1982. "Government Negotiations with Foreign Investors: Organizational Patterns in South and Southeast Asia." Unpublished draft manuscript, Harvard Business School, Boston, Mass.

Enos, John. 1984. "Government Intervention in the Transfer of Technology: The Case of South Korea." *IDS Bulletin* 15, 2:26–31.

Evans, Peter B. 1979. *Dependent Development: The Alliance of Multinational, State and Local Capital in Brazil*. Princeton: Princeton University Press.

Evans, Peter B. 1982. "Reinventing the Bourgeoisie: State Entrepreneurship and Class Formation in Dependent Capitalist Development." *American Journal of Sociology* 88:210–247.

Evans, Peter B. 1985. "Transnational Linkages and the Economic Role of the State: An Analysis of Developing and Industrialized Nations in the Post World War II Period." In Evans, Dietrich Rueschemeyer, and Theda Skocpol, eds. *Bringing the State Back In*. New York: Cambridge University Press.

Evans, Peter B., and Michael Timberlake. 1980. "Dependence, Inequality and Growth in Less Developed Countries." *American Sociological Review* 45:531–552.

Fields, Gary S. 1984. "Employment, Income Distribution, and Economic Growth in Seven Small Open Economies." *Economic Journal* 94 (March):74–83.

Fitzgerald, E. V. K. 1976. *The State and Economic Development: Peru since 1968*. Cambridge: Cambridge University Press.

Fitzgerald, E. V. K. 1977. "On State Accumulation in Latin America." In Fitzgerald, E. Floto, and A. D. Lehmann, eds. *The State and Economic Development in Latin America*. Center for Latin American Studies, Occasional Paper 1, University of Cambridge.

Flynn, Peter. 1978. *Brazil: A Political Analysis*. Boulder: Westview.

Gereffi, Gary. 1983. *The Pharmaceutical Industry and Dependency in the Third World*. Princeton: Princeton University Press.

Gereffi, Gary, and Peter Evans. 1981. "Transnational Corporations, Dependent Development, and State Policy in the Semiperiphery: A Comparison of Brazil and Mexico." *Latin American Research Review* 16, 3:31–64.

Gold, Thomas. 1981. "Dependent Development in Taiwan." Ph.D. diss. Harvard University.

Gold, Thomas. 1984. "Differentiating Multinational Corporations: American, Japanese and Overseas Chinese Investors in Taiwan." *Chinese Journal of Sociology* 7:267–278.

Hamilton, Nora. 1982. *The Limits of State Autonomy: Post-Revolutionary Mexico*. Princeton: Princeton University Press.

Jain, Shail. 1975. *Size Distribution of Income: A Compilation of Data*. Washington, D.C.: World Bank.

Kim, Eun Mee. 1983. "Dependent Development in Korea: A Preliminary Examination." M.A. thesis. Brown University.

Kim, Joong Min. 1983. "Growth with Equity in Taiwan and Korea: The Contribution of Agriculture to Industrialization and Income Distribution." M.A. thesis. Brown University.

Knight, Peter. 1981. "Brazil's Socio-economic Development: Issues for the Eighties." *World Development* 9, 11/12:1063–1082.

Koo, Hagen. 1984. "The Political Economy of Income Distribution in South Korea: The Impact of the State's Industrialization Policies." *World Development* 12, 10:1029–1037.

Kronish, Richard, and Ken Mericle. 1984. *The Political Economy of the Latin American Automobile Industry*. Cambridge: MIT Press.

Lim, Hyun-Chin. 1982. "Dependent Development in the World System: The Case of South Korea, 1963–1979." Ph.D. diss. Harvard University.

Newfarmer, Richard S., ed. 1985. *Profits, Progress and Poverty: Case Studies of International Industries in Latin America*. South Bend: University of Notre Dame Press.

O'Donnell, Guillermo. 1973. *Modernization and Bureaucratic-Authoritarianism: Studies in South American Politics*. Berkeley: Institute of International Studies, University of California.

O'Donnell, Guillermo. 1978. "Reflections on the Patterns of Change in the Bureaucratic Authoritarian State." *Latin American Research Review* 13, 1:3–38.

Palma, Gabriel. 1978. "Dependency: A Formal Theory of Underdevelopment or a Methodology for the Analysis of Concrete Situations of Underdevelopment?" *World Development* 6, 7/8:881–924.

Snow, Robert. 1984. "The Bourgeois Opposition to Export-Oriented Industrialization in the Philippines." Paper. Oxfam America, Boston.

Stepan, Alfred. 1978. *The State and Society: Peru in Comparative Perspective.* Princeton: Princeton University Press.

Zeitlin, M.; W. L. Neuman; and R. Ratcliff. 1976. "Class Segments: Agrarian Property and Political Leadership in the Capitalist Class of Chile." *American Sociological Review* 41, 6:1006–1029.

Coalitions, institutions, and linkage sequencing—toward a strategic capacity model of East Asian development Frederic C. Deyo

The East Asian NICs have sustained continuing and relatively equitable industrial growth over two decades. They have adapted flexibly to changing internal and external circumstances through rapid shifts in strategy and economic structure, including an early turn toward export-oriented development based on light industry and a more recent diversification into high technology and heavy industry. Structural imbalance has given way to diversified and increasingly integrated domestic economies with growing producer goods sectors, all within a context of extensive reliance on foreign capital, markets, and, increasingly, technology. The contributors to this book suggest a number of factors underlying the East Asian "economic miracle," including expanding world markets in the 1960s, ready access to loan and equity capital, a historical legacy of substantial investment in human and physical infrastructure, and an entrepreneurial and manufacturing base constructed during earlier periods of industrialization. Of particular importance have been a flexibility and responsiveness in reorienting both policy and economic structure to changing economic circumstances: early loss of momentum for a development strategy based on import-substituting industrialization and, later, oil price increases, declining export competitiveness in labor-intensive manufacturing, shrinking world markets, and growing protectionism in core economies (Hasan, 1984). Given the extent to which these small and relatively open economies rely on foreign markets, capital, and technology, responsive flexibility may indeed be the fundamental explanation for their continued economic growth.

The chapters in this volume suggest that contrary to earlier, neoclassical accounts (e.g., Balassa, 1981), one crucial factor explaining rapid growth and structural flexibility in three of the East Asian NICs—South Korea, Taiwan, and Singapore—has been a strong, developmentalist state. The

I thank Gary Gereffi, Stephan Haggard, Peter Katzenstein, and Robert Wade for helpful comments on earlier drafts of this chapter.

state's commitment to economic expansion and, more important, its *capacity* to implement well-chosen development strategies differentiate these NICs from other developing countries better endowed in natural resources, scale of domestic markets, and other economic assets.

In this concluding chapter I organize the arguments in this book around a "strategic capacity" model of development. The model seeks to explain East Asian success in promoting change in the domestic economic structure and in responding flexibly to change in external developmental circumstances. It draws into a single analytical framework the institutionalism of much modernization theory, on the one hand, and the coalitional and interest-based arguments that inform dependency theory, on the other.

Institutions and interests: contrasting approaches to development

Much of the modernization literature starts from the assumption that the sources of growth are to be found in institutional factors. Development involves a differentiation among economic, political, and other institutional orders. Economically, this process differentiates financial systems, labor markets, firms, and other economic institutions from kinship and the religious and political spheres of social life (Eisenstadt, 1966; Smelser, 1976; Moore, 1979). Secularized cultural values emerge which support "rational" economic behavior. This institutionalist approach is perhaps most explicit in the work of institutional economists, who emphasize the importance of economic institutions and culture for technological adaptation and change (e.g., Gordon, 1982; Street and Dilmus, 1982). And it could even be argued that institutionalist assumptions are shared by neoclassical writers, for whom the institutionalization of "free" (secularized, rational, structurally autonomous) markets in labor, capital, and goods determines the possibility and sustainability of growth.

If orthodox scholars see institutional rationalization as the major developmental problematique (Moore, 1979), Marxist and dependency writers working within a political economy framework emphasize the interplay of interests among social classes and political groups, both domestic and foreign. Dependency writers, in particular, identify the roots of growth in the interplay of interests and ideologies among dominant local classes or class segments, on the one hand, and core states and firms, on the other.

It should be noted in passing that one commonly posed distinction, between a presumed emphasis on external development factors among dependencistas and a greater emphasis among modernization theorists on internal factors, is less useful than this contrast between interest-based and institutional models. For modernization theorists, after all, external factors play an important positive role in initiating change, and for dependency theorists, the play of interests recognizes no national boundaries. Fernando Cardoso and Enzo Faletto, authors of the definitive early statement of dependent development, are most explicit in this regard: "We conceive the relationship between external and internal forces as forming a complex whole whose structural links are not based on mere external forms of exploitation and coercion, but are rooted in coincidences of interests between local dominant classes and international ones, and, on the other side, are challenged by local groups and classes" (1979:xvi).

We must, of course, temper the distinction between the institutionalism of orthodox theory and the emphasis on the conflict of interests among those working within a political economy framework, by recognizing the complexity of argumentation within each tradition. Modernization writers have stressed the importance of a consolidation of power in the hands of those committed to development and a corresponding shift of control over economic resources to those willing to direct such resources to productive investment (Rostow, 1962; Black, 1966). Similarly, those working with an interest-based perspective recognize that institutions play an important role. Whether they talk of capitalism, unequal terms of trade (Amin, 1974), or bureaucratic authoritarian political regimes (Collier, 1979), all refer to institutions that have figured prominently in writings on political economy.

More central to the theoretical distinction between institutional and interest-based approaches is the definition of the central problematique in theories of development. For most orthodox writers, the political creation of strategies through coalition formation and conflict among social groups, organizations, and classes provides what is largely a backdrop for the more focused discussion of processes of institutional change. Even C. E. Black's careful analysis of the "consolidation of modernizing leadership" centers less on the conflicting strategic interests of competing groups than on differential commitments to modernization in general and to the institutional reforms that follow a change in leadership in particular. Conversely, both Marxists and dependencistas see institutions as largely deriving from the larger play of power and interests; they understand them to function as instruments of domestic and international domination. Their attention focuses on the clash of interest, mainly economic, among powerful social actors and the definition of ruling strategies through group conflict.

Orthodox scholars are less concerned with interests and strategy conflict, in part because they assume that external linkages are benign and developmentally supportive and that long-term development generates economic improvement for most social groups and classes. These assumptions suggest few major interest clashes across political boundaries or social classes; they also imply the relevance and integrating power of a "developmental consensus." Similarly, dependencistas assume that domestic development may be inhibited by the interests of foreign firms and states and that local accumulation may require the continued economic exclusion of social groups and classes. These assumptions lead to a greater emphasis on conflict and domination and a correspondingly lesser emphasis on consensus.

Although neither approach necessarily invokes statist views of development, modernization writers have increasingly emphasized statist solutions to developmental obstacles in population control, for instance, industrial promotion, and agricultural modernization. Of particular importance are the institutional bases of effective strategy implementation through centralized planning organizations and coherent policies (Black, 1966; Moore, 1979; Sears, 1982; Ness and Ando, 1984; Johnson, this volume) and political institutions or regimes through which to implement development strategies and policies, to absorb increasing political pressures generated by social change, and to legitimate state rule and policy (Huntington, 1968).

Similarly, dependencistas clearly emphasize the strong, developmental state as sole repository of national economic interests in economies characterized by a weak bourgeoisie and dominated by powerful foreign corporations. Here, of course, we encounter the difficult issue of relative autonomy. Dependency writers seek to understand the process through which broad, strategic orientations emerge from the interplay of ideologies and interests among local and foreign classes and organizations (Cardoso and Faletto, 1979; Evans, 1979; Gereffi, 1983; Evans, this volume). But along with recent modernization writers, they are also led to stress the developmental importance of the relative autonomy of states from social classes and specific, private economic interests. A partial resolution of this dilemma is afforded by the recognition that the autonomy of the developmental state involves not so much the coalitional origins of general strategic priorities as the capacity to translate these general priorities into a coherent, operational program for development which will pass without challenge within the limits defined by the existing coalitional "pact of domination" (Cardoso, 1979; also see Petras, 1983:110–11, and Wallerstein, 1984:33). Such bounded autonomy provides the basis essential for developmentalist intervention and economic reconstruction where otherwise class or organizational forces might seek to abort strategic restructuring.

Interest-based and institutionalist approaches to the question of strategic capacity suggest two corresponding preconditions for strategy-led development: political closure and economic institutional consolidation.

Political closure refers in part to the external autonomy that permits domestic developmental coalitions in formulating strategy to assert national over foreign interests in cases where these diverge (see Gereffi, 1983). Closure refers, also, to the confining of strategy determination to a manageably narrow political coalition of dominant groups—a coalition able to deny domestic political opponents a voice in economic decision making and thus to effect rapid and coherent strategy shifts in response to changing economic circumstances. The narrowness of the coalition depends in part on the breadth of interests served by selected development strategies (Kaufman, 1979). Third, closure refers to the extent to which nonstate groups, even those constituting the ruling coalition, are excluded from the actual policy processes through which strategy is operationalized in policy and subsequently implemented (Johnson, 1982). And finally, closure specifies the need for broader exclusion of (or restricted access of) popular-sector groups from strategy to insulate technocratic economic planning from the vagaries of populist politics.

Coalitional political closure relates most closely to the emphasis among nonorthodox theorists on conflicting interests among elite factions. The broader exclusion of popular-sector groups from political processes forces us to consider the political *institutions* through which such exclusion may be achieved. At this point, interest-based and institutionalist arguments converge. For both modernization and dependency writers, the statist model based on strategic capacity poses a dilemma between effectiveness and legitimacy. Economic intervention by modernizing political elites through centralized planning institutions fosters both resistance and social disruption (Smelser, 1976). And as development proceeds, growing pressures for political participation exert ever stronger demands on planners for reform and redistribution. Early modernization writers typically asserted the merits of the pluralist, democratic solution to these pressures; more recently, however, a growing commitment to statist models, and a corresponding need for the political insulation of technocratic planning, has encouraged their successors to espouse more restrictive legitimating structures. Single-party and corporatist regimes have generally been portrayed as the most effective means for organizing and institutionalizing political participation without politicizing the planning process (Huntington, 1970).

The effectiveness-legitimacy dilemma is more difficult for dependency writers, for whom developmental constraints evoke a fuller, more fundamental, and more enduring political exclusion of popular-sector groups. Constrained possibilities for local accumulation reduce the latitude for enhanced social welfare; foreign investors demand protection from the uncertainties of domestic politics and industrial conflict; inegalitarian growth triggers political protest; and external indebtedness is accompanied by outside pressure for domestic austerity and stabilization. Dependencistas believe that the growing crises associated with dependent development encourage the total elimination of popular-sector groups from political life. This line of argument is developed by Robert Kaufman and other contributors to David Collier's excellent volume (1979) on the bureaucratic authoritarian regimes that emerged in the relatively industrialized countries of Latin America during the 1960s and 1970s. That book also suggests the more fundamental and unresolved dilemma between political effectiveness and legitimacy. Guillermo O'Donnell (1979), in particular, anticipates and explains the more recent failure of bureaucratic authoritarianism, noting its inability to generate legitimation structures. Mexico, whose dominant mass party has preserved a modicum of legitimacy in a context of dependent, economically exclusionary development, stands as the exceptional "success."

Economic institutional consolidation shifts attention from the politics of strategy choice to the policies and structures through which strategies are implemented (Katzenstein, 1978; White, 1984). It is clear that economic institutions may severely constrain strategy through their implications for policy feasibility just as strategies typically seek to alter such institutions to make desired choices possible. Nevertheless, the distinction between strategies and institutions usefully identifies two quite different phases of developmental capacity.

The institutional configuration most conducive to the effective implementation of strategy characteristically centers on a few powerful state agencies that closely link decisional and operational authority in strategy-relevant policy issues (see Johnson, 1982). Such agencies perform essential functions: external brokerage, policy implementation, and political control. The policy implementation and control functions of these agencies are self-evident. Less often recognized is the function of external brokerage—state mediation of access by local firms to external capital, markets, and technology. Such mediation is an essential precondition for the state management of external economic linkages on behalf of strategic goals for development.

Strategic capacity is further enhanced by the existence or creation of peak organizations in the private sector, organizations through which state actors can effectively redirect the disposition and organization of capital, labor, and physical resources. Such organizations, which might include industry associations, oligopolized industries, and trade union federations, are "strategic levers" for policy implementation (Katzenstein, 1978; Gereffi, 1983).

Singapore, Taiwan, and South Korea: the paradigmatic cases

Strategic coalitions and political closure

State intervention in Singapore, South Korea, and Taiwan has presupposed a degree of autonomy from foreign and domestic groups sufficient to permit elites and politically insulated technocrats to formulate coherent development strategies. The sources of state autonomy and power are to be found in the geopolitical context of early export-oriented industrialization, the policy institutions available to state elites, and the structural and social class consequences of sustained industrialization.

In South Korea and Taiwan early export-oriented industrialization was initiated by authoritarian, anticommunist regimes that enjoyed political and military backing from the United States (Cumings, this volume). Equally significant was British and subsequent ANZUS support for ruling elites in

Singapore. Such external political linkage suggests possibly negative consequences for state decisional autonomy in economic policy matters, of
course, and in fact "political dependency" did give core states some leverage over policy. Especially apparent was U.S. and UN encouragement of
development based on private enterprise, land reform, and, later, export-
oriented strategies in South Korea and Taiwan. But this influence seriously
compromised neither economic autonomy nor development itself. National
security and the containment of communism were the paramount considerations in U.S. and British foreign policy for much of the period. As a
consequence, political interests took precedence over economic ones, and
security interests themselves dictated economic assistance to create economically viable and politically stable regimes even where such goals required
neomercantilist policies.

If East Asian states looked out on a politically and economically supportive world state system, they looked in on relatively weak domestic social
classes. Bruce Cumings and Hagen Koo both point out in this volume that
colonial rule in Korea and Taiwan and land reform in the 1950s had already
reduced the political influence of landlord classes in these two agrarian
societies. But what of the industrial bourgeoisie nurtured during the import-
substituting industrial development of the 1950s? Could the new bourgeoisie
not have been expected to challenge reduced tariff protection, devaluation,
and other economic reforms taken in the transition to export-oriented industrialization? Stephan Haggard and Tun-jen Cheng (this volume) point to the
positive consequences for export industrialization in these countries of experienced groups of entrepreneurs who had emerged during import substitution
and who provided an alternative to direct foreign investment. But Koo,
Peter Evans, and I all suggest that the *political* weakness of the bourgeoisie
enhanced state strength and autonomy. In Singapore this weakness stemmed
from the brevity of import substitution and the major role played by foreign
companies there. In South Korea early postwar industrialization greatly
enhanced the political influence of private business, it is true, but the political discrediting of corrupt businessmen following the fall of Syngman Rhee
in 1960, along with the growing dependence of businesses on government
promotion and loans, greatly reduced the independence of the bourgeoisie.
Similarly dependent were Taiwanese businessmen, whose insular origins
further ensured them a politically subordinate position in a mainlander-
dominated society. Thus the state was able largely to disregard bourgeois
opposition to the policy measures it took at the outset of export-oriented
expansion, measures that opened major economic sectors to international
competition.

Equally weak were groups in the popular sector. In none of these countries were peasants united or politically organized, partly because smallholder agriculture predominated. Nowhere were labor movements able to
challenge state authority. Only in South Korea and Singapore was labor

strong enough even to provoke repressive measures from the state in the early phases of export development, and in neither case was labor's resistance sustained or effective.

Supported by external allies and insulated from domestic pressures, state technocrats were free to employ largely technical and economic criteria in development planning. But how did subsequent export-oriented industrialization affect the position of East Asian states and domestic social groups? First, capital and trade relations between the Asian NICs and core firms and investors have deepened over time. The continuing export penetration of core markets has generated political friction, of course, but deeper relations have increased core economic stakes in Asian security and thus strengthened the security alliances that buttress Asian political regimes against internal dissent.

Singapore's continuing extreme reliance on foreign investment has effectively marginalized the domestic bourgeoisie, both economically and politically. Industrialization in South Korea and in Taiwan, on the other hand, has generated an economically powerful domestic bourgeoisie. From the extensive state support for bourgeois interests and from state policies that seek to shield those interests from extensive foreign penetration and competition, one might infer that these groups command substantial political influence. For both bourgeoisies, however, it is clear that their subordination to elite-determined national development goals is far more significant than their political role in the formulation of those goals (Lim, 1982). Bourgeois penetration of high-level economic decision making is largely confined to leadership of strategy-*implementing* peak organizations, such as economic agencies, banks, and industrial associations and conglomerates, where the public sector and the private sector merge and interpenetrate. This political subordination in matters of strategy can be explained in part by the fact that preemptive political controls were established before a strong bourgeoisie emerged, that the bourgeoisie lacks political institutional access to national decision making, and in Taiwan that it is ethnically subordinate.

The paradoxical juxtaposition of economic power and political acquiescence is explained by several structural transformations. Especially important have been the implications of dependence on a world market. Continued access to foreign markets has depended on the ability of state agencies to negotiate effectively on behalf of local industries for liberal trade policies in core countries. Medium- to small-scale domestic firms in South Korea have depended on state-sponsored trading companies to facilitate exports and have required bureaucratic assistance to obtain loan and equity capital, export licenses, and foreign exchange. Korean firms generally have high debt-to-equity ratios and depend for their very survival on continued access to loan funds channeled by government-controlled banks and other agencies from foreign sources to local companies. Similarly, the China External Trade Development Corporation assists Taiwanese exporters through foreign advertising, trade fairs, provision of information about local suppliers to prospective foreign buyers, and maintenance of overseas offices. In both countries, export manufacturers have been helped by export incentives and subsidies, a target for protectionist sentiment in core countries. In these and other ways a continuing dependence on state largess for protection and support has encouraged bourgeois acquiescence to state policy (Haggard and Cheng, this volume).

If export-oriented industrialization has been associated with an erosion of the potential of business classes to provide political opposition, what of its consequences for labor? We might expect the rapid expansion of an industrial proletariat to generate new social forces of class opposition. But in practice export-oriented development has been accompanied by continuing weakness in East Asian labor movements, a weakness rooted both in political controls and in economic structural changes. Asian light-export industries, the basis for early export development, depended for their competitiveness on effective use of cheap, disciplined labor. In countries that lacked the linkage between wages and market demand found in Latin America under import-substitution industrialization, wage suppression was both costless and desirable. And so in countries where labor demonstrated a capacity to challenge domination by employers at the level of the enterprise, such as South Korea and Singapore, state intervention was swift and ruthless. Early political controls, effected through state-controlled trade union federations, preceded extensive proletarianization and thus preempted the sort of independent organizational opportunities normally available to labor at early stages of development (Winckler, 1984).

If Latin American industrialization created an urban proletariat of workers in heavy industry and settled working-class communities where labor movements could find a "natural" social base, East Asian export industrialization created a transient, mobile labor force of workers in light industry who had shallow proletarian roots. In such a context the absence of enduring bonds of solidarity among coworkers and working-class neighbors provides a significant impediment to independent unionization and collective action. The impact of economic restructuring on labor is of course uncertain, although it should be noted that economic restructuring since 1974 has not substantially altered the occupational structure of these East Asian countries.

Economic institutions and developmental intervention

Developmental intervention in Singapore, South Korea, and Taiwan has gone beyond macroregulative policies to policy instruments targeted on economic decision making in particular sectors and firms (Wade, 1985). Recent restructuring efforts, moreover, have been associated with a deepening of state intervention and with increased state equity participation in heavy industry and high-technology sectors (Chen, 1981; Myers, 1984; Haggard and Cheng, this volume). Even the government of Hong Kong has involved itself in the expansion and diversification of the dynamic finance sector. Both Haggard and Cheng and Chalmers Johnson in this volume suggest the importance of public-sector bureaucratic agencies—public enterprises, planning boards, development banks, savings institutions, research institutions, and so on—in generating coherent policies that conform to overall strategy as well as in implementing those policies. Of particular importance here is the insulation of these organizations from political penetration from below and an integration of function and decision making to allow them to pursue coherent, unitary policy (Hasan, 1984; Evans and Alizaheh, 1984).

Industrial policy has depended on hierarchical linkages, both institutional and organizational, between these bureaucratic agencies and a multitude of private-sector organizations. State-controlled, credit-based financial systems have been of special importance (Johnson, this volume; Wade, 1986). In South Korea and to a lesser extent Taiwan relatively high debt-to-equity ratios render decisions on industrial investment exceptionally responsive to the policy-based lending priorities of state-owned or state-controlled banks (Schmitz, 1984; Wade, 1985; Haggard and Cheng, this volume). More generally, public agencies have exerted economic influence through subsidies, import and export licensing, discretionary enforcement of regulations, subcontracting, foreign exchange controls, and other incentives and controls in developmentally strategic industries. Although we cannot reduce state influence over private-sector decision making to the magnitude of state financial control (Wade, 1986), we can find one indirect indicator of the economic power of the state in a significant growth during recent years in the ratio of government revenue to gross domestic product (Barrett and Chin, this volume).

The important role played by peak organizations in the private sector is seen in the implementation of export and industrial policies through general trading companies, conglomerates, and industry associations. The effective harnessing of these private organizations to national development strategies has encouraged a close interpenetration of organization and personnel across public and private sectors. Low levels of differentiation between these two sectors, illustrated in joint public-private ventures, parastatal boards, and state-supported trading companies and associations (see Evans and Alizaheh, 1984; White and Wade, 1984), are perhaps best exemplified by national trade union federations, whose dual developmental roles of political exclusion and economic mobilization have typically received support from extensive bureaucratic penetration and personnel overlap.

The state, to facilitate policy implementation, has in many cases played an important role in promoting institutional consolidation. Johnson, for example, notes the success of state efforts to foster general trading companies as instruments of export promotion. More recently South Korean authorities have encouraged a unification and consolidation of production in heavy industry to reduce competition and overproduction, as well as a reorganization of small firms in strategic export industries. In both cases the state has in effect allocated production of manufactured goods among pre-determined groups of firms to "rationalize" national production.

This pattern of institutional consolidation across public and private sectors is clearest in South Korea. But though Taiwan has pursued the course of promoted concentration less actively, its far larger public enterprise sector suggests a functionally equivalent institutional configuration in several economic sectors (Wade, 1985). Indeed, economic restructuring has been associated with an expansion of public enterprise or public participation in directly productive activities, or both, in all three countries.

Strategic capacity: the management of external capital linkage

Strong East Asian states have been able both to restrict and to manage external capital in ways that support strategic goals. In South Korea wholly owned foreign subsidiaries are permitted in only a few industries, while Taiwan has placed greater emphasis on joint-venture participation by foreign capital. In addition, and to varying degrees, the external position of domestic firms in the two countries has been enhanced by government-supported trading companies, official trade representation in major cities around the world, internationally negotiated access to core markets, and subsidized loans. In some instances state enterprise or direct equity participation in joint ventures has preempted direct foreign investment in industries deemed strategically important and beyond the reach of private domestic capital (Myers, 1984). And finally, in Singapore as well as in Taiwan and South Korea, the creation of development banks and other financial institutions subject to state control has enhanced domestic capital mobilization (Johnson, this volume).

Singapore, where foreign firms have played a dominant role in industrialization, suggests that the management of external capital provides a basis for development as important as simple restriction (Simon, 1985). Taiwan, South Korea, and Singapore all exercise extensive public control over the sectoral distribution and economic behavior of foreign capital. In these countries state-determined development strategies have both guided and been strengthened by the effective positive management of external linkages. Such management takes various forms: mediation, screening, and regulation.

State *mediation* of dependency involves the institutional channeling of most external linkages through bureaucratic agencies that are thereby enabled to introduce strategic criteria into the construction of foreign market, technology, and capital relationships (Haggard, 1986). The role that state-controlled South Korean banks play in mobilizing and allocating foreign capital illustrates this type of dependency management; so do selective import and export controls exercised through duties, licensing, and foreign exchange restrictions (Wade, 1985). Mediation also provides a necessary precondition for *screening*, the imposition of development considerations in determining the sectoral and other characteristics of direct foreign investment. In general, early preference went to labor-intensive export production; later, encouragement was given to investment in heavy and high-technology fields. Finally, state *regulation* of the behavior of multinational corporations has followed initial screening. Such regulation, including domestic sourcing requirements, profit-repatriation restrictions, production and marketing regulation, technology sharing, and so on, has reduced the enclave nature of foreign production by encouraging domestic linkage with local firms. State brokerage of relationships between domestic and foreign capital provides the major avenue for linkage management; an increase in direct participation in joint ventures with foreign capital now provides the state with more direct and powerful control.

If effective management of foreign capital rather than containment better describes the external developmental role of strong states in Singapore, South Korea, and Taiwan, then the East Asian NICs present strong reasons for our rejecting the call by some dependencistas (e.g. Senghaas, 1984; Chirot, 1977:205–8) for autarky or at least a reduction of external dependency as a prerequisite for sustained autonomous development. Only in rare cases can economic withdrawal achieve such a goal. Far more important has been the political and institutional capacity to direct such resources on behalf of strategic development goals and, just as fundamentally, to generate flexible strategies that foster developmentally favorable linkages to a changing world economy (see also Haggard, 1986).

Linkage sequencing and strategic capacity

For dependency writers, the outer limits of development are posed by the periphery's structural relations with the core, which define the developmental constraints to which strategies must attend. Strategy is thus directed to the management of dependency relations in their external manifestations as trade, investment, and technology flows as well as their internal manifestations as structural distortions, class relations, and decisional penetration (Evans, this volume).

Modernization theorists see the external environment as more benign, though they do now respond to dependency critiques by recognizing external environmental constraints to which strategies must adapt (Smelser, 1976:148). More generally, they see the international system as the source of ideas, technologies, and capital whose positive impact modernizing elites enhance through domestic institutions and planning. A more extreme perspective on the relationship between strategy and external factors is that of Wilbert Moore (1979), who argues that strategy may determine external trade and investment relations. His position is close to recent discussion of the ways in which state strategies seek actively to create and alter external opportunities and relations through trade, investment, and foreign exchange policies (Yoffie, 1983; Haggard, 1986; Wade, 1985). Such arguments presuppose far looser outer limits to development than dependency accounts typically assume.

The conceptual and empirical problems involved in assessing developmental limits render unlikely an early resolution of these issues. It is obvious that late developing Third World countries are often more strongly affected by events in core countries than vice versa. It is also clear, however, that these important external linkages to the core may be negative or positive in their developmental impact. Thus the chapters in this book suggest the constraints on and crises of development as well as the narrow range of feasible strategies for the small, externally vulnerable states of East Asia. But they also suggest ways in which the world system has energized local development. Neoclassical works have stressed the importance of the world market for domestic growth; this volume suggests the importance of external geopolitical factors in fostering the domestic political and institutional capacity to manage external economic relationships. This argument suggests a middle ground between dependency and strategic autonomy. By demonstrating the positive effects of external political ties for subsequent capacity to manage developmental processes on behalf of strategic goals, it integrates the notions of constraint and choice, political and economic linkage, and the positive as well as the negative effects of linkage.

Foreign markets, capital, and technology, it has been noted, have played an important role in East Asian development. In addition, it is clear that external political linkages have been important for the formulation of development strategy, political structure, and external finance. But this book suggests a more systematic approach to understanding the development consequences of external linkages. This approach, centering on a consideration of the sequencing and interaction of particular phases of external linkage, permits a fuller understanding of the external underwriting of strong, developmentalist states in East Asia. The cases of Taiwan and South Korea bear many similarities and may be treated together. Though it departs in significant respects from the experience of Taiwan and South Korea, Singapore also conforms to the overall pattern identified in these two countries.

The nuclear leveling of Hiroshima and Nagasaki in 1945 signaled at once the collapse of a Japan-centered regional empire in which South Korea and Taiwan played important roles and the political insertion of both countries into a U.S.-dominated world state system that preceded by some years their reintegration into the world economy (Cumings, Koo, this volume). U.S.

interests after the war centered on the containment of communism and the suppression of insurgency inside these front-line states. As a consequence the United States established and supported exclusionary, authoritarian states while at the same time destroying or suppressing leftist groups in both countries. This political rather than economic mandate in U.S. policy dictated substantial development assistance, both in financial terms and in planning, whose goal was to create economically viable dependencies. It was during these years that the United States assisted in the establishment of central planning agencies, which were to play an important role in development in later years. Tolerance for import barriers and inward-looking policies of import substitution, as well as access to U.S. markets, followed from these considerations (Evans, this volume). The new economic strategies initiated in the early 1960s in response to pressure from AID and World Bank missions signaled reintegration into the world economic system, including an opening to private foreign capital and deepened involvement in world markets. By this time, however, strong developmentalist states and substantial planning machinery were in place. In addition, the progressive erosion of U.S. hegemony in Asia, accompanied by the economic ascendancy of Japan and culminating in the U.S. withdrawal from Vietnam, ensured a gradual reduction of the previously dominant role played by U.S. political agencies in East Asian developmental coalitions; the consequence was to enhance domestic economic autonomy. Suggestive of a growing autonomy are increases in export-partner diversification, a greater capacity for internal capital mobilization, and increased diversity in the national origins of foreign investors (Barrett and Chin, Haggard and Cheng, this volume).

Koo argues in this volume that the externally fostered emergence of strong exclusionary states before extensive industrialization or linkage to foreign capital permitted East Asian governments to impose preemptive controls over both emergent social classes and external capital. Postwar states faced a bourgeoisie whose economic power followed rather than preceded authoritarian regimes. Labor unions were controlled from the outset, so subsequent unionization conformed to established corporatist principles. Similarly, foreign capital confronted states able and predisposed to determine the magnitude, sectoral distribution, and operating conditions of investment. This sequence clearly differentiates the Asian NICs from their counterparts in Latin America, where less effective bureaucratic authoritarian controls were instituted after the emergence of powerful labor unions, growth of an entrenched bourgeoisie, and extensive penetration by foreign capital.

Parallels between Singapore and the two former Japanese dependencies are striking. Under British colonial rule, and especially between 1945 and 1965, the destruction of the political left along with external backing for moderate, anticommunist political leaders encouraged a strong state to emerge which combined political centralization with an efficient bureaucracy. The British military and political disengagement late in the 1960s increased the developmental autonomy of ruling elites. As a consequence the reemergence of trade unionism, which had been destroyed in the 1960s, could easily be contained within state-dominated corporatist structures. Moreover, the massive increase in direct foreign investment during the 1970s could readily be subordinated to the development goals of the ruling party.

Preemptive sequencing similarly explains political contrasts *among* the East Asian NICs. Though in this chapter I have been emphasizing the relative developmental homogeneity of this small group of Third World countries, Bruce Cumings elsewhere in this volume points to strong contrasts between South Korea and Taiwan in the ease and effectiveness with which they have deployed political and strategic capacity. Taiwan has a political stability and a lack of significant opposition to ruling groups and strategy which strongly contrast to South Korea, where more repressive regimes have been imposed in response to sometimes violent opposition from middle-class intellectuals, students, and workers. While Korean opposition has proved ineffective in comparison with opposition in Latin America, it is more intense in Korea than in Taiwan or Singapore, and the variation may be explained in part by differences in developmental sequencing. After the war the United States pushed harder, and to greater effect, for democratic institutions in South Korea than in Taiwan. Second, more extensive early industrialization and a more developed anticolonial resistance movement encouraged higher levels of political mobilization before President Park imposed martial rule in 1961. Third, and perhaps most important, greater competition among elite factions, coupled with the emergence of a relatively stronger industrial bourgeoisie during the 1950s, presented greater opportunities for an opposition to mobilize. Fourth, structural differences in the nature of industrial transformation (e.g., heavy industry and concentration of the work force) have given independent trade unions somewhat greater opportunities for mobilization in South Korea than in Taiwan, as I argue elsewhere in this volume. And finally, the somewhat fitful and uneven nature of Korean economic growth has helped activate this potential for opposition. These differences are not so great as to suggest we group South Korea with Brazil and Argentina, but they do explain why South Korea has experienced less success than Taiwan in the preemptive management of political participation and correspondingly relied more on police control than on a political party apparatus. Similarly, Singapore's early period of leftist political mobilization during the Malayan Emergency and under the relatively open democratic regime of the late 1950s and early 1960s would seem to suggest a Korean political trajectory, but the greater effectiveness of preemptive political controls there is probably best explained in terms of substantial elite unity and the lack of a strong domestic bourgeoisie along with relatively even growth. These tentative observations go some distance to explain a ''softer'' authoritarianism (Johnson, this volume) in Taiwan and Singapore than in South Korea's higher-tension polity, where greater opposition meets greater repression.

The developmental consequences of strategy: the case of economic equality

The association of economic dependency with sustained growth poses one challenge to dependency theory; another is suggested by the relatively favorable equity record of East Asian growth. Dependencistas, after all, would expect the moderately high levels of external economic reliance seen in the East Asian NICs to be accompanied by similarly high levels of inequality. One response is to argue, as do several contributors to this volume, that the characterization of Asian development as equitable has been overdrawn and must be substantially qualified. But there can be little argument regarding the contrast with Latin America's extremely high levels of inequality. As in the case of growth, Peter Evans points out elsewhere in this book that the relative equity of East Asian growth can be explained in part by levels of economic dependency somewhat lower in Asia than in Latin America. Bruce Cumings and Hagen Koo both refer also to the inequality-moderating impact of early land reform programs.

Whether one sees high or moderate levels of dependency in East Asian development, one of the major sources of inequality for dependencistas, authoritarian exclusionary political regimes, are as widespread in East Asia as they are in the high-inequality NICs of Latin America. We are left with a paradoxical association between authoritarian regimes seeking to contain labor costs on behalf of export-led growth, on the one hand, and relatively egalitarian development patterns, on the other. We can in part resolve the paradox by reference not to dependency per se but to economic strategy and structure. Export-oriented strategies have fostered early and massive employment of multiple wage earners from low-income households and a consequent narrowing of interfamily inequalities as measured by Gini ratios (Barrett and Chin, Deyo, this volume). Progressive declines in unemployment have pushed wages upward (Haggard and Cheng, this volume). Export-oriented industrial development has not resulted in the highly segmented and inequality-generating labor markets that characterize the Latin American NICs. Finally, more recent restructuring has demanded an ever fuller economic mobilization of labor, the major development asset possessed by these resource-poor countries. This in turn has encouraged continuing investments in education, housing, and health to maintain internationally competitive labor costs as determined by wage-productivity ratios. Such investment has led to a further reduction in levels of absolute poverty.

Despite the political marginalization and outright repression of East Asian workers, the chosen export-oriented development strategy has fostered efforts to maintain low labor costs, but its structural consequences have been precisely the opposite: it has brought economically marginal families into the developmental mainstream, if only at low levels of consumption and security.

Hong Kong: exception or confirmation?

A deliberate adherence on the part of Hong Kong's colonial elite to laissez-faire principles of political economy seems to preclude application of the strategic capacity model I have suggested. Indeed, one could argue that industrial dynamism in this small colony derives in large measure from a continuing Schumpeterian process of adaptive innovation, imitation, and creative destruction among the colony's multitudinous small firms. Nevertheless, the recent experience of sluggish industrial transformation alongside rapid growth in finance sectors suggests the usefulness of the model for even this exotic case. First, it should be remembered that the strategic turning points for import substitution and export orientation in the other countries were sanctioned or actively promoted by foreign tutelary states for reasons of geopolitics. More critical for the argument is the recent industrial move into high-technology and heavy industry. In this instance foreign states and firms have been far less supportive, so the impetus and capacity for industrial transformation have had to come from within. If developmentalist states facilitate such structural transformations during economic crises, as Chalmers Johnson argues, then their importance should become especially apparent when restructuring is needed but external support is lacking. Thus we might explain, first, Hong Kong's response to the economic crisis of the 1970s, which was sluggish and ineffectual relative to that of the other East Asian NICs, as seen in the continuing dominance of textiles and other labor-intensive, low-technology manufactures; and second, the growing role of the state in current efforts to diversify and restructure.

Second, the success that *has* been achieved in restructuring Hong Kong's economy underscores the earlier suggestion that peak developmentalist organizations need not necessarily be confined to public or state sectors. Haggard and Cheng, for example, argue that the major banks, especially through their peak association, and large trading companies have played important development roles in investment capitalization, penetration of foreign markets, and so forth. These and other powerful organizations within a socially and commercially dense institutional context have in effect assumed the roles played elsewhere by state development agencies. It is interesting to note here that the strong state argument of Alexander Gerschenkron in fact referred not so much to strong states per se, though his historical examples dealt with state-led industrialization, as to centralized economic institutions among late developers: "The more backward was a country's economy, the greater was the part played in its industrialization by special *institutional* factors designed to increase the supply of capital to the nascent industry and, in addition, to provide it with *less decentralized* and better informed entrepreneurial guidance (1963:428, italics added).

But what of the generation of strategy? In what sense may strategy emerge from private-sector institutions? It seems clear that the peak economic associations in Hong Kong have in fact assumed a role of economic tutelage in the development of the colony, which is not surprising if one takes into account the social cohesiveness and unity of commercial, financial, and industrial leaders, on the one hand, and colonial authorities, on the other. Although small manufacturing firms predominate, economic and political concentration is assured by an extreme concentration of financial institutions, by interlocking directorates, and by extensive subcontracting. Power, wealth, and social status converge on a tiny colonial elite that commands substantial power to direct the larger economy (Hofheinz and Calder, 1982). Colonial authorities view their role largely as a matter of creating conditions under which the private enterprise system may flourish. Their close, personal relations with economic leaders, cemented through membership in exclusive clubs, educational ties, intermarriage, and, among fellow Britons, pride of culture in a Chinese world, ensure at least a compatibility if not a fusion of public and private economic morality which is functionally equivalent to the weak differentiation of political leadership from bureaucracy in the other Asian NICs. Implicit development strategies thus emerge as pervasive, shared assumptions among members of a closed establishment regarding the needs of the colony. And both the generation and the implementation of these strategies are politically insulated from the demands of small business, organized labor, and other nonestablishment interest groups by an exclusionary, authoritarian colonial state—a state that is in turn nurtured and sanctioned by a greater China whose economic interests it serves.

Further suggestive of the usefulness of a strategic capacity model in understanding Hong Kong's development is the observation that finance, rather than manufacturing, is leading Hong Kong's economic transformation. There is a far greater concentration and institutional consolidation in finance than in industry; peak banking organizations are more firmly linked to smaller financial institutions than to manufacturing firms; and the state plays a greater developmentalist role in this sector than in others. Thus, it is not surprising that Hong Kong's recent economic dynamism has centered on its role as a center for regional finance.

We lack sufficient documentation of the developmental role of Hong Kong's major banks and trading companies to give a definitive treatment of the relationship between foreign and domestic capital there. One might nevertheless suggest that such a role has extended to the mediation and screening, if not the regulation, of external dependency. In the colony predominantly small manufacturing firms secure capital from major financial institutions, which in turn mobilize capital in world markets. Such firms generally produce under subcontracting arrangements that the major trading firms arrange and organize. Similarly, small financial institutions participate in regional finances through their relationships with the major banks. Hong Kong's peak private economic organizations thus occupy a position filled elsewhere by public-sector bureaucracies in the developmental management of economic dependency and domestic restructuring.

References

Amin, Samir. 1974. *Accumulation on a World Scale*. New York: Monthly Review Press.

Balassa, Bela. 1981. *The Newly Industrializing Countries in the World Economy*. New York: Pergamon.

Black, C. E. 1966. *The Dynamics of Modernization*. New York: Harper & Row.

Cardoso, Fernando. 1979. "On the Characterization of Authoritarian Regimes in Latin America." In David Collier, 1979.

Cardoso, Fernando, and Enzo Faletto. 1979. *Dependency and Development in Latin America*. Berkeley: University of California Press, 1979.

Chen, Yu-hsi. 1986. "Dependent Development and Its Socio-political Consequences: A Case Study of Taiwan." Ph.D. diss. University of Hawaii.

Chirot, Daniel. 1977. *Social Change in the Twentieth Century*. New York: Harcourt Brace Jovanovich.

Collier, David, ed. 1979. *The New Authoritarianism in Latin America*. Princeton: Princeton University Press.

Eisenstadt, S. N. 1966. *Modernization: Protest and Change*. Englewood Cliffs: Prentice-Hall.

Evans, David, and Parvin Alizaheh. 1984. "Trade, Industrialization, and the Visible Hand." *Journal of Development Studies* 21, 1:22–46.

Evans, Peter. 1979. *Dependent Development: The Alliance of Multinational, State and Local Capital in Brazil*. Princeton: Princeton University Press.

Gereffi, Gary. 1983. *The Pharmaceutical Industry and Dependency in the Third World*. Princeton: Princeton University Press.

Gerschenkron, Alexander. 1963. "The Early Phases of Industrialization in Russia and Their Relationship to the Historical Study of Economic Growth." In Barry Supple, ed. *The Experience of Economic Growth*. New York: Random.

Gordon, Wendell. 1982. "Institutionalism and Dependency." *Journal of Economic Issues* 16, 2:569–575.

Haggard, Stephan. 1986. "The Newly Industrializing Countries in the International System." *World Politics* 38:343–370.

Hasan, Parvez. 1984. "Adjustment to External Shocks: Why East Asian Countries Have Fared Better than Other LDCs." *Finance and Development* 21 (December):14–17.

Hofheinz, Roy, and Kent Calder. 1982. *The Eastasia Edge*. New York: Basic.

Huntington, Samuel. 1968. *Political Order in Changing Societies*. New Haven: Yale University Press.

Huntington, Samuel. 1970. "Social and Institutional Dynamics of One-Party Systems." In Huntington and Clement Moore, eds. *Authoritarian Politics in Modern Society*. New York: Basic.

Johnson, Chalmers. 1982. *MITI and the Japanese Miracle*. Stanford: Stanford University Press.

Katzenstein, Peter. 1978. "Conclusion: Domestic Structures and Strategies of Foreign Economic Policy." In Katzenstein, ed. *Between Power and Plenty: Foreign Economic Policies of Advanced Industrial States*. Madison: University of Wisconsin Press.

Kaufman, Robert. 1979. "Industrial Change and Authoritarian Rule in Latin America: A Concrete Review of the Bureaucratic-Authoritarian Model." In David Collier, 1979.

Lim, Hyun-Chin. 1982. "Dependent Development in the World System: The Case of South Korea, 1963–1979." Ph.D. diss. Harvard University.

Moore, Wilbert. 1979. *World Modernization: The Limits of Convergence*. New York: Elsevier.

Myers, Ramon. 1984. "The Economic Transformation of the Republic of China on Taiwan." *China Quarterly* 99 (September):500–528.

Ness, Gayl, and Hirofumi Ando. 1984. *The Land Is Shrinking: Population Planning in Asia*. Baltimore: Johns Hopkins University Press.

O'Donnell, Guillermo. 1979. "Tensions in the Bureaucratic-Authoritarian State and the Question of Democracy." In David Collier, ed., 1979.

Petras, James, with Stephen Gundle. 1983. "A Critique of Structuralist State Theorizing." In Petras, ed. *Capitalist and Socialist Crises in the Late Twentieth Century*. Totowa, N.J.: Rowman & Allanheld.

Rostow, Walt W. 1962. *Stages of Economic Growth*. 2d ed. New York: Cambridge University Press.

Schmitz, Hubert. 1984. "Industrialization Strategies in Less Developed Countries: Some Lessons of Historical Experience." *Journal of Development Studies* 21, 1:1–21.

Sears, Dudley. 1982. "The New Role of Development Planning." In B. Jalan, ed. *Problems and Policies in Small Economies*. London: Croom Helm.

Senghaas, Dieter. 1984. "The Case for Autarchy." In Charles Wilber, ed. *The Political Economy of Development and Underdevelopment*. New York: Random.

Simon, Denis. 1985. *Taiwan, Technology Transfer, and Transnationalism*. Boulder: Westview.

Smelser, Neil. 1976. *The Sociology of Economic Life*. 2d ed. Englewood Cliffs: Prentice-Hall.

Street, James H., and James D. Dilmus. 1984. "Institutionalism, Structuralism, and Dependency in Latin America." *Journal of Economic Issues* 18, 2:633–641.

Wade, Robert. 1985. "The Role of Government in Overcoming Market Failure: Taiwan, South Korea, and Japan." Paper.

Wade, Robert. 1986. "The Organization and Effects of the Developmental State in

East Asia.'' Paper presented at a conference on Development Strategies in Latin America and East Asia, University of California at San Diego, 4–6 May.

Wallerstein, Immanuel. 1984. *The Politics of the World Economy*. Cambridge: Cambridge University Press.

White, Gordon. 1984. ''Developmental States and Socialist Industrialization in the Third World.'' *Journal of Development Studies* 21, 1:97–120.

Winckler, Edwin. 1984. ''Institutionalization and Participation on Taiwan: From Hard to Soft Authoritarianism.'' *China Quarterly* 99 (September):481–499.

Yoffie, David. 1983. *Power and Protectionism: Strategies of the Newly Industrializing Countries*. New York: Columbia University Press.

Index

Library of Congress Cataloging-in-Publication Data

The Political economy of the new Asian industrialism.
   (Cornell studies in political economy)
   Includes index.
   Contents: Export-oriented industrializing states in the capitalist world system / Richard
Barrett and Soomi Chin–The origins and development of the Northeast Asian political
economy / Bruce Cumings–State and foreign capital in the East Asian NICs / Stephan
Haggard and Tun-jen Cheng–[etc.]
   1. East Asia–Economic policy. 2. Korea (South)–Economic policy. 3. Taiwan–
Economic policy. 4. Singapore–Economic policy. 5. Hong Kong–Economic policy. I.
Deyo, Frederic C. II. Series.
HC460.5P65   1987   338.95   86-29103
ISBN 0-8014-1948-4 (alk. paper)
ISBN 0-8014-9449-4 (pbk. : alk. paper)